David O. Selznick's

GONE WITH THE WIND

By Ronald Haver

WINGS BOOKS

NEW YORK • AVENEL, NEW JERSEY

This edition is published by Wings Books, distributed by Outlet Book Company, Inc., a Random House Company, 40 Engelhard Avenue, Avenel, New Jersey, 07001, by arrangement with Alfred A. Knopf, Inc.

Random House
New York • Toronto • London • Sydney • Auckland

Printed and Bound in Mexico

Library of Congress Cataloging in Publication Data
Haver, Ronald.
    David O. Selznick's Gone with the wind.
    1. Gone with the wind (Motion picture)   I. Title.
PN1997.G59H38   1986   791.43′72   85-31801
ISBN: 0-517-60677-1
        0-517-61532-0 (Deluxe Edition)

Designed by Thomas Ingalls

13   12   11   10   9   8

Margaret Mitchell Marsh, the Atlanta housewife and 35-year-old author of the most popular American novel ever written.

Introduction

I WOULD HAZARD A GUESS that most people who have seen David O. Selznick's *Gone With The Wind* have never read Margaret Mitchell's *Gone With the Wind* —which is unfortunate because her book is one of the most satisfying reading experiences one can have with twentieth century fiction. Fifty years ago this was something that practically every literate person in the United States seemed eager to prove. For once, critics and public seemed to agree that the book was, in the words of J. Donald Adams in the *New York Times Book Review,* ". . . one of the best . . . it is, in narrative power, in sheer readability, surpassed by nothing in American fiction."

The overwhelming fame and acceptance of the novel in 1936–37 paved the way for the unprecedented financial and critical success of the 1939 motion picture. As the book's sales waned over the years, conversely the film's popularity grew, and due to carefully handled revivals every seven years, achieved the status of, if not "the greatest motion picture ever made," then, certainly, the most beloved and popular movie ever made.

The primary reason for this long-term appeal of the film *Gone With The Wind,* aside from the elements it took from the novel, was the picture's chief author, producer David O. Selznick. Selznick was one of that small band of legendary men known as "creative producers"— Samuel Goldwyn, Irving Thalberg, Darryl Zanuck, and Hal Wallis— men who reshaped the look, style, and impact of the American motion picture in the years following the introduction of sound. In so doing, they gave a new definition and authority to the term "producer," as well as giving their films the stamp of their own individual personalities, an achievement usually reserved for stars and directors. But it was Selznick who carried the function of the producer to its logical extreme; he delighted in the process of movie making, in the glamour, the excitement, and the razzle-dazzle of the film industry of his time. He was deeply, almost obsessively involved in every aspect of his films, from the writing of the screenplay, through casting, set design, costuming, photography, editing, and the hundreds of other details that go into the making of the modern motion picture. He was, in a sense, the first auteur-producer, for, more often than not, his pictures reflect his own sensibilities and attitudes more than they do those of the craftspeople who helped him achieve his ends.

By the time he bought *Gone With The Wind* in 1936, these sensibilities and attitudes had been shaped by his cultural and ethnic roots; an upper-middle class Jewish background, with its strong tradition of reverance for the past and a belief in the unity and strength of the family. This was overlaid with a childhood love of classic liter-

ature, instilled in him by his father, who read to him the works of Charles Dickens, Leo Tolstoy, and Emily Brontë. Coupled with this were the exciting new forces of twentieth century popular culture: theater, silent film, radio, mass circulation magazines, and the graphic arts, all of which had an impact on the adolescent Selznick, and would emerge later in the look, feel, and sound of his films.

Selznick's love affair with the movies, which was equalled in its time only by his audience's, was practically a lifelong romance. His own career, in fact, remarkably parallels that of the American film business. He was the third son of a Russian emigre turned jeweler, Lewis J. Selznick. Born on May 2, 1902, in Pittsburgh, David Selznick was three years old when the world's first nickelodeon opened for business, several doors away from his father's jewelry store.

The Selznick family moved to New York in 1912, just as the infant motion picture industry was becoming an economic force, and Lewis J. Selznick became one of the legendary figures in the film business of the time, training two of his sons, Myron and David, in all phases of motion picture financing, production, advertising, and distribution. By the time he was thirteen, David was in charge of his father's advertising department, overseeing campaigns for all of the Selznick products and being awestruck by the first New York screenings of *The Birth of a Nation.* (*The Birth of a Nation* was one of the young Selznick's primal movie-going experiences and impressed him to the point where thirty years later he was patterning sections of his *Duel in the Sun* after the Griffith masterwork.)

With the collapse of the family fortunes in the mid-1920s, due to over expansion and under capitalization, the twenty-four-year-old David followed the film industry west to Hollywood where he went to work at the bottom of the ladder as a reader in the story department of the two-year-old MGM organization. Within a year his knowledge, enthusiasm, and aggressiveness had advanced him to the point of supervising some of the company's low-budget films.

His subsequent career took him all over Hollywood. He was assistant to Benjamin P. Schulberg (father of Budd), production head of Paramount Pictures when sound was introduced in 1928. Selznick was one of the first creative individuals to experiment with the new technology, quickly adapting the best of silent technique to the possibilities of the new medium and creating, almost overnight, an entirely new method of story-telling—less poetic, but more affecting in its ability to move and involve an audience.

Selznick eventually left Paramount because he disagreed with their assembly-line method of production which was geared to turn out a

(Left John ("Jock") Hay Whitney and David O. Selznick on the Atlanta set of their *Gone With The Wind* (1939).

picture a week. He believed that each film should be carefully thought out as to story, appeal, and casting, with as much time as possible being spent on every aspect of production; and that one man should have complete authority over each project, carrying it through from beginning to end. He had the opportunity to put this theory into practice on a limited basis when he took over as production head of RKO Pictures in 1931. There he produced a series of smart, literate films that bore out the wisdom of his ideas. At RKO he was able to introduce new talent on both sides of the camera—George Cukor and Katharine Hepburn did some of their best early work with Selznick, while Fred Astaire was put under contract at his urging. And Selznick was the only executive in Hollywood with the imagination to back Merian C. Cooper in his outsize fantasy, *King Kong*.

Leaving RKO in a dispute over who had final say in production matters, Selznick rejoined MGM, this time as an autonomous producer, responsible only to his father-in-law, Louis B. Mayer. In the two years of his tenure, he produced eleven features, five of which—(*Dinner at Eight, Viva Villa, Anna Karenina, David Copperfield*, and *A Tale of Two Cities*)—are acknowledged classics of the time.

But it was at his independent studio, Selznick International, formed in 1935, that Selznick came into his own. Financed largely by the prominent Whitney family of Long Island, with John Hay Whitney playing an active role in the operation of the company, Selznick produced an unbroken string of outstandingly successful pictures ranging from literary works such as *Little Lord Fauntleroy, The Prisoner of Zenda, The Garden of Allah, The Adventures of Tom Sawyer*, and *Rebecca* to the archetypal Hollywood myth *A Star Is Born*; from the quintessential "screwball comedy" of the time *Nothing Sacred* to the apotheosis of the romantic cinema, *Gone With The Wind*.

There has long existed the misconception that David Selznick's *Gone With The Wind* is Margaret Mitchell's *Gone With the Wind*. But all Selznick took from her work was the title, a few characters and some of the plot points. And yet so strong are these aspects of Miss Mitchell's novel that the film has firmly maintained its hold on the popular imagination, while its protagonists have attained legendary status for several generations of moviegoers and, now, video addicts.

Margaret Mitchell wrote a very realistic account of the War Between the States and its aftermath in and around Atlanta. It was a dense, richly detailed account of the life and times of Scarlett O'Hara, and the changes that affected her and her numerous family and acquaintances. The manner of the telling was wry, insightful, and not particularly admiring in its dissection of the psychology of Scarlett O'Hara. Merian C. Cooper, an old friend of Selznick's and one of his partners in the Selznick International company, referred to Scarlett as a "first class bitch," and indeed in Mitchell's depiction of her she does

deserve the "accolade."

Scarlett was shrewd, stubborn, calculating, acquisitive, self-centered, and not particularly bright or beautiful. But she had courage, loyalty of sorts, and an amazing single-mindedness and resiliency which makes her able to survive anything. She rises above war, Reconstruction, the Ku Klux Klan, attempted rape, miscarriage, and any other number of misfortunes which were set against an engrossing and complex historical background, giving the story its epic qualities and a compelling narrative thrust.

Selznick realized at once that the narrative richness of the book could not be captured by his film; all he could hope for was to keep the highlights of the basic plot and some of the dialogue. He eliminated most of the characters, almost all the history, softened and glamorized the remaining characters and situations.

Scarlett O'Hara was not beautiful in Miss Mitchell's world, but she was in David Selznick's. The author described Tara as "ugly and sprawling," but Selznick's depiction of the O'Hara home has become a symbol of the romance and mythology of the Old South. He replaced Miss Mitchell's realistic view of the world as seen through Scarlett's eyes with a florid, highly charged romanticism that was his particular style. Selznick's *Gone With The Wind* has a kinetically opulent splendor that achieves its effectiveness by the inter-workings of script, design, carefully naturalistic but dramatic lighting, and settings that are faultlessly correct as to look, feeling, and psychology.

The orchestration of color, design, and lighting to create a mood was carefully supplemented by the elaborate use of music as an additional emotional force. The careful attention paid to makeup, lighting, and hairdressing of the women stars is particularly effective in an era when sexuality could not be blatant; it was carefully expressed in a way that would appeal not only to the men in the audience, but more importantly to the women, who were the arbiters of taste in most American households during the thirty years of Selznick's most active period.

In utilizing this stylistic approach to *Gone With The Wind*, Selznick created his own work, building on the foundation laid by Margaret Mitchell. She privately disapproved of many aspects of the Selznick treatment, remarking tartly to her friend Susan Myrick, who oversaw the technical details of the production, that the film had a falsely romantic tone. She particularly objected to the forward title that opened the story and talked about "cavaliers and gallantry." "I certainly had no intention of writing about cavaliers . . . [it] dislocat[ed] one of the central ideas of the book."

But even she, with her reservations, was a devoted fan of the film, writing Selznick in 1943 that, "I have seen the film five and one half times now . . . and each time I like it better . . . each time [it] reaches out . . . to lead me down paths that seem ever new for I forget in watching that I was the author and am able to view it with fresh eyes."

It has been nearly fifty years since the first screenings, but David Selznick's romantic, glossy style of moviemaking has kept *Gone With The Wind* the standard by which Hollywood and the American film industry measure their efforts. Its particular combination of excellences still attract and satisfy audiences on a scale that cannot be matched by many contemporary films, let alone any other that is almost half a century old.

What you will read and see here is the story of the making of David O. Selznick's *Gone With The Wind*. It's an account that has been exhaustively researched, making full use of the Selznick archives, including all original source material on the production of the film and its subsequent history. Added to this are interviews with many of the craftspeople who worked with Selznick on the picture. It is as accurate an account of the production as time, money, resources, and dedication will allow. I hope it offers an instructive and entertaining look at how David Selznick made his masterpiece. If you want Margaret Mitchell's *Gone With the Wind*, you'll have to read her book. And I'll hazard another guess. When you do read it, you'll like it even more than the movie.

RONALD HAVER
Hollywood
February, 1986

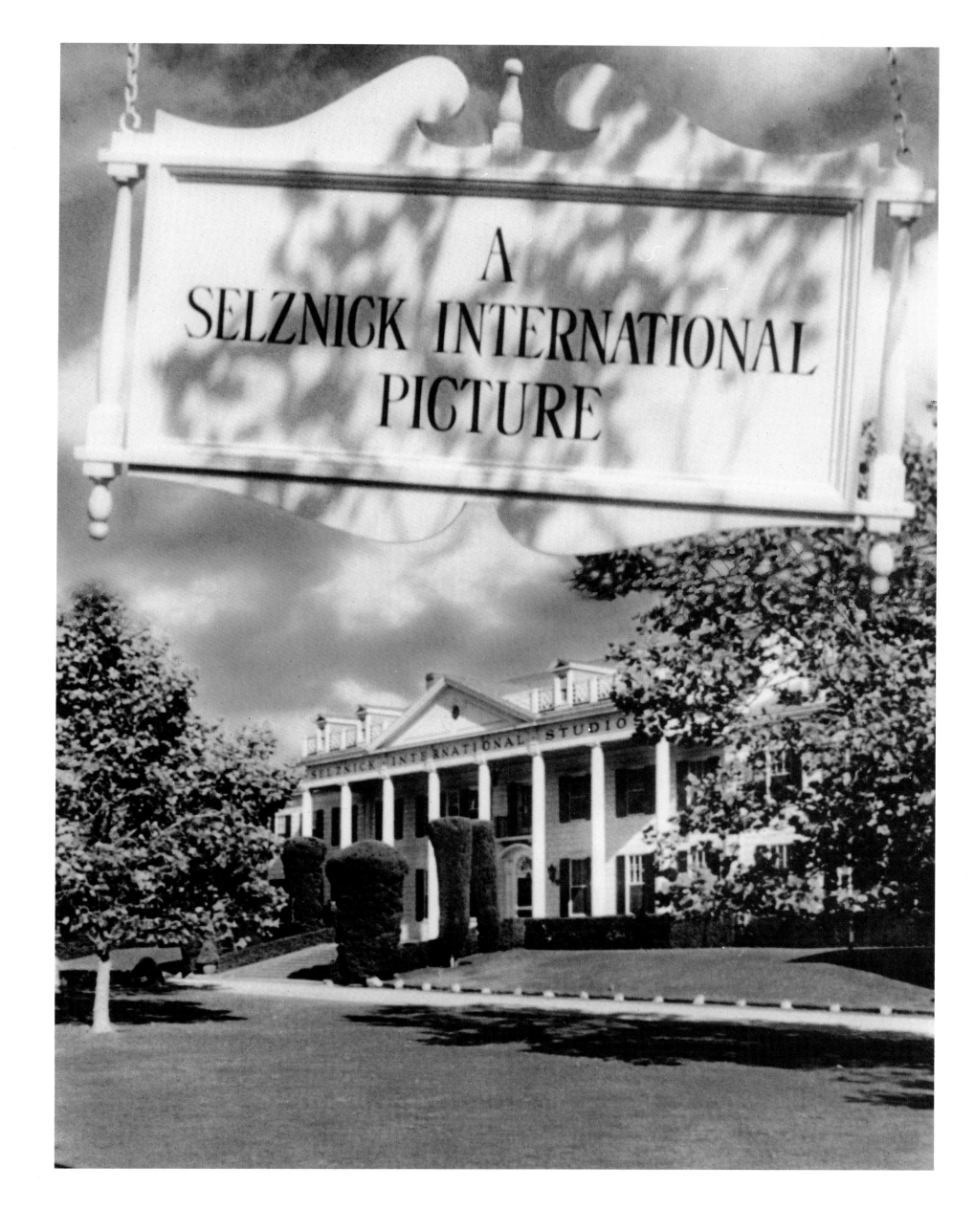

These sketches illustrate the traditional Hollywood treatment of classic or best-selling books. As originally conceived, *Gone With The Wind* was to begin with a shot of the book, showing its distinctive jacket; the cover opens, the pages turn, and the camera moves in to a close shot of the first line of the novel: "Scarlett O'Hara was not beautiful, but men seldom realized it when caught by her charm as the Tarleton twins were...." The line dissolves into a close-up of Scarlett, and the story is under way.

Gone With The Wind

ACCORDING TO David Selznick's daily activity log for May 20, 1936, at 1:28 P.M. he was in a projection room looking at edited sequences from *The Garden of Allah* when the teletype in his office clattered out a message from Kay Brown in New York: "... have just airmailed detailed synopsis of *Gone With The Wind* by Margaret Mitchell, also copy of book.... This is an absolutely magnificent story ... a great literary property and we must have it.... The book is 1,000 pages long and I have only gotten through half of it, it is one of the most lush things I ever read.... I am absolutely off my nut about this book.... I beg, urge, coax and plead with you to read it at once.... I know that after you do you will drop everything and buy it."

The novel she was so enthusiastic about had been the talk of the New York publishing world for the last two months; executives of the Macmillan Company, one of the oldest and most respected firms in the business, had let it be known that they felt they had something extraordinary in this first novel by a thirty-five-year-old Atlanta housewife and ex–feature writer for the Atlanta *Journal*. In 1926, largely to amuse herself while recuperating from a broken ankle, she had begun to write the story "of a girl who was somewhat like Atlanta, part of the old South, part of the new South; how she rose with Atlanta and fell with it and rose again; what Atlanta did to her, what she did to Atlanta and the man who was more than a match for her. I took them and put them against a background which I knew as well as my own background." Off and on for the next several years she continued to "hit the story a few licks," as she put it, through the last years of the twenties, the crash and depression of the early thirties, finally, in 1935, bringing her pile of unfinished manuscript out of the storage closet to which she had consigned it and, in a self-confessed weak moment, turning it over to Harold Latham, a Macmillan editor who was scouring the South for publishable material. By the time the story was ready for publication in early 1936, it ran to 1,037 pages covering twelve years in the life of its heroine, Scarlett O'Hara—spoiled, prideful, willful, and resilient—set against a meticu-

lously detailed background of the last of the plantation days, the Civil War, and Reconstruction as lived in Atlanta during that whole turbulent period of social and economic change.

Because of the high cost of printing, the book would carry a $3.00 price tag on its scheduled May 5 publication date, 50 cents higher than usual for fiction. Ten thousand copies of the book was the first print order from Macmillan, but then a sudden and unexpected acceptance of the novel for its July 1936 selection by the Book-of-the-Month Club (then ten years old) boosted the original print order by 40,000 copies, forcing Macmillan to move the official publication date to June, but also allowing it to send actual bound books instead of galley proofs, as was the usual custom, to the story departments of the various motion picture companies. Each received the 2½-pound volume in mid-May from the publisher's agent, Annie Laurie Williams, who sent along a note stating that the asking price would be $100,000, quite a sum for a first novel by an unknown author, but one that the shrewd Miss Williams reckoned would get everybody's attention, automatically giving an aura of importance to the book.

Katharine Brown at Selznick International was only one of the women in the New York motion picture world who went "off their nut" over the fortunes of Scarlett O'Hara. At Universal, Elsa Neuberger, before she left to join the Selznick forces, was highly vocal in her praise of the book to the new head of the company, Charles Rogers, who wired her back: "I told you no costume pictures." In the Burbank, California, studios of Warner Bros., Jack Warner had been briefed on the synopsis and the opinions of the New York people that the book would be big; he dangled the role in front of his recalcitrant young star Bette Davis, who turned up her nose and decamped hastily for England to try to break her contract. When she went, so did Warner Bros.' interest in the book, narrowing Annie Laurie's potential field down considerably. There was MGM, where she hoped Irving Thalberg might be intrigued with it as a vehicle for his wife, Norma Shearer. Paramount was already out of the

1936—David O. Selznick in his office, engrossed in something that could very well be *Gone With The Wind.*

running; it was their disastrous picture version of *So Red the Rose* the previous year that was cited as evidence that the Civil War was not to be messed with. RKO noted the "unsympathetic nature of the heroine," and felt that "so many involvements of plot and background . . . the censorable material . . . and the period in which it is laid would make it prohibitively expensive." So RKO dropped out, but not before the studio's biggest female star, Katharine Hepburn, read the book and immediately began badgering the heads of the company to reconsider. Darryl Zanuck of 20th Century-Fox, after reading the synopsis, seriously considered making an offer, but was put off by Annie Laurie's asking price.

Meanwhile, in Kay Brown's office at Selznick International, a young woman named Franclein Macconnel had promptly begun the delicate task of synopsizing the massive story. In four days she had finished a fifty-seven-page condensation that managed to convey much of the strength of the plot and characters. It was this that Kay Brown sent to David Selznick on May 20, paving the way with her strongly worded teletype message. Both the synopsis and the book arrived at the Culver City studio on May 22. But Selznick, preoccupied as he was with the troublesome *Garden of Allah,* did not have time to read even the synopsis, prompting the anxious Kay Brown to send a copy of the book to Jock Whitney in the hope of getting faster action from him. So far the only nibble had come from Zanuck, who had offered $35,000, which Annie Laurie disdainfully turned down, much to Kay Brown's relief and Margaret Mitchell's shock. Kay Brown bombarded Selznick with daily telegrams, teletypes, and memos, exhorting him to "just pick up the book and read from chapter 21 to 26 . . . it is something that would 'tear the heart out of a body' . . . I am going to try to do everything in my power to keep this from being sold until you make up your mind. . . . I know Mr. Whitney will let me spend the money for this book if you will." "The money" had now come down considerably, from $100,000 to $65,000. Finally moved by her incessant badgering, Selznick read the synopsis on May 24 and wired her: "Have carefully thought about *Gone With The*

Wind . . . think it is fine story and understand your feeling about it. If we had under contract a woman ideally suited to the lead I would probably be more inclined to buy it than I am today . . . feel that its only showmanship values would be in either such star casting or in a tremendous sale of the book. . . . I do not feel we can take such a gamble . . . therefore most sorry to have to say no in the face of your evident enthusiasm."

Selznick had not reckoned with Kay Brown's determination, however. If she couldn't convince him head on, she would outflank him, and for this tactic she enlisted Jock Whitney, who was reading the book and whose enthusiasm was becoming as rabid as hers. While she worked on Whitney, Selznick was having second thoughts, for he wired her the next day: ". . . feel there is excellent picture in it . . . suggest you call this to Cooper and Whitney's attention for possible Pioneer color picture, especially if they can sell the very colorful man's role to Gary Cooper. . . . Were I with MGM . . . I would buy it now for . . . such combination as Gable and Joan Crawford." So far, Selznick had heard only from Kay Brown and knew the story only from the synopsis. By now his own interest began to be piqued, and he re-read the synopsis, this time with an eye to buying the story as a vehicle for Ronald Colman, with whom he had one more picture to make. Throughout most of June, Selznick vacillated between interest in the story and concern over the cost and the casting resources necessary to make it properly. While he waffled, Katharine Hepburn, who had finished the book, intensified her efforts to get RKO to buy it for her, and negotiations were tentatively reopened by studio chief Sam Briskin, which Annie Laurie dutifully reported to Kay Brown. Frantically, she brought up her big guns, beseeching Jock Whitney to convince David. Whitney needed no additional prodding from her; he had finished the book. According to Selznick, "Jock wired me that if I was nervous about paying the price, that he would personally buy the book and hold it for the company, if we decided we wanted it. . . . I couldn't risk letting him have the last laugh on me. . . ." So he instructed Kay Brown to make a firm final offer of $50,000 for the rights, saying: "I cannot see my way clear to paying any more...." RKO's last offer had been for $45,000. Annie Laurie decided the $50,000 would probably be the best she could get and advised Miss Mitchell accordingly. Mitchell quickly accepted, much to Kay Brown's relief.

By late June laudatory reviews of the book were beginning to appear in growing numbers, climaxed by front-page notices in the book review sections of *The New York Times* and the *Herald Tribune*. The effect of all this was to start a stampede by the picture companies to Annie Laurie's door. RKO was now determined to get the property for Hepburn, and on Miss Mitchell's arrival in Manhattan on July 29, the studio hierarchy spent several hours trying to persuade her to change her mind and accept their offer of $55,000. But she came from a long line of people who believed that once you gave your word, you kept it, and she turned them down flat. The next day, Miss Mitchell met with Kay Brown and the other "Selznickers," as she called them, and warned them that she was selling the book against her better judgment as she was positive that it would be impossible to make a picture out of it, saying: "It had taken me ten years to weave it as tight as a silk pocket handkerchief. If one thread is broken or pulled when they begin cutting, they will have technical problems they never dreamed of." With that warning she signed her contract, giving Selznick International Pictures the right to "the exclusive, complete and entire motion picture and broadcasting rights, including television, in the property known as *Gone With The Wind*... [furthermore] the owner shall not be responsible for any additions, adaptations, substitutions or other changes the purchaser may make, or for any words or any delineation or interpretation of character different than that contained in the property."

By July, bookstores could not keep up with demand; they began reordering in huge numbers. In mid-August, two printing plants were working on the book in three eight-hour shifts a day, and entire freight cars were filled with copies to be delivered all over the country; the book was selling an average of 3,700 copies a day. By the end of September, over 330,000 copies had been sold. Nothing like this had ever happened in the publishing world before. The book began to be joked about on the radio, editorialized about in newspapers, used as the basis for sermons, becoming one of the first popular-culture media events, a massive, spontaneous demonstration of word-of-mouth advertising as men and especially women took the story for their own. For this Scarlett O'Hara and her saga were something new in American fiction: a vital, determined, courageous, and dominating heroine who used every resource at her command to meet adversity and beat it on its own terms. To a generation of women, *Gone With The Wind* represented the first time that a twentieth-century woman's voice had spoken to them about their lives and their beliefs, giving them a sense of themselves and their place in American society.

While the gale force of the novel's popularity began to build, Selznick, off on vacation in Honolulu, finally read the book and was alternately ecstatic and apprehensive about what he had gotten himself into. The synopsis had given some indication of the scope and relationships of the story, but nothing had prepared him for the pictures conjured up in his mind by Miss Mitchell's prose, nor for the absorbing and detailed characterizations and their complex interworkings. He hadn't been so excited by a project since *David Copperfield*, but he realized at once the enormous problems inherent in undertaking something of this magnitude. Months, perhaps years of careful, meticulous planning would be needed; the mass of material contained in the novel would have to be condensed, much of it eliminated, if it were to be brought into manageable proportions. This was made even more obvious when Selznick returned to Culver City in August and found the stacks of mail from readers all over the country, imploring him not to change the story "like the movies always do," and giving him the first hints of the controversy that would surround the casting of the central roles. Lydia Schiller was given charge of organizing this correspondence, keeping track of who the favorites were. She kept them in a file marked "Scarlett Letters," and the names seemed to change on a monthly basis. "The first few months had Miriam Hopkins and Margaret Sullavan leading the suggestions," she recalls, "with many people very strong for Ronald Colman as Rhett." As October approached, sackfuls of mail continued to plague Selznick with vociferous suggestions and demands about most of the central characters, but always

about Scarlett, and it wasn't just the public that had joined Kay Brown in going "off their nut" over the story. In Hollywood, seemingly every female performer between the ages of Shirley Temple and May Robson decided she must have the part, and the Selznick studio offices on both coasts were inundated with photos, letters, telegrams, and phone calls from anxious agents and ambitious actresses—a situation the studio press chief Russell Birdwell gleefully reported to the trade and national press, building a publicity campaign out of the unprecedented interest that was beginning to astound even the most hardened veterans of the Hollywood press corps.

All this fuss was gratifying to Selznick, but it was very premature because he had still not settled on a writer to do the script. After his return from Hawaii he had tossed the choice back and forth in his mind between Ben Hecht and Sidney Howard, and finally decided to offer the assignment to Sidney Howard because "he is the best constructionist around right now." The distinguished Mr. Howard had won the Pulitzer Prize in 1924 for his play *They Knew What They Wanted*, and he had subsequently added to his reputation with *The Silver Cord* and stage versions of *Yellow Jack* and Sinclair Lewis's *Dodsworth* (just adapted by him to the screen for William Wyler and Sam Goldwyn). Howard was an old friend of Merian Cooper's, the two had flown together during the war, and Selznick asked Cooper to help Kay Brown in convincing Howard to take the job. Cooper gladly did so, as he too was under the spell of the book; he commented in a letter that it was "the story of a bitch and a bastard ... and the most supreme book written on courage in the English language." Cooper's persuasiveness and his own perusal of the book convinced Howard to take on the job, which he did in mid-October 1936. Selznick immediately began a campaign to have Howard come to Culver City to do the script, telling Kay Brown: "I have never had much success with leaving a writer alone to do a script without almost daily collaboration with myself and [the director]." Howard, however, preferred to work on his farm in Massachusetts, free from conferences, distractions, and the endless discussions he knew would go on with Selznick.

Frustrated at having Howard out of immediate earshot, but dashing off instructions by mail, Selznick was also beginning a series of daily conferences with George Cukor, who had just come from MGM where he had directed Greta Garbo in *Camille*, following on the heels of his work on the prestigious Thalberg production of *Romeo and Juliet*. They had both been large, complex projects, two of MGM's biggest pictures of the year; *Gone With The Wind* would be his first picture for Selznick International. Cukor had read the book just as it began its phenomenal climb to popularity and he candidly admitted years later, "I didn't think it was the second coming of Christ.... It was an effective, slightly crappola thing, but a damn good story with some very original things in it.... In spite of its faults it had vitality and was a very picturesque, good rich book." Cukor's favorite for Scarlett was Hepburn, who was furious with RKO for not buying the property for her. She and Cukor were now close friends and they waged a heavy campaign to convince Selznick that she was perfect casting, but he didn't agree. In his mind, and that of the by now millions of readers, Scarlett O'Hara was an extremely feminine, seductive girl-woman, shrewd but not bright, and despite Margaret Mitchell's opening disclaimer, she had to have the kind of beauty and sex appeal that would make Rhett Butler's twelve-year pursuit of her convincing to moviegoers. Hepburn could play all these things, indeed *had* played all these things before, but that, as far as Selznick was concerned, was the basic problem with casting her or any other leading actress in the part: the pre-identification that they would bring to the role, whether it be Hepburn, Margaret Sullavan, Bette Davis, or Miriam Hopkins. Casting any one of these would alienate too many of the potential audience, and ultimately relegate the picture to the status of a star vehicle rather than giving it the fresh new feeling he wanted it to have. This meant a talent search, and, as Selznick wrote to Kay Brown, "an entire cast of new faces... *Copperfield* and *Tom Sawyer* have been child's play by comparison. You had better get yourself prepared accordingly."

To do this, Brown organized a three-prong reconnoitering operation: casting director Charles Morrison was to cover the Western states; one of Selznick's assistants, Oscar Serlin, would cover the Northern half of the country, while Brown herself led an expedition through the deep South, searching through high school and college drama departments and the hundreds of local little theatres. In Atlanta, they auditioned five hundred people in one day, and Miss Mitchell, in spite of her efforts to keep her distance, was so intrigued that she seriously considered disguising herself and watching the proceedings. Some idea of the pressure that Kay Brown and her small crew operated under can be gained from her wire to Selznick: "We are in Atlanta, barricaded in our rooms. The belles turned out in droves. For the most part they were all healthy mothers who should have stayed at home; the rich debutantes are all offering to pay us to play Scarlett, and all the mammys in the South want to play Mammy. I feel like Moses in the Wilderness. . . . I need a drink and Georgia is a dry state."

While the search went on, the board of directors of Selznick International was holding its annual meeting and contemplating how best to deal with the problems entailed by its prize property, not the least of which was the expense of producing it properly. The company had a fluctuating working capital of only about $3 million. It was obvious to both Selznick and Cooper, the only two picturemakers on the board, that the production problems of script, length, design, and special effects would boost the cost of the picture considerably beyond the company's present resources—to upwards of $2 million, a staggering sum in the uncertain days immediately following the depression. Considerable discussion and argument took place at the November 1936 board meeting about the wisdom of the company's tackling the project at all, with Henry Ginsberg trying to persuade Selznick and Whitney to accept one of the lucrative offers that were coming in for the rights to the book (the last offer had been for $1 million) and take a hefty profit. Selznick persuasively argued against this, saying that "making *Gone With The Wind* was exactly the kind of challenge I had been searching for since *David Copperfield,* and I was determined that our little company . . . should take this story that would strain the resources of the largest of the studios and . . . try to make it the biggest picture of all time."

It was suggested that they could use just half the book, as Warner Bros. had recently done with *Anthony Adverse,* but Jock Whitney was adamant in backing Selznick's desire to follow the whole story from beginning to end, or as much as could be strung together dramatically. Selznick said later of Whitney's involvement in the project: "He was probably more active in connection with the production of *Gone With The Wind* than any man in his executive position as head of the company has ever been before. Throughout all the time we were preparing it his faith never wavered; never for a moment did he have any doubts about the outcome, or worry about its cost, assuring the members of our Board that he was confident of the final result and that he would share responsibility with me for it." Putting his money where his mouth was, Whitney and his immediate family ponied up another $5 million, some of it coming from Pioneer, for it was at this meeting that the two companies were formally merged and the decision made to take over the entire RKO-Pathé studio, not only because of the expanded production schedule but also because of the looming necessities of *Gone With The Wind.*

On December 14, 1936, Selznick received from Sidney Howard a fifty-page memorandum entitled "Preliminary Notes on a Screen Treatment of *Gone With The Wind.*" Not a script, not even a treatment, it was Howard musing his way through the dramatic pathways of the book. He broke the story down into seven main sequences, following the structure of the novel very closely, using the "warm, simple opening scene, fading in on the . . . Tarleton twins . . . as they visit Scarlett on the porch at Tara." Howard eliminated all of Miss Mitchell's detailed backgrounding of the subsidiary characters, the flashbacks involving Scarlett's parents, the parallel between Scarlett and Atlanta being the same age and the same type—young, vigorous, and pushy—but kept the emphasis on Scarlett's Irish heritage, her "love of the land," as her father puts it. The twin love stories of Scarlett-Rhett, Ashley-Melanie were developed throughout the outline just as they had been in the novel. In his treatment of Rhett Butler, Howard found himself "troubled throughout the war section of the book by the lack of both variety and invention in what Rhett does as he makes various appearances . . . perhaps we should show him doing his stuff as a blockade runner . . . we should take this liberty because it is vitally important to dramatize Rhett's activities very clearly and at once." To work in the war background, Howard suggested a series of six

These three pictures were taken by a research photographer who accompanied director George Cukor and Hobe Erwin, the film's original interior decorator, on their trip through the Clayton County section of north Georgia in mid-1937. Margaret Mitchell conducted them on a tour of the area, pointing out portions of the territory where she had placed the fictional plantations of Tara and Twelve Oaks. Remnants of the plantation era were still to be found, including (top) this modest ante-bellum dwelling. The clapboard house (middle) is very similar to Margaret Mitchell's childhood home and is probably much closer to her description of Tara in the novel than what finally emerged in the film—in character, at least, if not in design. The cotton fields (above) were typical of this section of the country.

Oct. 19, 1938

Mr. David O. Selznick
Selznick International Pictures, Inc.,
9336 W. Washington Blvd.,
Culver City, Calif.

Dear Mr. Selznick:

    Mr. Neville Reay, of your
publicity department, has asked me to write
you, giving the results of our "Scarlett O'Hara"
contest.

    Unfortunately, no exact
tabulation was made, but the following information will give you what you want, I believe.

    Out of approximately 70,000
letters, Bette Davis, the favorite, polled close
to half the votes. Katharine Hepburn was second,
with approximately 13,000. Miriam Hopkins ran
third - Margaret Sullavan, fourth - Joan Crawford,
fifth - Barbara Stanwyck, sixth. A great number
of people voted for an unknown actress to play
the role of "Scarlett," and a handful mentioned
Carole Lombard.

    Best regards,

    Sincerely,

    Jimmie Fidler

Dear Sirs —

Please don't spoil "Gone
With the Wind" by putting
Cary Grant in it as Rhett
Butler. What about Frederic
March ?

Yours sincerely —
Sue James

A sampling of the thousands of letters that deluged the studio immediately after it became known that Selznick had purchased the motion picture rights to *Gone With The Wind.* Jimmie Fidler was a gossip columnist whose radio show was popular nationwide.

different montages illustrating the declining fortunes of the South, with vignettes of food and medical scarcities in Atlanta, battle scenes, and the eventual collapse of the Confederacy, with Scarlett midwifing Melanie's baby in a hot, dry, deserted Atlanta, after having run to Dr. Meade for help, only to find him surrounded by the dying remnants of the Confederate Army. Howard ended the first half of his outline with Scarlett returning to Tara, finding her mother dead, her father half mad, and the once verdant land almost totally destroyed. Here he suggested a seventeen-scene montage showing the hazards and back-breaking toil and constant foraging for food endured during the final days of the war by Scarlett and her family and those of the servants left, with her vowing quietly to herself that "as God is my witness, we're going to live through this and when this war is over I'm never going to be hungry again," whereupon she immediately kills a marauding Yankee cavalryman, saying afterwards, "Now we've got a horse and some money and we can get something to eat and some cotton seed to plant." Following the intermission, Howard found himself "seriously troubled with laying out the material of the second half.... Our chief difficulty will come from the lack of organization of the material ... something Miss Mitchell herself is only partially successful at concealing.... In making this Reconstruction part of the picture as vivid as I should like ... the introduction of the Ku Klux Klan is [especially difficult].... Because of the lynching problems we have on our hands these days, I hate to indulge in anything which makes the lynching of a Negro in any sense sympathetic." Scarlett's return to Atlanta for the tax money to save Tara, her rejection by an imprisoned Rhett, her marriage to Frank Kennedy and his death, and Rhett's proposal were all covered quickly and efficiently by Howard. For the final sequence, he wrote that

> unfortunately for our purposes, the novel at this point has nearly two hundred pages of disjointed incident covering some five years and the marriages of Scarlett and Rhett ... the birth and death of Bonnie, the death of Melanie and Scarlett's realization of her imaginary love for Ashley, and her learning that Rhett is through with her ... I have tried my utmost to avoid this doubling of deaths at the end by omitting Bonnie ... but I use her because Rhett's explanation on Page 1031 of the book has, I think, something very like tragic profundity: "... I liked to think that Bonnie was you, a little girl again, before the war and poverty had done things to you. She was so like you, so willful, so brave and gay and full of high spirits, and I could pet her and spoil her—just as I wanted to pet you. But she wasn't like you—she loved me. It was a blessing that I could take the love you didn't want and give it to her ... when she went, she took everything."

Selznick spent most of the Christmas season and the first week of 1937 going over these notes, comparing them with his breakdown of the novel and discussing them with Cukor, replying to Howard on January 6, telling him:

> I am very happy over your approach to the story, rough as it is.... I recognize, perhaps even more than you, the problem of length. I am prepared for a picture that will be extremely long ... as much as 2½ hours . . . but even getting down to this length is going to be tough.... We must prepare to make drastic cuts and these must include some of the characters.... One of the problems we have in *GWTW* is that it is so fresh in people's minds.... I urge you very strongly indeed against making minor changes ... which may give us slight improvements, but there will be five or ten million readers on our heads for them; where for the most part, they will recognize the obvious necessity of our making drastic cuts. I am embarrassed to say this to you who have been so outstandingly successful in your adaptations, but I find myself a producer charged with recreating [the] best-beloved book of our time, and I don't think any of us have ever tackled anything that is really comparable to the love that people have for it.... I certainly urge most strongly against including any sequences in which Rhett is shown "doing his stuff" as a blockade runner. We will be forgiven cuts if we do not invent sequences.... The fact that the book and the picture may be somewhat out of balance in stressing Scarlett for two thirds and Rhett through the last third doesn't worry me.

What was worrying Selznick was the financial investment that seemed to be mushrooming. Howard's preliminary notes had brought home the realization that the unofficial estimate of $2 million might miss the mark by a wide margin.

While waiting for Howard to deliver his first draft, Selznick and his staff were preoccupied with the preparation and production of the next three pictures on the release schedule: *A Star Is Born, The Adventures of Tom Sawyer,* and *The Prisoner of Zenda.* As these moved out of the offices, onto the stages, and finally into the theatres, work proceeded simultaneously on several aspects of *Gone With The Wind.* Barbara Keon, Selznick's script secretary, Lydia Schiller, and several of the other women in the office began breaking the novel down, indexing every major event and action, cross-indexing this for time periods, seasonal changes, the historical background, and then making separate indexes for characterizations, dialogue topics, character relationships, clothing, descriptions of interior and exterior sets, so that even before there was an official script, there were ten detailed reference scripts that could be used as guides in the extensive pre-production work that was obviously going to be necessary. This was still late 1936, and the production department had not yet shaken down into the smooth efficient operation that Selznick hoped it would become. The location problems and the cost overruns on *The Garden of Allah* had frightened Selznick into the realization that the making of *Gone With The Wind* could be a fiasco without a production manager who was considerably more than merely capable. It was early in 1937 that Selznick first began thinking seriously of offering the job to Ray Klune. Klune too had read the book and, "It scared the hell out of me.... There were so many characters, all those relatives and Scarlett had all those kids, you know. But then after I got over my initial shock, and David assured me that they were going to eliminate a lot of the people, I settled down and read it again.... Now I knew we were going to make the picture, nobody, not even David, seemed to know exactly when . . . which I was glad for, because I began thinking about the various methods we could use to get it done and I realized that it was just a vast job of preparation."

In trying to arrive at a reasonable approximation of a budget without a script, Selznick asked each of the department heads to go through the book and break it down into what they considered to be the absolute minimum needed for sets, costumes, and performers. As head of the art department, Lyle Wheeler, with his architectural and illustrative background, not only made a budget for his department but also began working with the illustrators in sketching his ideas for the sets. Over at RKO, Walter Plunkett, with whom Selznick had worked on the beginnings of *Little Women,* was busy on the costumes for *Mary of Scotland* with Katharine Hepburn; at her urging, he had read the book when word filtered out that Selznick had bought it. Plunkett, as he later recalled, "wrote [Selznick] a note begging for the costuming job. An immediate reply asked me to sign a contract, and as soon as I did, Selznick said right at the beginning that I was to work only with him. He didn't want anyone to see the sketches I was going to do. I read the book two more times, making notations of every line and passage containing a reference to clothes or related subjects. Then my secretary read the book to catch any items I might have missed, then we made a script of these notes, and it worked out that there would be almost 5,500 separate items, all of which would have to be made from scratch." Complicating Plunkett's task further was the fact that styles of clothing in the book, especially women's fashion, underwent two visible metamorphoses, from the prewar plantation days with their distinctive billowing hoop skirts, through the improvised look of the impoverished war years, to the bustles of the Reconstruction era. Plunkett's initial breakdown of the story, added to Wheeler's estimate for settings and Klune's projections of the manpower involved in front of and behind the camera, added up to a rough total of $2.5 million—or the entire year's production budget for Selznick International. The figure gave Selznick momentary pause, and he immediately discussed it with Jock Whitney, who bolstered him up by reiterating what he had told him earlier: "The important job we have to do is to make the picture properly and in accordance with public expectation."

According to the publicity fact sheet for the completed picture, "The first script prepared at Selznick International was finished February 20, 1937." But there is no trace of this first draft screenplay in any of the

Val Lewton, Selznick's story editor and the nephew of actress Alla Nazimova. A cultured, literate man, his opinion of the studio's prize property is almost visible in the carefully masked expression on his face: he remarked to several of his associates that the book was "ponderous trash" and thought Selznick was making the biggest mistake of his career. Lewton later went on to greater fame as the producer of *The Cat People* and *I Walked with a Zombie* (which sound like trash but aren't).

Director George Cukor and Sidney Howard, the Pulitzer Prize–winning dramatist to whom Selznick gave the seemingly impossible task of wresting a filmable script from the 1,037 pages of Miss Mitchell's novel. This photo was taken in mid-1937, when Howard was in Culver City working on the third draft of his adaptation with Selznick and Cukor. Howard ended up making three separate trips to Culver City to work on revisions. As late as April 1939, while the film was in production, he was called in by Selznick to work on the construction and dialogue of the second half of the film.

GABLE AS RHETT

PHOTOPLAY THROWS ITS HAT IN THE RING

Herewith we enter the Great Casting Battle of "Gone with the Wind," because to our mind there is but one Rhett—Clark Gable. So sure were we of our choice that we had Vincentini paint this portrait of Clark as we see him in the rôle: cool, impertinent, utterly charming. We like all the other handsome actors mentioned as Rhett—only we don't want them as Rhett. We want Gable and we're going to stick to that regardless

of any kind is nowhere more evident in this script than in the scenes of Scarlett's return to Tara to find her mother dead, her father crazy, her sisters near death, and the plantation devastated. Howard illustrated all this by having Scarlett ask her father, "Where's Mother?" Her father replies, "We buried your mother yesterday." This was followed by an immediate dissolve to Mammy and Pork, the two remaining house servants. As Mammy strokes Scarlett's hands and notices the calluses, she lectures her on the fact "dat you can allus tell a lady by her han's." Whereupon Scarlett lashes out with:

> Fiddledee-dee! What good are ladies now? What good are gentleness and breeding? I came home for Ma's comfort and guidance and she isn't here to give them, and nothing she ever taught me will help me now. Better I'd learned to pick cotton like a darky. Mother was wrong! We were all wrong, Mammy! We've all got to work now! And plow and sow and weed and pick cotton like field hands. . . . Anyone who won't work here can go with the Yankees! Tara's all I've got left and I'm going to keep it . . . if I have to break every back on the place! It's like my Pa once said to me—after all, land *is* the only thing that lasts!

Here the sequence faded out, Howard having jettisoned his first choice of Scarlett's vow in favor of this more subdued climax.

This bothered Selznick greatly, for he felt that the whole core of Scarlett's character and her transformation lay in these sequences, and that if they did not match up to the indelible impression left by the novel, then no matter how much effort they put into every other aspect, the picture was doomed to failure. It was imperative, he felt, to capture the essence of the twenty-eight pages that it took Miss Mitchell to describe, in some of the best writing in the book, the hopelessness of Scarlett's situation, which begins with her absolute, pathetic defeat at finding

> Tara . . . acres desolate, barns ruined, like a body bleeding under her eyes. . . . This was the end of the road, quivering old age, sickness, hungry mouths, helpless hands plucking at her skirts. And at the end of this road, there was nothing—nothing but Scarlett O'Hara Hamilton, nineteen years old, a widow with a little child. . . . She was seeing things with new eyes for, somewhere along the long road to Tara, she had left her girlhood behind her. She was no longer plastic clay, yielding imprint to each new experience. The clay had hardened, some time in this indeterminate day which had lasted a thousand years. . . . She was a woman now and youth was gone. . . . When she arose at last and saw again the black ruins . . . her head was raised high and something that was youth and beauty and potential tenderness had gone out of her face forever. What was past was past. . . . There was no going back and she was going forward. . . .

The scene ends with Scarlett saying: "As God is my witness . . . the Yankees aren't going to lick me. I'm going to live through this, and when it's over, I'm never going to be hungry again. No, nor any of my folks. If I have to steal or kill—as God is my witness, I'm never going to be hungry again."

It was this sense of futility, of change and determination and courage writ in romantic theatrical images, that Selznick felt was missing not only in this crucial section but throughout the entire screenplay, and he was determined to keep working with Howard until all these elements were somehow captured. So Howard reluctantly made the trip westward to Culver City, spending most of the spring and summer of 1937 in daily sessions with Selznick as the two men struggled to reconcile their opposing styles and to merge the best of their dramatic instincts.

As Howard traveled west, George Cukor was swinging in a wide arc through the South retracing Kay Brown's trail, looking at promising potential Scarletts and Melanies and spending several days in Atlanta, where Margaret Mitchell took him on a tour of the various locales of the story in and around the city. Cukor's passion for research and atmosphere was well served by Miss Mitchell, who spent several days showing him and his two assistants the distinctive red earth of Clayton County and some of the old homes that had been built before Sherman marched through Georgia, giving them a tour of the area outside Jonesboro to the approximate locations of both Tara and Twelve Oaks.

Cukor was accompanied on this trip by Hobe Erwin, one of the

Selznick files; the earliest script in the collection is dated August 1937, and it is probably as close to Howard's original as there is. This "first completed version" follows the story from the opening with sixteen-year-old Scarlett and the Tarleton twins at Tara to the ending twelve years later in Atlanta with Rhett leaving Scarlett after telling her: "I wish I cared what happens to you, but I don't." Scarlett then turns for comfort to Mammy, who assures her, "He'll come back . . . ain' I always been right before?"; and Scarlett tells Mammy, "We'll go home to Tara, Mammy . . . I'll get strength from Tara and I'll think of some way to get him back. After all, tomorrow is . . . another day." It was largely a straightforward literal rendering of the book. The scenes were primarily dialogue sequences, with the dialogue usually taken from Miss Mitchell's original. As a dramatist, Howard did not care for the large gesture or heavily dramatic moments, and the script is largely a succession of almost polite conversations and understated drama—an interesting, intimate, and spare version of the story, but to Selznick, not theatrical enough; he felt it missed the high emotionalism and heady romanticism that permeated the novel. An even greater problem was discovered after Hal Kern had broken the script down scene by scene, timing these individually: when added up, the estimated running time of the picture was almost five and a half hours.

But in spite of its shortcomings, this script was a beginning and Selznick liked enough of it to know that at least they were on the right track. As with every other one of his projects it needed, he felt, extensive rewriting, eliminating some sequences and some of the seventy-nine separate speaking roles that Howard had written in. Conversely, although he was pleased with Howard's handling of the main narrative line for Scarlett, Melanie, Rhett, and Ashley, Selznick was disappointed with the lack of impact in the war scenes in and around Atlanta. Howard's penchant for throwing away drama and avoiding ringing climaxes leading interior decorators in the country, who had a respected, prosperous business in New York. Erwin dabbled in motion pictures; he had worked with Cukor on *Little Women* and had gained his confidence and respect. After a period of protracted negotiations, Erwin was signed to an unusual contract that gave Selznick "the right to consult with [Erwin] in the East between now and the date we designate for starting [production] without compensation. After start of production we will guarantee him $5,000 for ten weeks work," his salaried services to commence "not earlier than August 1, 1937, and no later than July 15, 1938," a clause that indicates when Selznick hoped to start and finish the production. Cukor and Erwin, through the efforts of Miss Mitchell, were given access to some of the more outstanding houses in Atlanta. But after touring them through the outlying regions of the city, Miss Mitchell commented in a letter to Kay Brown:

> I am sure they were dreadfully disappointed . . . for they had been expecting architecture such as appeared in the screen version of *So Red the Rose* . . . and this section of North Georgia was new and crude compared with other sections of the South, and white columns are the exception rather than the rule. I besought them to please leave Tara ugly, sprawling, columnless and they agreed. I imagine, however, that when it comes to Twelve Oaks they will put columns all around the house and make it as large as our new city auditorium.

As Cukor wound up his tour, Walter Plunkett began his. If Cukor had an appreciation for research, Plunkett had a perfectionist's devotion to it. He loved discovering the details of craftsmanship, the look and feel of the past as expressed by the styles, the fabrics of clothing and its accessories. Selznick knew of Plunkett's mania for perfection and had not been above taking advantage of this zeal. The contract he negotiated with Plunkett called for the designer to work on the research and designs for three months with no compensation, and after production started, to work for $750 weekly. Plunkett's trip to Atlanta was entirely at his own expense and on his own initiative; he took along his notes on costumes and discussed them at great length with Margaret Mitchell and, as he recalled, "she was very amused when I showed her that she had described almost every dress of Scarlett's as green." Miss Mitchell arranged meetings for him with some of the more notable dowagers of Atlanta society, a number of whom had trunks full of clothing of the pre- and post–Civil War periods. Plunkett was in his element, "handling and sketching these museum pieces"; he was even allowed to clip sample swatches from the seams of the garments so that the fabric could be reproduced for use in the picture. "One woman in Charleston," recalls Plunkett, "even sent her children out to gather a box full of thorns from a tree native to that area . . . because during the blockade days of the war, there were no metal pins and clothing was held together by these thorns."

As Plunkett completed his research and left the South, word came in May 1937 that Margaret Mitchell had been awarded the Pulitzer Prize for fiction. This, coupled with an earlier announcement that *Gone With The Wind* had been selected as the most distinguished novel of 1936 by the American Booksellers Association, created a second stampede to the bookstores, so that by the middle of 1937, one year after publication, sales of the novel had reached the astonishing figure of 1,375,000, with no let-up in sight, confirming the book's unofficial status as a modern classic. In mid-1937 Selznick noticed an increasing number of demands that the part of Rhett Butler should be played by Clark Gable. Earlier, there had of course been the calls for Ronald Colman, some for Fredric March, and surprisingly even for Basil Rathbone, whom numerous Southerners, according to Margaret Mitchell, considered perfect for the part. (Miss Mitchell, who managed to maintain a sense of humor about this national mania, commented privately that she personally would like to see Rhett played by either Groucho Marx or Donald Duck.) But it was Gable who began to dominate the daily flood of mail throughout 1937, especially after the widespread success of *San Francisco* in which his character of Blackie Norton had much the same appeal as that of Rhett Butler—a proud, iconoclastic outcast; rough, tough, but with a touch of class about him and a final vulnerability that allowed him to be humbled by his love for a woman. MGM had Gable tightly locked under contract; when Selznick first approached Louis B. Mayer to investigate the possi-

Drawings by Vincentini

IS THIS SCARLETT?

Again Vincentini scores—with this picture of Scarlett, as Photoplay conceived her. The prime requisite was, we told him, that Scarlett must be in Gable's arms, for, you see, we still insist on Clark as Rhett. For the rest, she must have the fire of Paulette Goddard; the acting ability of Shearer; the voice of Alicia Rhett, Southern girl candidate, whose name is really identical with the hero's. The artist, we believe, has endowed her with all these qualities, and a few individual charms of her own, for isn't she still Scarlett O'Hara, Miss Unknown? Now turn the page and read her story

bilities of Gable playing the part, he was told it could be arranged in one of two ways: Selznick could come to MGM and make the picture as an MGM production; or MGM would loan Gable to Selznick and put up half the estimated $2.5 million cost of the film in return for distribution rights and 50 percent of the net proceeds for seven years. Neither of these options was particularly appealing to Selznick, although the second proposal was not absolutely out of the question. But he was under contractual obligation to release his pictures through United Artists until 1939, which meant a delay of almost two years if he wanted Gable badly enough. Warner Bros. offered to give him Errol Flynn, Bette Davis, and Olivia de Havilland for the principal parts, asking only 25 percent of the profits, but this was not given more than momentary consideration by Selznick. Bette Davis was not Scarlett O'Hara by any stretch of his imagination, and he remarked to intimates that he would give the part to Katharine Hepburn before he'd give it to Davis. The only other real possibility for Rhett was Gary Cooper, and that might be arranged, as Cooper was under contract to Sam Goldwyn, who in addition to being a close friend of Selznick's was also tied up in the United Artists fold. As to the differences in suitability of Gable and Cooper for the part, Selznick later commented: "They were the two great symbols of their time . . . they each had different appeals. Clark was the great sex image, as well as having an extremely virile appeal . . . whereas Gary was the symbol of America. The extraordinary thing about both was that men liked them as well as women, so there was no resentment by the men at women in the audience falling in love with them. . . . And more importantly, at least as far as the underlying character of Rhett Butler was concerned, both Gable and Cooper were always gentlemen in the true sense of the word." So Selznick, and ultimately Jock Whitney, began working on Goldwyn to let them have Gary Cooper. But Goldwyn, for reasons that have never

These costume sketches by Walter Plunkett were done in early 1938 on the basis of his several readings of the novel and the first Sidney Howard script. Plunkett's attention to detail is evident not only in the design of the costumes but in his careful renderings of the personalities of the various characters as described by Miss Mitchell, and they probably influenced Selznick's ideas of what the performers should look like. Almost all of these designs were used in the final picture.

been made clear, was opposed to the idea and let the negotiations die of neglect, leaving Selznick with no choice but to try to make a more equitable deal with Mayer and MGM.

One of the schizophrenic aspects of Hollywood has always been the way in which the closest of friends, even blood relations, would give no quarter in their business dealings with each other. These men were completely unsentimental, using personal knowledge of each other's affairs and misfortunes to try to get the upper hand and squeeze every single possible benefit and concession to themselves out of their deal-making. Selznick, no slouch when it came time to be ruthless, found himself outmatched by the intractability of Mayer's terms. As Merian Cooper explained it: "We couldn't make the picture and satisfy the public without Gable.... The Whitneys didn't need Metro's money and we didn't need their distribution . . . but because of Gable, we were forced into making a deal with them." Cooper errs in stating that they didn't need MGM's distribution; next to Gable, it was the most attractive and ultimately valuable aspect of the eventual MGM contract. United Artists, because of poor organization, insufficient manpower and resources, never did have the kind of selling organization that inspired Selznick's confidence. If he and Whitney were going to risk several millions of their dollars, their reputations, and years of their lives, then a deal with MGM at least would minimize the possibilities of not collecting all the money there was to be had in the movie marketplace. So in mid-1938, after months of negotiations, soul-searching, and debates back and forth with Whitney and the other executives, Selznick resignedly chose to take MGM's offer, deciding that Gable, half the production costs, and the distribution set-up might be worth 50 percent of the profits.

All during 1937 and well into 1938, Selznick and Sidney Howard had labored together and separately, in Culver City and New York, over the second, third, and fourth drafts of Howard's original, with the avowed intent of getting it down to filmable proportions. In an effort to gain another perspective, Selznick asked Hal Kern to go over the latest version and recommend where cuts might be made. Kern recalls that

"David asked me to do this . . . and he had Metro's script department do an estimate too. Timing scripts is a process involving taking the shooting script, sitting down with a stopwatch, and conjuring up the action and reading the dialogue out loud, much as you'd visualize it being done from what you know of pace and speed in the staging. On *Gone With The Wind,* the script David gave me in mid-1938 I estimated would run about 26,000 feet, or something like four hours and twenty minutes. MGM's estimate was 29,000 feet, and David asked me why theirs was so different from ours, and I had to tell him that they were timing at what they knew to be Cukor's tempo, which was invariably slower than most, while I was just timing at what I thought would be the ideal tempo, one that allowed us to do a picture without too much drag in it. He wanted to know if there was anything I felt we could cut, and I told him that I had spent hours at home going over it, trying to come up with something that I could tell him was too long." Kern felt the cuts would have to come in the subsidiary characters, and the background events of the Civil War. This latter was covered by six montages in the latest script, put in largely at Selznick's insistence to illustrate the worsening fortunes of the South, its defeat and surrender, Lincoln's assassination, and the subsequent arrival in the South of the perils of the Carpetbaggers, the military occupation, and the humiliation of Reconstruction.

The biggest problem with making these suggestions was the confusion they caused Selznick: he truly did not want to drop anything that was already in the script; he just wanted to tighten and improve it, and especially the dialogue, insisting that Howard not invent new dialogue but use Miss Mitchell's whenever possible. When Howard demurred, Selznick would put it in himself, and Howard, finally wearying of the mess of day-long conferences, constant changes of mind and approach by Selznick, fled disgustedly to New York in October. Selznick followed him to Manhattan, where he insisted the two continue working while Howard rehearsed his new play, *The Ghost of Yankee Doodle.*

In Culver City, keeping track of the permutations of the various drafts and alternate versions of scenes became the task of Lydia Schiller, who recalls

being more and more roped into the enormous detail of things . . . following one character throughout the book, sitting in on story conferences, taking notes. Then I was assigned as script girl and moved into George Cukor's office and worked with him on pre-production, and worked with Eric Stacey, the assistant director, on breaking down the script, laying all the sequences out on a production board, and all those thousands of details. As time passed, we were all amazed at how the thing kept mushrooming. David's ideas were very costly . . . what he planned to do, it seemed, would absolutely break the company. . . . He didn't have the backing of any of his executives . . . they all called it Selznick's folly. . . . Whitney gave him support and his wife Irene, he leaned a great deal on her opinions . . . but everybody else, I think even Danny O'Shea [Selznick's attorney] thought that this was the greatest mistake he'd ever made.

Selznick too was very aware that one false and unconsidered move could result in the kind of mistake that Lydia Schiller talks about. After the script, the casting remained the most troublesome aspect, especially insofar as his announced decision to "give the American public a new girl, if possible. To this end," said Selznick, "I have spent close to $50,000. . . . Between George Cukor and myself we have seen practically every bit player and young actress that was even remotely a possibility . . . as well as hundreds and even thousands that were not. . . . We have had readings, we have made tests, we have trained girls who looked right, but whose talent was uncertain. Not only that but we have had the cooperation of every other studio in town trying to find a new girl, since I promised . . . that if they succeeded in finding me a girl they could have an occasional picture with her. . . ." In June 1938, evidently weakening in his own resolve, Selznick sent up a trial balloon announcing to the press that Clark Gable and Norma Shearer would be playing the leads in the picture. The reaction was much worse than he anticipated: Shearer, said the letters and columnists, was too old, she was too reserved and ladylike, too much the screen *grande dame* to play the part. Shearer listened to her fans and turned down Selznick's tentative offer, saying, "Scarlett is a

thankless role; the one I'd like to play is Rhett." Terrified lest the publicity backfire and turn public opinion against the project, Selznick gave orders that no more information was to be sent out on the picture, "not one single word . . . that is not an official and final announcement."

All during the spring and summer of 1938, while he was spending five hours a day with Howard working on the script, and wrestling with the Gable-MGM decision, Selznick was still actively occupied with the two pictures he had in production, *The Young in Heart* and *Made for Each Other.* Both were relatively simple to make in that, being fairly economical modern stories, they did not demand the hours of attention that he was devoting to *Gone With The Wind.* Selznick had Lyle Wheeler and his illustrators begin roughing out sketches not only of the sets, but also of the lighting compositions and the camera angles, in the belief that this would save time and money. The idea had come to Selznick when he had heard Merian Cooper relate what Walt Disney was doing on his feature-length cartoon *Snow White and the Seven Dwarfs.* Cooper had been impressed with Disney's "story-boarding" technique and remembered having done somewhat the same thing with *King Kong.* Selznick's decision to have a live-action feature script done completely in sketch form was innovative, although the approach had been used for years on individual sequences and on musical numbers or other scenes that needed careful organization and special effects.

Selznick now began looking for someone who could take over the coordination of the composition and color design of the entire picture. He found him in mid-1937 in the person of William Cameron Menzies, one of the industry's pioneer art directors, who had designed the silent Fairbanks fantasy *The Thief of Bagdad,* and had gone on to become one of the most influential visual talents working in the American film industry. Selznick detailed his plans for Menzies in a memo to Jock Whitney in September 1937:

I feel we need a man of Menzies' talent and enormous experience on the sets of this picture and on its physical production. . . . What I want on *Gone With The Wind* and what has been done only a few times in picture history (and these times mostly by Menzies) is a complete script in sketch form. . . . This is a mammoth job that Menzies will have to work on very closely with Cukor. I also want him to design and lay out and in large degree actually direct the montage sequences. In short, it is my plan to have the whole physical side of the picture . . . personally handled by one man, and that man Menzies . . . who may turn out to be one of the most valuable factors in properly producing this picture.

Selznick was also deep in discussion with Henry Ginsberg and Ray Klune about the limitations of their present studio set-up. The company was still leasing production space from RKO-Pathé on a picture-by-picture basis, but after they took over Pioneer's commitments, it was obvious that this arrangement would be inadequate. Accordingly, Selznick International leased the entire studio for one year beginning in mid-1937. A year later, regardless of a $33,000 loss from this operation, the agreement was renewed over the opposition of Sonny Whitney and other board members who wanted to go back to the old, less expensive arrangement. Selznick, however, contended that "it would be impossible to produce *Gone With The Wind* under the old basis because of the size of the picture and the inadequacy of the equipment of the Pathé studio. Accordingly, I think we should exercise our option on the studio for another year . . . and proceed to build up our key personnel and purchase essential equipment with the view to having sufficient capable people and equipment to tackle a picture of the magnitude of *Gone With The Wind.*"

One of these "key" people Selznick was referring to was Jack Cosgrove of the small but vitally important "special effects," or—as it was usually referred to in the industry—"trick" department. Every major studio of the time had one, and it was their existence that made possible much of the scope and grandeur of pictures of that era. By use of paintings, glass shots, double exposures, process backgrounds, and a whole range of other technical tricks, they made it possible for just about anything that could be dreamed up by a writer and director to be put onto film convincingly—the most celebrated case of this being *King*

(Top, right) Production manager Raymond Klune, Daniel T. O'Shea, David Selznick, and his executive secretary, Betty Baldwin, in one of their few nonfrantic moments, going over still another draft of the script. (Above) Jack Cosgrove, the special effects wizard to whom fell most of the task of supplying *Gone With The Wind* with its epic production values, shown here with one of the two specially built machines that enabled him to accomplish this. This modified 35 mm projector had a light source several times more powerful than any projector then in existence, allowing him to beam the image from one machine directly into the lens of another and making possible the copying of color process plates and matte paintings with no appreciable loss of color. (Top, left) Art director Lyle Wheeler and David Selznick going over some of the sketches drawn by Wheeler and his staff. (Above, left) Wheeler and William Cameron Menzies, the guiding genius behind the dramatic Technicolor look of *Gone With The Wind*. It was Menzies who gave the film its carefully stylized visuals, tying the disparate sequences together with his eye for color and composition. His sketches indicating color mood and lighting design were gone over carefully by Lyle Wheeler, who turned them into workable master drawings, adding to them his detailed renderings of both exterior and interior set designs. (Left) Wilbur Kurtz, a walking encyclopedia on the Civil War in north Georgia. He was also a close friend of Margaret Mitchell and at her suggestion had been hired by Selznick International to oversee the details not only of the history but also of the sets. He gave Selznick, Wheeler, and Cukor detailed descriptions and drawings of the city of Atlanta, farm implements, and household items; among other things, he wrote a 32-page description of a typical Southern barbecue of the pre–Civil War era. It was Kurtz who supplied the studio construction staff with the blueprints for the distinctive barrel-vaulted Atlanta train station. A skilled architect and illustrator, Kurtz is seen here with one of his renderings, a painting of Twelve Oaks, which he did not design but whose conception benefited from his suggestions.

Twelve of the 1,500 production sketches made to guide the director and cinematographers in obtaining the proper look and feel of *Gone With The Wind*. (First row) Menzies sketched this version of the opening scene, showing Scarlett and the Tarleton twins on the porch of Tara; Gerald O'Hara's evening gallop home from Twelve Oaks and the family at prayer were done by J. McMillan Johnson. (Second row) Scarlett eavesdropping on the staircase at Twelve Oaks was done by Dorothea Holt; it underwent considerable revision before it was used in the film. The waltzing couples at the Atlanta bazaar and Scarlett trying on the green bonnet given to her by Rhett are both the work of Dorothea Holt. (Third row) The population of Atlanta waiting in front of the telegraph office for news from Gettysburg and the sketch of the battlefield through which Scarlett travels on her way back to Tara are by Johnson. Scarlett being greeted by her half-crazed father is by Menzies. (Fourth row) Scarlett and Melanie hovering over the body of the Yankee cavalryman Scarlett has just shot is also by Menzies. The sketch of Rhett and Scarlett's Atlanta home under construction is by Johnson, and Scarlett's ornate, garish bedroom in the house is the work of Dorothea Holt.

Kong. As Selznick grew more deeply immersed in the production aspects of *Gone With The Wind,* it became apparent to him that "I could not even hope to put the picture on the screen properly without an even more extensive use of special effects than had ever before been attempted in the business.... In the preparation of the script... I made it part of my business to look for and to conceive opportunities for furthering the spectacle values and improve [*sic*] the production design of the picture.... I calculate that there will be over one hundred trick shots in *Gone With The Wind* ... so we had better be prepared to invest substantial amounts of money to upgrade our equipment in this department."

While, at Selznick's urging, Cosgrove was experimenting with ways of extending the effectiveness of Technicolor trick work, Ray Klune and Lyle Wheeler looked for ways to economically accomplish the production of the hundreds of sketches that were coming out of the Menzies department. Wheeler recalls that the Menzies sketches "were difficult technically . . . they were very stylized . . . but we strove to keep that feeling . . . and still make it real enough so that you thought you were there.... David was very particular because he had certain scenes that were in his mind, certain color feelings, shadows, realistic or unrealistic, that he wanted . . . so we did an awful lot of tests just to see how these color and lighting effects would work out."

One of the biggest hurdles faced by the art department was in locating accurate photos and other visual evidence of Atlanta's past, since so much had been destroyed by the fire of November 1864. The research department of Selznick International was headed by a woman named Lillian Deighton, who was diligent and exhaustive in her labors, but the material was just not there. For help, Selznick turned to Miss Mitchell, who despite her desire not to become involved was nevertheless anxious to do everything she could to help make the picture as historically accurate as possible. She had remarked that she "didn't care what they do to the story, I just hope [they] don't distort the history.... Southerners are indignant when our history is portrayed improperly." So when Selznick's request reached her, she responded by saying she could be of no help herself but strongly recommended that Selznick get hold of Wilbur Kurtz of Atlanta, whom she considered the greatest authority on the Civil War in the area, and who also had a fine collection of early Atlanta pictures. Kurtz was brought out to the studio in January 1938 and stayed for several weeks, helping Menzies and Wheeler with the visual layouts of Atlanta and the fictional plantations. In his diaries, Kurtz relates, "As to Tara . . . Mr. Cukor, who had seen Clayton County . . . knew that plantation houses down there at best were nothing wonderful, but since Tara was also fictional . . . they both indicated that the house should be 'warmed up' a bit. 'After all,' said Mr. Selznick, 'the Atlanta and Clayton County audiences are a very small percentage.' This indicated . . . to me . . . that he was taking the larger view of things and playing up—or down—somewhat to the general . . . preconceived ideas of the world-at-large about things Southern. Maybe he's right...."

By now almost two years had elapsed since Selznick had bought the book, and while he had been active on other projects, George Cukor had not made a picture since *Camille.* Through most of this period, he had been occupied with preparations for *Gone With The Wind*—an expensive layoff, for Cukor had been on salary at Selznick International all that time at the rate of $4,000 a week, making it likely, as Selznick pointed out, that

we are in danger of paying him about $300,000 for his services on *Gone With The Wind....* Regardless of his great abilities... I am fearful that he is [becoming] an expensive luxury.... George's statement is that this is not his fault . . . that he could have done pictures . . . but we have not forced him to do pictures.... When I first tackled *A Star Is Born,* I spoke to George about doing it and he didn't feel that he wanted to do a Hollywood picture . . . when we took H. C. Potter off *Tom Sawyer* . . . George didn't want to do it . . . when we needed him for another picture he preferred to direct Garbo.... I think the biggest black mark against our management to date is the Cukor situation and we can no longer be sentimental about it.... We are a business concern and not patrons of the arts....

What Selznick failed to mention here was his own constant reiteration

The two sketches above show different versions of the staircase in the postwar Atlanta house of Rhett and Scarlett and give a good example of Selznick's and Wheeler's insistence on re-doing the drawings until each was satisfied. The final version (below) was modeled by Lyle Wheeler after a grand staircase from a mansion in the Nob Hill section of San Francisco, possibly the Flood or Crocker home. Dramatically compelling, it became the focus of much of the action of the last third of the film. (Property man Arden Cripe is on the staircase with Vivien Leigh, Cammie King, and Hattie McDaniel.)

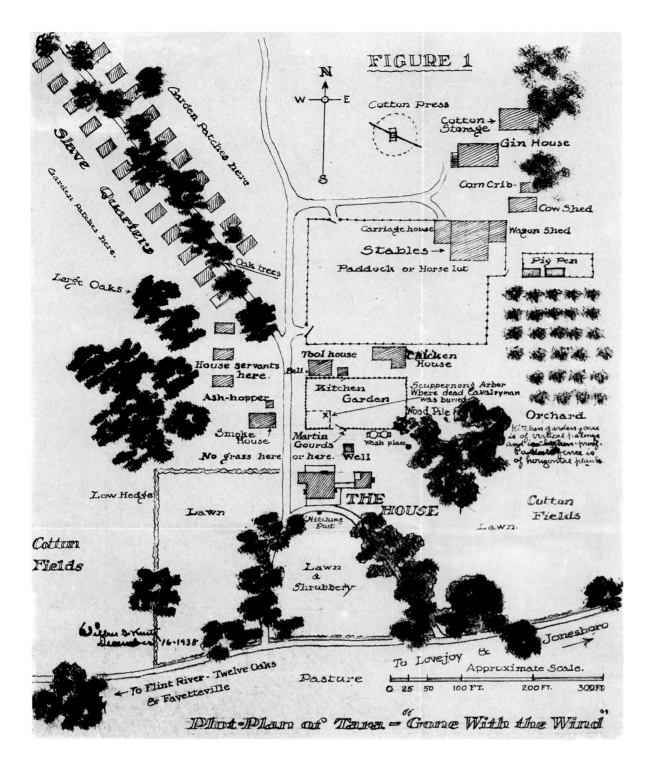

FIGURE 1

N
W·E
S

Plot-Plan of Tara – "Gone With the Wind"

Wilbur Kurtz drew up this plot plan of Tara and its environs from descriptions provided by Margaret Mitchell. It played an important part in giving a proper sense of direction in the staging of all of the scenes at the plantation, keeping the art director and cameramen and directors consistent in their use of sunlight, arrivals and departures, and camera angles.

that *Gone With The Wind* was to go into production "shortly," and his reluctance to let Cukor take on any outside projects that might conflict with the somewhat vague starting date. As the winter of 1937–38 gave way to spring and Selznick still did not have a satisfactory script or even a hint of a Scarlett O'Hara, he resolved part of his financial worries about Cukor by lending him to Columbia Pictures to direct Katharine Hepburn and Cary Grant in an adaptation of Philip Barry's play *Holiday*.

While Cukor was off at Columbia, Selznick was suddenly confronted with a long-simmering, potentially unpleasant controversy concerning *Gone With The Wind*—both the book and the picture to be made from it. Around the studio this was euphemistically referred to as "the Negro problem," and it had its origins in the feelings of many blacks about the way in which their history and sensibilities had been portrayed in the novel. As early as April 1937, Selznick had started receiving clippings from the many Negro newspapers and magazines of the time, which were not exactly hospitable to the work. One criticism from Dora Popel in *The Journal of Negro Life* commented that "the general outline of the history is true . . . but Miss Mitchell's presentation of Civil War and Reconstruction problems is unwarrantedly biased. . . . In her array of 'Mammies,' 'Cookies,' 'Porks,' and 'Sams' one sees only ebony black Negroes . . . who had been docile and childlike as slaves become suddenly impudent and vicious as 'free issue' Negroes." Another reviewer,

L. D. Reddick in *The Journal of Negro History,* stated: "This book no doubt is honestly written . . . but at the same time . . . it is written with a passionate sectional and racial bias. It is almost painfully weak in the handling of the larger social forces implicit in the materials." Selznick and Howard had gone out of their way to see that in the picture, at least, "Negroes come out on the right side of the ledger," removing the Ku Klux Klan and any other scenes that could be remotely construed as anti-Negro propaganda. Unfortunately, however, the script that they had prepared made use of the anathematic term "nigger" in the dialogue scenes, and the few readings that had been held to cast Mammy and the other black character parts had quietly enraged the performers who had been forced to utter the term. Their outrage had been transmitted to the headquarters of the National Association for the Advancement of Colored People, which promptly launched a campaign against both the picture and Selznick, with editorials in all the leading black papers exhorting their readers to boycott the picture and to write letters demanding that all the black characters in the picture be removed. This was not quite the tempest that it would be today, for at that time blacks were at the very bottom of the economic and social spectrum, except for the privileged few who made good in the entertainment and educational worlds and were considered "a credit to their race."

Selznick was certainly no bigot, but he did subscribe to the prevailing liberal ethic of the time, which treated blacks with "dignity" yet kept them in their place. When the first wave of letters and editorial protests broke over his head, he was surprised, bewildered, and a little angry—and also a little fearful. He had a long memory of the race riots over *The Birth of a Nation,* and the thought of any such controversy surrounding *Gone With The Wind* caused him anguish on both a personal and a corporate level. "I feel this particularly keenly," he wrote to Jock Whitney,

> because it might have repercussions not simply on the picture and not simply upon the company and upon me personally, but on the Jews of America as a whole among the Negro race. . . . I think these are no times in which to offend any race or people. . . . I feel so keenly about what is happening to the Jews of the world that I cannot help but sympathize with the Negroes in their fears, however unjustified they may be, about material which they regard as insulting or damaging. I personally think it most important that we should go after prominent space in all the Negro journals, both local and national, to not merely obviate the possibility of further trouble and resentment but contradict and cure any impression that presently exists . . . that the picture will be derogatory. . . . We must explain how sympathetic we are and that the only Negro characters in the picture . . . are treated with great dignity . . . and that the only liberties we have taken with the book . . . is [*sic*] to improve the Negro position in the picture . . . that we have not characterized any of the Negroes as mean or bad and that they have nothing to worry about as far as a pro-slave angle is concerned or anything else and that we have the greatest friendship toward them and their cause. *I am most anxious to remove any impression (which I am sure is very wide-spread) that Gone With The Wind, this company and I personally are enemies of the Negroes* [Selznick's emphasis].

A number of influential black reporters were brought out to the studio and personally assured by Selznick that all offensive terms would be removed from the script; he hedged a bit on their suggestion that he hire a black technical adviser because, as he remarked in a memo to Whitney, "we're surrounded now on all sides by advisers . . . one more will only confuse us . . . and such a person would probably want to remove what comedy we have built around the Negroes . . . no matter how lovable we have made them." The reporters left the studio extolling their treatment and assuring Selznick that the 3 million readers of the Negro papers would "give us their blessings and pray for us nightly." For the time being, at least, as Selznick remarked, "the situation seems to be well in hand."

Cukor, having finished *Holiday* quickly, reported back to the studio and immediately began an intensive round of screen tests trying to find the elusive Scarlett. These tests were valuable for two reasons: first, Cukor's direction of them was his own sort of homework/rehearsal, to see how the scenes played, how they could be blocked and staged, which portions of the script would work and which needed further refinement. They were also helpful in that they gave Selznick and Hal Kern an indication of the tempo and pacing that the picture would be played in, and in this respect Selznick was greatly worried, for as he pointed out to George, "I hope you will realize more fully than you do, just how far I have to go in cutting the script and just how far you have to go with tempo. . . . I am frantic to learn that the latest test of the Scarlett-Ashley paddock scene is not shorter than the last time you did it . . . but actually is twenty feet longer." Pace and tempo aside, however, the most important aspect of these tests was still to turn up an actress who was young enough, fresh enough, and talented enough to play the part. So far, Selznick felt that

> the failure to find a new girl is the greatest failure of my entire career. . . . It would be shocking if the starting date rolls around and we have found neither a Scarlett nor a Melanie nor an Ashley and have to resort to people that have been dug up from high schools and God knows where else. . . . Certainly I would give anything if we had Olivia de Havilland under contract to us so that we could cast her for Melanie. . . . It is a long time since George has seen her sister Joan Fontaine . . . she certainly should have readings. . . . Our best Melanie

to date is, I think, Dorothy Jordan. I am . . . depressed about the Ashley situation and I feel our snobbish attitude about newcomers may have cost us a great performance by a great star. . . . I suppose our best possibilities, depressing as it seems, are Leslie Howard and Melvyn Douglas. . . . All we have to do is line up a complete cast of such people . . . and we can have a lovely picture for release eight years ago. Concerning Scarlett, I think our best possibilities at the moment are Jean Arthur, Loretta Young, Doris Jordan, Katharine Hepburn and Paulette Goddard.

This was written in late July 1938, and Paulette Goddard was just finishing her first major role for Selznick in *The Young in Heart,* her only other part of any importance prior to this having been in Chaplin's 1936 *Modern Times.* She and Chaplin were living together, supposedly as man and wife, a situation that no one looked into too closely. She was attractive, intelligent, with a kind of sparkling insouciance about her personality that carried over into her screen appearances. In her tests, she was the most appealing of all the women they had tested so far, and both Cukor and Selznick felt that with considerable coaching she might make a credible Scarlett. Around the studio, she was considered by most of the staff to be the probable choice. But not everybody was delighted with this idea. Russell Birdwell, in particular, had harsh words about the choice:

> Strictly from a publicity standpoint, I can not go too strongly on record in opposing the proposed selection of Paulette Goddard for the role of Scarlett O'Hara. . . . I must warn you of the tremendous avalanche of criticism which will befall us and the picture should Paulette be given this part. . . . It will throw us under the shadow of such a resentful press that all of our good public relations work of the past will be completely dissipated. I have never known a woman, intent on a career dependent upon her popularity with masses, to hold and live such an insane and absurd attitude toward the press and her fellow man as does Paulette Goddard. . . . The girl who gets the part . . . must be prepared to have her life laid bare in cold black type. This, Goddard is neither willing nor able to do. Briefly, I think she is dynamite which will explode in our very faces if she is given the part.

If Selznick vacillated and felt like a failure over Scarlett, he was at least positive about Rhett Butler, and in August 1938 he announced at a very formal contract signing that he had arranged with MGM to borrow Clark Gable for the part. On the day of the signing he sent a special memo to every department at the studio, assuring them that "the contracts that have been signed with Loew's, Inc. for the release of *Gone With The Wind* in no way affect its identity as a Selznick International picture or its production on this lot. You will, accordingly, please continue uninterruptedly on your work on this picture, which will definitely start production between November 15 and January 15." Separately, in a small handwritten note to Cukor, Selznick advised him to "Please call Clark Gable on your own, and tell him how happy you are, etc. Start that relationship!"

Gable's contract stipulated that Selznick pay him $4,500 per week plus a bonus of $16,666. Gable had not wanted the part, commenting that

> everybody had their own idea of what Rhett should be like. . . . It was annoying to have people look painfully surprised when I said that I hadn't read [the book]. When I finally did read it, I saw very clearly what I was in for . . . and I was scared stiff. . . . Miss Mitchell had etched Rhett into the minds of millions of people . . . it would be impossible to satisfy them all. . . . The public interest in my playing Rhett puzzled me. . . . I was the only one, apparently, who didn't take it for granted I was going to play the part. . . . I knew what was coming the day that David called me. . . . He put his cards on the table . . . he was going to try to get me from MGM if he could . . . but I like to pick my spots and now found myself trapped by a series of circumstances over which I had no control . . . it was a funny feeling. . . . I think I know now how a fly must react after being caught in a spider web. . . . Rhett was simply too big an order. . . . I didn't want any part of him.

As an actor Gable was, in spite of his phenomenal fame, still extremely insecure. It was only after being persuaded by Carole Lombard, with whom he was romantically involved, and MGM's lure of the large

August 24, 1938—Louis B. Mayer and David Selznick sign the contract by which MGM gave Selznick $1.25 million and the services of Clark Gable for the role of Rhett Butler. In return MGM obtained the distribution rights to the picture for five years plus 50 percent of the profits, while Loew's, Inc., MGM's parent company, got 15 percent of the gross receipts for distributing the picture. Al Lichtman, who negotiated the deal, smilingly hovers over Mayer. Gable received his salary of $4,500 weekly plus a $50,000 bonus for signing, which he used in divorcing his second wife so that he could marry Carole Lombard. MGM insisted that Selznick pay one-third of the bonus in addition to Gable's salary.

bonus and the promise to assist him in his divorce proceedings with his wife, that he decided to take on the role. Once the deal was made, however, Gable said no more and resigned himself to the inevitable. He had to finish one more picture for MGM, *Idiot's Delight,* after which he would take his six-week vacation and report to Selznick International, according to the contract, "not later than January 5, 1939 . . . for a period reasonably necessary to complete the role."

This setting of the start date by MGM forced Selznick into the realization that he had only four months to resolve all the details that were still unsettled, and that the time had now come when he would have to make all the postponed decisions regarding the settings, the costumes, and the casting, both in front of and behind the camera. The many postponements had already cost him the services of Hobe Erwin, who had agreed to extension after extension, until finally, in October 1938, he wrote Selznick, "I think we should terminate the contract now . . . the postponements have cost me more than I could possibly make on the picture." Erwin suggested a replacement, Joseph Platt, decorating consultant for the prestigious *House & Garden* magazine, a man who was, in Erwin's words, "not only my peer, but in lots of ways exceeds me. . . . He is a great designer, illustrator, painter . . . and will be able to handle the assignment beautifully." Meanwhile, Klune, Menzies, and Wheeler were wrestling with one of the biggest headaches in the script, what was called "the burning of Atlanta" although, as Wilbur Kurtz pointed out to them and Selznick, "Scarlett left Atlanta on September 1st, and the city wasn't burned by Sherman until November 14th or 15th." However, Miss Mitchell had spent four paragraphs describing the destruction of the Confederate munitions warehouses, and it was this that Selznick and Howard had written into the script, expanding the conflagration beyond all recognition of what was described in the novel until it took on the proportions of a burning city. Lyle Wheeler, meanwhile, had been spending a great deal of time on the 40-acre back lot, going over the plans for the transformation of the standing sets into the streets of Atlanta.

In order to build Tara and the Atlanta railroad station, the area in front of the standing sets had to be cleared of a number of leftover settings, and the area directly behind these street sets was still dominated by the huge wall that had been re-dressed for *King Kong,* in front of which stood the remnants of the native village from the same picture. Wheeler got the idea that it might be easier to burn those sets down than to bulldoze them. He reasoned that if they gathered all the sets they wanted to get rid of, put false fronts on them, built a shell to suggest the railway station and the freight yards, and then burned them, it would probably work very well for the fire scenes. The idea was brought up at the next production meeting; Selznick was dubious, but Wheeler, Menzies, and Klune were all for it and persuaded him that it should be tried, that the area had to be cleared anyway and this was one way of doing it. Selznick reluctantly gave approval while he now came to grips with his most pressing problem other than finding a Scarlett: the script. In all the months of preparations, he had not exactly lost sight of the fact that the script was not complete. Indeed, he'd continued to work on it almost daily, first with Sidney Howard, until he quit in disgust, then with Barbara Keon, reworking each scene countless times until the only way that order could be brought out of the chaos was to start a separate file for each sequence, circling the bits that he liked from each version in red pencil. This formless mass of revisions took up almost an entire four-drawer file cabinet, and by October, Selznick realized he would now, somehow, have to wrest a workable script out of this mess. To do this at the studio, with its continual distractions, was obviously impossible, so Selznick decided to take four packing cases full of the various drafts and go to Bermuda, a trip he hoped he could "talk Margaret Mitchell into taking at our expense . . . such a trip might not frighten her as much as one to Hollywood." She wasn't frightened, she just wasn't interested. So Selznick took Jo Swerling, who had just finished revising the script of *Made for Each Other,* with him to Bermuda. They labored for almost two months, and when they returned to New York, the script was in no more manageable shape than when they had left, something that Selznick attributed to Swerling's inability to come to terms with the material. From Bermuda, he wired Kay Brown that he would need a new writer as

(Above) William Cameron Menzies's sketches for the burning of the Atlanta munitions warehouses, vividly described by Miss Mitchell in four paragraphs in the novel. Selznick turned this incident into one of the most spectacular and dramatic scenes in the film, as Scarlett, Rhett, Melanie and her newborn baby, and the slave girl Prissy escape besieged Atlanta by fleeing through the burning railroad yards. The sequence had originally been designed to be shown on a screen twice normal width; it was filmed using a special double-mounted camera, and tests were made on a 60-foot wide screen at one of the studio sound stages. But Whitney and MGM both convinced Selznick that the picture didn't need this gimmick, and the plan was dropped. Some idea of the scope of Selznick's approach can be gained from the drawing at the bottom, which shows the approximate proportion of the enlarged-screen idea.

(Right) The Selznick International back lot, called "Forty Acres," looking north toward Washington Boulevard with the Santa Monica mountains in the background, in early 1938. The towering structure in the foreground is what was left of DeMille's *King of Kings* set and *King Kong's* wall and gate. This and all of the surrounding sets were equipped with false fronts and stood in for the burning munitions warehouses in *Gone With The Wind.*

Filming the burning of the Atlanta munitions depot, Saturday night, December 10, 1938. Twenty-seven cameramen operated seven Technicolor cameras, three of which are under the corrugated sheeting in the center. The fellow with his hand in his pocket wearing the topcoat, hat, and sweater directly in front of these makeshift sheds is art director Lyle Wheeler. At the extreme left, wearing a dark hat and holding a microphone in front of his mouth, is William Cameron Menzies, who directed the sequence. This shot was taken during a lull in the proceedings. Director George Cukor, wearing a white scarf, is above Menzies, talking to Daniel O'Shea. In the circle is Selznick, standing next to Vivien Leigh, to whom he had been introduced earlier in the evening by his brother Myron. Laurence Olivier, wearing a scarf and a dark topcoat, is standing slightly ahead of them with his hands in his pockets.

soon as he arrived in New York: "Not interested Sidney Howard, but understand Oliver Garrett's play is a terrible flop so we should be able to get him cheaply . . . want him to do continuity certain sequences, maybe throughout picture if price right . . . would want him familiarize himself with book and script and prepare work en route home and at studio." In New York, in addition to Oliver H. P. Garrett, the growing company of Gone With The Winders was joined by Atlanta historian Wilbur Kurtz, who would later be going out to the studio to oversee all the historical details of time and place. While they were conferring on the new screenplay in New York, the question of Ashley's Christmas leave in Atlanta came up: Was it before or after Gettysburg? Kurtz said it was before; Selznick said no, it was the Christmas after. Relates Kurtz, "I insisted I was right and David countered with a bet of ten cents! I took him up and he looked through the pages. . . . I was weakening before he turned to the marked page—but he was getting too much fun out of it. Finally he found the page and triumphantly told me that I owed him a dime. 'No one can ever accuse me of not having read the book,' he declared."

The Selznick party left New York on November 28, on board the Super-Chief bound for Los Angeles. Oliver Garrett spent most of the trip in his stateroom, pounding away at the sixth revision of the script. While the train roared westward across the wintry landscape, Ray Klune and his staff in Culver City were hard at work on the final preparations for the spectacular fire sequences. Klune realized that it would be impossible to keep the flames burning for more than forty minutes. During that time, they would have to photograph the action of the escaping Rhett and Scarlett, with several dramatic bits of business that were called for by the script. And they would have to catch the fire from every conceivable angle, using as many cameras as possible. Since Technicolor had only seven cameras at the time, the work would have to be scheduled for a day when all of them were available; the earliest date was Saturday, December 10, which gave them approximately two weeks to work out the logistics of the sequence. "We planned the whole thing sort of as a football rehearsal," recalls Klune. "We built a miniature of the whole damned thing and kept it under lock and key, because it was an expensive one and we didn't want anyone messing around with it. . . . We rehearsed for about ten days, every move, every camera position—we decided during these rehearsals that instead of changing lenses on the cameras, which was a brute of a job on those Technicolor things, we'd move the cameras instead. We'd move the camera from position one to position five—different lenses on each camera because we wanted to get a medium shot, a long shot, and a close shot from almost every position. So we had all the camera positions indicated on the model, and the camera crews." Klune wanted as much control as possible over every aspect of the scene; he knew how dubious David was about the whole idea, and he was determined that every detail of the potentially hazardous venture would be gone over minutely to minimize the chance of the operation becoming a useless fiasco and, even more important, of the fire itself getting out of control. The studio was surrounded by the Culver City suburbs, and the height of the main set plus the age of the material caused him to worry that flying fragments could cause a major disaster. The Culver City Fire Department had been alerted, but they had only two pieces of equipment, and Klune wanted the entire area ringed with fire trucks, including the section behind the main set facing the Baldwin Hills. The cooperation of the Los Angeles Fire Department was enlisted, and they promised thirty-four pieces of equipment for the night, which eased his mind a bit on that score. But Klune was still concerned about

The end result of all the pyrotechnics: Yakima Canutt, the stunt man for Rhett Butler, leads a wagon through the inferno with Dorothy Fargo, one of the two doubles used for Scarlett O'Hara.

the length of time needed to move each camera from one position to the next, set it up, and start photography, all of which would be going on while the fire raged; and it could only rage for so long. He began trying to find some way to control the actual fire, so that it would perform on demand. To achieve this, he brought in Lee Zavits, "the best special effects man in the business," as Klune called him. Zavits devised an ingenious and unprecedented method of solving the problem. Behind the false fronts of each of the sets, they constructed an intricate double network of pipes, one of which would carry a mixture of kerosene and coal oil, and the other, larger one, water. The two would be force-fed from two main pumps set off to one side, each manned by two men. The pipes with the oil mixture were equipped with electric valves to shut off the fuel, at which point the water pumps would take over and douse the flames, giving Klune the control he wanted.

Selznick and the rest of his party arrived back in Culver City on December 2, one week before the big event. But when Klune briefed him on what they'd been doing and took him on a tour of the back lot, showing him the false fronts and elaborate piping, and running through the planned camera moves, Selznick suddenly got cold feet. "Are you sure that this is the best way to do this?" Klune recalls him asking. He

reassured him; but several days later, Selznick was at him again. "He was very nervous about it. He said, 'You're positive everything is ready?' I told him, 'David, we're as ready as we're ever going to be. Another day and we'll be overtrained. We've got everything scheduled for tomorrow night, we've got all the fire companies we can get, insurance is covering everything; everybody is keyed up to a fever pitch. If we postpone it, we might as well not do it, we could never crank up our enthusiasm again.' So we got the go ahead to do it as planned."

At about four o'clock on the afternoon of Saturday, December 10, the sun went down, and the temperature, which had been in the mid-seventies, dropped to 30 degrees. The last of the Technicolor cameras arrived from the studios where they were being used and were put into place. Fire tests were made on some small foreground structures, light tests were made by meters from various distances, and Klune called for one last rehearsal, with cameras, actors, and position switches. According to Wilbur Kurtz: "Property men were lugging things around and the cameramen and electricians were weaving about in a most businesslike fashion. The place swarmed with firemen . . . and fire trucks." At 6:30 there was a ninety-minute dinner break, after which everybody returned to the set and waited for Selznick to arrive. He had sent out a number of

The Temple of Jerusalem and the great gate from *King Kong* come crashing down in fiery splendor as the wagon with Rhett, Scarlett, Melanie, and Prissy crosses in front. The wagon and its occupants were added later by Jack Cosgrove, who superimposed the separately filmed action of the wagon onto the footage of the collapsing building.

invitations to friends and relatives to come watch the proceedings, the start of which was set for eight o'clock. By that time nearly everybody had arrived, including Selznick's mother. When Selznick's limousine finally arrived with him and George Cukor, there were almost two hundred people behind the ropes that Klune had set up back of the cameras. This bothered Klune, "because with all those people, it could get very confusing, if everyone got to screaming and yelling at one another. So to ensure that there would be no misunderstanding, I took the public address system and talked to all the guests, including David, and asked them to please not talk during the whole thing that was to follow, that we expected that it would be burned out within 45 minutes, and that during that time we wanted absolute quiet, because this was either going to come off or it wasn't." Everything was ready, awaiting Selznick's okay, but he asked Klune to delay a while longer; his brother Myron still had not arrived. Lydia Schiller recalls:

I was rushing from camera to camera, keeping track of which one was where, which lens they had, what angles they were shooting.... We had some buried cameras, some close to the fire ... so my work for the night was to watch the action very closely, to match the principals

when we changed positions, and to watch the progression of the wagon through the fire, and make sure that [the stunt man and woman playing] Rhett and Scarlett were always in the right positions.... I was standing right with Mr. Selznick and he was very angry with Myron for being late, he held up the start of the burning because he wanted him to be there.... Finally we saw Myron coming ... he had two people with him and Mr. Selznick said, "Let 'er go, Ray," and then all his attention was focused on the action.

Klune gave the signal to Menzies, who relayed it to Lee Zavits behind the fire break to one side of the large *King Kong* gate. The grips started the pumps feeding the oil mixture through the network of pipes. Zavits had wired the sets in various strategic places so that by pressing a contact switch, sparks would ignite the gasoline; he counted sixty seconds, then pressed the switch. Instantly there was an ear-splitting whoosh as the fire ignited the oil-soaked timbers and surged upward 300 feet into the night sky. To Lydia Schiller "it was just suddenly the holocaust ... it scared all of us ... it was like a whole town suddenly going up in flames.... Just as this ferocious thing happened, up comes Myron with these two people ... all three seemed to be a few sheets to the wind and Myron said

This early sketch of Tara makes it look like a suburban home, circa 1938. It was Wilbur Kurtz who suggested replacing the slender wooden posts with whitewashed square brick columns, copied from one of the research photos.

something to Mr. Selznick but he just shook him off, he was so engrossed in the fire." A battery of huge searchlights—white and amber—were mounted on platforms; in front of some of these were asbestos tables on which fires were lit, giving out a thick black smoke, which streamed across the field of light making irregular patches of fast-moving shadow, as if a blaze were in progress in back of the cameras. As soon as the fire had started, Menzies called "action," and Rhett and Scarlett drove a wagon across the front of the inferno. The stunt man didn't really do the driving, however; on the floor of the wagon, out of camera range, was another driver who controlled the horse by two slender wires passed through a small opening in the front of the wagon and attached to the horse's bit, enabling him to control the horse's rearing and plunging. In the middle of the first take, the wagon suddenly lost its left front wheel, the horse sat down, and Klune called for Zavits to douse the flames. At this point, Lydia Schiller remembers that "Mr. Selznick turned to Myron and said, 'What did you say?' and Myron replied, 'Here's your Scarlett,' and introduced him to Vivien Leigh. . . . I don't think Mr. Selznick was suddenly electrified." But Selznick later remembered: "When my brother introduced her to me, the dying flames were lighting up her face. . . . I took one look and knew that she was right—at least right as far as her appearance went . . . and right as far as my conception of how Scarlett O'Hara looked. . . . I'll never recover from that first look."

While this exchange had been taking place, the cameras had been moved to their secondary positions, a gang of grips had moved out the faulty wagon, and a new one had been put in its place. Klune gave the signal and the fire began again. "It went beautifully," says Klune; "instead of the three or four burns, we got six or seven." As the inferno raged, the low-hanging clouds spread the reflection of the flames over most of Culver City, and for the hour and a half that the fire continued, the phone lines in Los Angeles were jammed with anxious callers, all of

whom seemed convinced that MGM was on fire. "When Selznick heard this," related Wilbur Kurtz, "he was tickled immensely." On the seventh take, Menzies gave the signal and an off-camera tractor tugged at the blazing remnants of DeMille's *King of Kings* and Cooper's *King Kong,* causing the structure to collapse spectacularly—a phoenix in reverse. Selznick, never particularly analytical about his own past, probably gave no thought to the ironies of the moment—or perhaps he did have a flashing thought of the times when he had seen these same sets as he took the bus to work during his first weeks at MGM, or of the dark days in 1932 when Cooper had come to him for the money to rebuild this set for a project that in the intervening years had been transmuted into the status of a legend. Later that night he wrote to his wife in New York: "The fire sequence was one of the greatest thrills I have had out of making pictures, first because of the scene itself, and second because of the frightening but exciting knowledge that *Gone With The Wind* was finally in work."

If it was an emotional moment for Selznick, it was even more intense for Ray Klune, who recalls: "After it was over, I just sat down exhausted. . . . I was sweating all over . . . and shaking from the strain, and David came over to me, put his arms around me and said, 'You were right, I'm sorry. This was one of the greatest things I've ever seen. I think you're the best production manager I've ever known.'" Forty years later, the memory of that moment was still strong and vivid enough to cause Ray Klune to be moved almost to tears as he related it in a voice suddenly thick with emotion, adding quietly: "It's something I'll never forget."

The cost of the entire operation had been only $24,715, just $323 more than the allotted budget, which according to Klune, "would probably run about half a million dollars if you did it today." The ninety

The final version of Tara, as it was built on the back lot, doesn't quite follow Miss Mitchell's description of "a clumsy, sprawling building . . . built by slave labor"; in fact, the result was judged classy enough to be featured in the November 1939 issue of *House & Garden,* for which this Kodachrome was specially taken. The landscaping of the plantation was done by Florence Yoch, a friend of the Whitneys', who had done some work on their Long Island estates.

minutes between the start of the fire and its conclusion saw the completion of one of the most important and ultimately memorable moments of the picture. But of even more consequence was the inadvertent turning up of Vivien Leigh. The twenty-five-year-old actress was in Hollywood on a quick holiday from London to see Laurence Olivier, laboring on Goldwyn's *Wuthering Heights.* Theirs was a passionate involvement, in spite of each being married to someone else. She had journeyed halfway around the world to be with him; in five days she would have to return to England for a contracted stage performance. Her determination to be with Olivier was coupled with an equal resolve to enter herself in the O'Hara sweepstakes. She had achieved some measure of success in English theatrical circles, being considered not only beautiful but an actress of great potential. Her several appearances in British films had not escaped the attention of Selznick, who had not been impressed, but Leigh, who had studied the part of Scarlett O'Hara in England, was convinced that if she had the opportunity she could make a favorable impression. Myron, who was Olivier's American agent, was her entree to David, and accordingly she was all charm, high spirits, and vivacity in the hours immediately following her meeting with him. Olivier, who was as frenzied about her as she was about him, had remarked to Myron: "Just look at Vivien tonight! If David doesn't fall for that, I'll be very surprised."

Fall he did, for the next day Selznick confided in a letter to his wife: "Myron brought Larry Olivier and Vivien Leigh with him to the fire. Shhh: she's the Scarlett dark horse and looks damn good. Not for anybody's ear but your own: it's narrowed down to Paulette, Jean Arthur, Joan Bennett and Vivien Leigh." All this enthusiasm on the strength of one reading, for she had not yet been given a screen test. The morning following the fire, she had read through the library scene for Cukor in which Scarlett proclaims her love for Ashley Wilkes. Where

most of the other actresses had played it as either coy and sentimental or arch and hysterical, Leigh had, as Cukor recalls, "a kind of indescribable wildness about her" that he found "very exciting." Her clipped British accent needed some work, which she assured him she would do. Twelve days later, Selznick abruptly canceled another test for Paulette Goddard; the actress, costumed and made up, was replaced by Vivien Leigh, who later recalled, "When I put the costume on it was still warm from the previous actress." After several days of tests and accent rehearsals, both Selznick and Cukor were convinced they had finally found the perfect Scarlett. But there was a problem: Leigh, in addition to being committed to a stage play in London, was under contract to Alexander Korda, and the negotiations involved were long and complicated. There were two other factors that had to be contended with: first, she was English, and the wrath of the South and indeed the entire country might conceivably rise up in nationalistic indignation; added to this was the moral outrage that could follow if it were learned that she and Olivier were involved in an extramarital affair. The American public liked its movie stars lusty and romantic on screen, and pristine and virtuous off. With Leigh, her acting ability and her physical rightness for the part made the risks worth taking; she was unknown in this country and her situation with Olivier could be handled discreetly and even turned into a romantic asset. All these problems whirled through Selznick's mind while the negotiations with Korda were carried on via cable and letter. Leigh, in a surge of optimism about her chances, had already freed herself of the stage commitment, then spent several days waiting for some news from Selznick. When word finally came, it was from Cukor, inviting her and Olivier to a Christmas party at his home. During cocktails, he took her aside and told her that the part of Scarlett had been cast. When she asked who had been given the part, he told her offhandedly, "I guess we're stuck with you."

GIRLS TESTED FOR THE ROLE OF SCARLETT

Name	Where From	Date Tested
Louise Platt	New York City	September 28, 1936
Talullah Bankhead	New York City	December 22, 1936
Mrs. J. H. Whitney	New York City	April 5, 1937
Lynn Merrill	New York City	May 24, 1937
Linda Watkins	New York City	June 3, 1937
Susan Fox	New York City	June 3, 1937
Adele Longmire	New Orleans; New York City	August 18, 1937
Haila Stoddard	New York City	November 9-10, 1937
Diana Forrest	New York City	November 9-10, 1937
Edith Marrener	New York City; Hollywood	Dec. 2, 1937; Dec. 6, 1937
Linda Lee	New York City	December 13, 1937
Dorothy Mathews	New York City	December 13, 1937
Ardis Ankerson	New York City	February 4, 1938
Paulette Goddard	Hollywood	February 9, 1938 Feb. 12, Feb. 19, Nov. 8-9-11, Dec. 8, Dec. 20-21, 1938
Terry Ray	Hollywood	Feb. 9-12-19, 1938
Anita Louise	Hollywood	Feb. 10, March 21-22-23, 1938
Em Bowles Locker	Richmond, Va.	Feb. 15, 1938
Margaret Tallichet	Hollywood	March 19, 21-22-23, 1938
Frances Dee	Hollywood	March 24, 1938
Nancy Coleman	Hollywood	Setp. 29, October 1, 1938
Shirley Logan	Hollywood	Sept. 29; Oct. 7, 1938

(Above) Jean Arthur with Hattie McDaniel. Arthur was the first established film star to do a complete test for the role. At the time, Selznick commented in a letter to his wife, "[She] has been no end of trouble. . . . I look at her as though I had never known her before!" (She and Selznick had had a brief romance in the late twenties, when they were both at Paramount.) Miss Arthur is reputed to have burned her screen test after losing the part. (Below) Makeup artist Monty Westmore and hair stylist Hazel Rogers prepare Paulette Goddard for her color test for the role of Scarlett O'Hara. Goddard was the leading contender for the part and the only actress besides Vivien Leigh who was given a Technicolor test for the role (bottom).

Page 2

Name	Where From	Date Tested
Doris Jordan	New York; Hollywood	October 17, 1938; Nov. 18, Nov. 29, Dec. 8, 1938
Marcella Martin	New York; Hollywood	Oct. 17, 1938; Dec. 21, 1938; Jan. 11, 1939
Fleurette DeBussy	New York City	October 17, 1938
Austine McDonnel	New York City	October 17, 1938
Mary Ray	Hollywood	Nov. 8-9, 1938
Lana Turner	Hollywood	Nov. 17-18, 1938
Dianna Barrymore	New York City	November 24, 1938
Jean Arthur	Hollywood	December 17, 1938
Joan Bennett	Hollywood	December 20, 1938
Vivien Leigh	London; Hollywood	Dec. 21-22, 1938

GIRLS SUGGESTED FOR SCARLETT BUT WHOSE TESTS WERE GENERAL

Name	Where From	Date Tested
Katharine Aldridge	New York City	October 17, 1938
Lyn Swann	New York City	Dec. 27, 1938

The official studio list of all the actresses tested for the role of Scarlett O'Hara.

(Top, left) Tallulah Bankhead was the first well-known actress to try out for the role. Her test was photographic only, as Selznick was mostly concerned about her ability to convincingly portray the sixteen-year-old Scarlett. (Top, right) Melvyn Douglas tested for the role of Ashley Wilkes opposite Lana Turner, who was trying out for Scarlett. Of Douglas as Ashley, Selznick remarked, "He gives the first intelligent reading we've had yet." Turner was physically right for the part, but her woeful inexperience dropped her out of the running early on. (Above, left) Douglass Montgomery (also known as Kent Douglass) as Ashley and Joan Bennett as Scarlett. Bennett gave one of the best readings of the role and was with Paulette Goddard one of the leading contenders for the part. Douglass Montgomery was the studio's in-house Ashley, testing with four different actresses, the last being Vivien Leigh. (Above, right) Model Edythe Marrener did several tests for Scarlett, on the strength of which she signed a contract with Paramount Pictures, changed her name to Susan Hayward, and had a very successful thirty-year career. She is seen here with Dorothy Jordan in the part of Melanie. Miss Jordan had given up a promising career to become Mrs. Merian C. Cooper and was coaxed out of retirement to test for the role of Melanie Wilkes. (Below, left and right) Vivien Leigh with Douglass Montgomery in her first screen test for the part of Scarlett O'Hara, playing the paddock scene, in which Scarlett tries to persuade Ashley to run away with her to Mexico. Cukor directed the scene and Ernest Haller photographed it.

(Top) January 14, 1939—David O. Selznick ends two and a half years of searching when he announces that Vivien Leigh, a little-known British actress, will play Scarlett O'Hara. Like the fictional heroine, Miss Leigh had an Irish-French ancestral background. At the same time Selznick finalized the casting of the two other central roles by signing the twenty-three-year-old Olivia de Havilland to play Melanie Hamilton and the forty-three-year-old British-American matinee idol Leslie Howard to play twenty-six-year-old Ashley Wilkes. Howard, considering the role foolish, had not wanted to play it, but Selznick finally persuaded the reluctant actor by promising to let him be associate producer as well as co-star of the studio's remake of the Swedish film *Intermezzo*. Olivia de Havilland, who had become one of Hollywood's leading ingénues after her appearance in the Warner Bros. 1935 success *Captain Blood*, was called by Selznick and George Cukor to read for the part of Melanie at the suggestion of her sister, Joan Fontaine. This had to be done in secrecy, as Miss de Havilland was kept on a tight acting leash by the head of her studio, Jack Warner, who didn't like his players to be too ambitious. Selznick and Cukor were impressed by the actress and approached Warner, who refused to consider lending her, his reasoning being that she would be too hard to handle after playing such a meaty role. Miss de Havilland took matters into her own capable hands and circumvented her boss by appealing to his wife, Ann, convincing her that it could only be to the studio's credit to have her play a plum role in the biggest picture of the year. Mrs. Warner agreed, and she convinced her husband. Warner loaned out de Havilland for a cash payment plus the services of James Stewart, with whom Selznick still had a one-picture commitment. Ironically, at Warner Bros. Stewart was cast as the lead in the film adaptation of *No Time for Comedy*, a role Laurence Olivier had created on Broadway. (Above) A party at Myron Selznick's home the week before filming was to start on *Gone With The Wind*. (Clockwise, from left) Vivien Leigh, Laurence Olivier, David Selznick, George Cukor, Irene Selznick, Jock Whitney, and Merle Oberon.

The final casting of the picture was formally announced on January 13, 1939, and it came as no surprise to most of the industry, as *The Hollywood Reporter* had run an article on January 5, quoting several unnamed sources to the effect that Vivien Leigh had been given the part, and that Olivia de Havilland was to be borrowed from Warner Bros. to play Melanie Wilkes, with Leslie Howard as Ashley. The expected storm of controversy over the selection of the British-born Miss Leigh turned out to be only a brief flurry, while her relationship with Laurence Olivier was discreetly cosmeticized by Selznick's insistence that the two live apart during the filming. With the public consciousness ministered to and tucked in for the duration of production, Selznick and his staff began the feverish round-the-clock activity that would finally put *Gone With The Wind* into actual work. Now that the cast was assembled, Walter Plunkett was at last able to begin constructing the more than two thousand costumes that had been designed for nonexistent actors. On the back lot, after the debris of the fire had been cleared away, the construction crew was building the shell of the Atlanta train shed in front of the already finished Atlanta streets. Behind the car shed and up on a slight grassy knoll, the foundation and the brick steps of Tara were being laid in place. On top of this the front facade only would be built, and part of the roof, the rest being added by Jack Cosgrove's special effects department. Trucks were delivering trees, bushes, and green sod to plant around the house, while a special crew was busy constructing oak trees out of telephone poles, barrel staves, chicken wire, plaster, and paint. The photographic problem of re-creating "the red earth of Tara" was ingeniously solved by the combined efforts of Menzies, Zavits, and Klune, who brainstormed into existence the use of pulverized bricks, which would be scattered not only over Tara but all of the Atlanta street sets.

In his inner sanctum, Selznick was plowing through the last series of decisions that needed to be made regarding the final technical staff. Earlier he had made up his mind that Lee Garmes would be the perfect person to photograph the picture. Garmes was a small, round, energetic man, who'd been in the business since 1916. He had pioneered the innovative "north light technique," derived from his study of the work of Rembrandt, whereby all the light sources came from one direction, giving his images a clean, luminous quality. Since 1937, he had been working in England; when he received a cablegram from Selznick asking him to come back and work on the picture, he said, "You could have knocked me over with a feather because I had been reading so much about it that I thought it was practically finished. I got my agent to accept and cut my salary almost in half to do it." By the time Garmes arrived in Hollywood, the picture was a week away from its starting date, and Garmes plunged right into work on the makeup and lighting tests of Vivien Leigh. To assist Cukor in making certain that the customs and attitudes of the story's era would be presented as accurately as possible, Selznick had brought to Culver City, at Margaret Mitchell's suggestion, Susan Myrick of Atlanta, who in addition to being a close friend of Miss Mitchell's was also an expert on everything pertaining to the manners, morals, and sensibilities of the South, past and present. Her unerring eye for details and her ear for the proper sound of Southern speech were put to good use by Cukor and Selznick in the weeks before shooting started.

As the days crept nearer to the starting date, Selznick made one more concerted effort to pummel the script into a semblance of finality, throwing writers at it like darts in the hope that one of them might hit a bull's-eye. In the two weeks preceding the January 26 target date, John Balderston, Michael Foster, Edwin Justus Mayer, John van Druten, and F. Scott Fitzgerald all tried their skills at cutting, pasting, writing, and rewriting; but on the day before the first scene was to be shot, Selznick admitted defeat in a long letter to Jock Whitney:

> Don't get panicky at the seemingly small amount of final revised script.... It is so clearly in my mind that I can tell you the picture from beginning to end, almost shot for shot.... I want to match up the best things from the book (and from the various scripts) as well as try to make cuts.... The job that remains to be done is to telescope all these into the shortest possible form.... A couple of nights ago I was sick with trepidation, but as of tonight—the night before we start shooting—I am filled with confidence ... but you will have to bear with me for the next couple of months, which will be the toughest I have ever

January 20, 1939—Cinematographers Lee Garmes, Wilfred Cline, and Karl Struss photographed these Technicolor makeup, hair, and costume tests of the performers in *GWTW.* This series of tests convinced Selznick that the color schemes for some of the costumes were too drab, that the hair styles were wrong, and that the makeup on the actresses was too light. Hazel Rogers, hair stylist at Selznick International, was assigned the lesser performers, and Sydney Guilaroff was brought over from MGM to re-design Vivien Leigh's hair; as it turned out, he did only the opening sequence of the film, and then Hazel Rogers was reinstated. Leslie Howard, after seeing his test in the Confederate uniform, remarked that he "looked like a fairy doorman at the Beverly Wilshire Hotel." Fred Crane and George Bessolo, the two actors testing for the Tarleton twins (third row, right), could not be made up to convincingly resemble each other, so it was decided that they would be the "Tarleton boys" instead. Selznick also wanted their hair to look redder, since they were described as "carrot tops" in the book. (During the course of the production, Bessolo changed his name to George Reeves—and years later took to changing his clothes in phone booths.) Evelyn Keyes (above, left) was a young actress from Atlanta under contract to Cecil B. DeMille. She had impressed photographer Max Munn Autrey with her beauty, and he had sent a letter to Selznick suggesting that she be tested for Scarlett. Selznick didn't like her for Scarlett but thought she would be effective as Scarlett's bitchy sister Suellen. Ann Rutherford (above, center), who had achieved a certain fame as Polly Benedict in the Andy Hardy series at MGM, was borrowed for the role of Scarlett's sweet younger sister, Carreen. Five-year-old Cammie King (above, right) was given the part of Scarlett and Rhett's daughter, Bonnie, after her sister, who had been tested six months earlier, outgrew the part. Miss King was the stepdaughter of Herbert Kalmus, the president of Technicolor.

(Above) Lyle Wheeler and his secretary with one of the models for the exteriors of the Atlanta street scenes. This was the largest setting ever built for a movie, with fifty-three full-size buildings and two miles of streets. (Below) Harold Fenton, construction superintendent, standing in front of the blackboard on which he kept a record of the progress of all of the ninety sets used in *Gone With The Wind* on the stages and on the back lot. At the same time, Fenton and his crew of 125 men were also readying the sets used in *Intermezzo* and *Rebecca*.

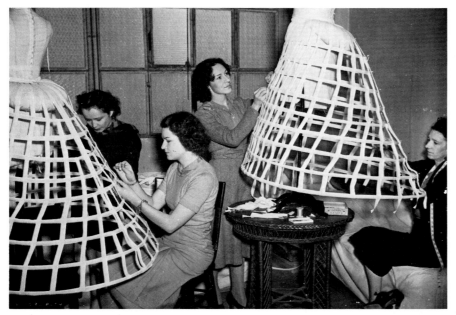

The costume department constructed the 5,500 separate items necessary to dress the performers, including the hundreds of hoop skirts, corsets, and other undergarments that were no longer in existence.

known, possibly the toughest any producer has ever known, which is the general opinion of the whole industry.... You have had faith in me to date, and I beg you to continue to have this faith until the picture is finished ... at which time if the picture isn't everything that everyone wants, I ... am willing ... and anxious to leave the whole goddam business.

The next morning, Thursday, January 26, at 8:00 A.M., on the front lawn of Selznick International, actress Mary Anderson ran the Confederate stars and bars up the flagpole, officially marking the start of filming. Vivien Leigh and the four other performers needed for the day's work had been at the studio since six, being costumed and made up. By 8:30, they were gathered on the steps of Tara on the back lot while George Cukor called for the blocking and camera rehearsal. The first scene scheduled was also the first scene of the picture, Scarlett and the Tarleton boys talking about the war and the upcoming barbecue at Twelve Oaks. It was a vital scene, for it unspooled the dramatic thread that would carry all through the story—Scarlett's discovery that Ashley, the man she loves, is to marry his cousin Melanie. The two actors playing the Tarleton boys were at worst amateurs and at best adequate. Directing them, for a perfectionist like Cukor, must have been frustrating, for his concentration was on Scarlett and her reactions to them, and also on the general air of the scene, which had to immediately conjure up a whiff of the Old South and its particular graces. Cukor had to spend an inordinate amount of time trying to bring the two actors down to the natural unforced kind of work neither of them had been trained in, and Leigh, though a gifted technician, was not above being rattled by having to stop constantly while Cukor tried to make the scene and the actors all blend together. The tension permeated the entire studio: "Everybody was nervous," recalls Ray Klune, "and it showed in the next day's rushes. George had Vivien on too high a key, way up there. David felt that she was playing it as though it were the first act of a dress rehearsal. The same thing with the boys ... they were overdoing it."

The light failed right after lunch, so Cukor and Vivien Leigh moved to the unfinished bedroom interior set, where they were joined by two seasoned actresses, Hattie McDaniel, playing Scarlett's shrewd Mammy, and Butterfly McQueen, a New York import who had been cast as the shrill, slow-witted servant girl Prissy, one of the main sources of comedy in the picture. Approximately one hundred people were jammed around the small set—carpenters, painters, grips, technicians, trying to finish it up. By 5:00 P.M. the set and the camera crew were ready. The scene involved Mammy getting the sixteen-year-old Scarlett ready for the barbecue, and it was the first good scene that Cukor had to work with. He labored over it gleefully, delicately touching up the finer points of the relationship between the two women, pulling McDaniel down from being just a little too broad and swift in her dialogue, giving the interplay between the two a richness and an honesty that resonated throughout the rest of the story.

The next day in the rushes, Selznick was disappointed with the first scene, realizing it would have to be retaken and shrugging the results off as first-day jitters. The bedroom scene was infinitely better, but Selznick was shocked to find that Cukor, without consulting him, had inserted a small bit of dialogue between Mammy and Scarlett, with Scarlett insisting that Prissy take all the food Mammy had prepared for her, "right back to the kitchen, I won't eat a bite," while Mammy insists: "Oh, yas'm, you is, you's gwine eat every mouthful." To Cukor this was necessary to smooth the way for what he felt was an abrupt and arbitrary change of mood in the script as written. He had lifted the dialogue almost verbatim from the novel, and Selznick, while realizing the value of it, was still unhappy with the fact that it had been done. In addition, Cukor's pacing of the scene bothered Selznick; it was full of pauses, glances, and reactions. He realized that it was these subtleties that made it work, but it ran one minute longer than it had in the tests, and it had needed shortening then. At the end of the first day's filming, with one and a half scenes completed out of a total of 692, the total amount of money spent on the picture was a whopping $1,081,465, out of a total budget estimate of $2,843,000.

As the first week wore on, Cukor continued to make David aware of his unhappiness with the fragmentary nature of the script. Cukor was a

The week before filming is to start, Selznick muses on the back lot, standing in the reconstructed Atlanta train station, with Tara in the background.

January 26, 1939—(Above, left) The original opening sequence as filmed by George Cukor. The Technicolor cameras turned the Tarleton boys into the aforementioned "carrot tops" to such an extent that the scene had to be re-shot because their hair was such a bright orange. (Above, right) Even though the Atlanta bazaar sequences were later extensively re-filmed by Victor Fleming, Cukor's shot of Rhett Butler's entrance remained in the final film. (Below) Cukor registering delight as he photographs the waltzing figures of Vivien Leigh and Clark Gable on a specially built camera platform that gave the illusion that the camera was moving among the dancers.

very fastidious director who relied on the script to anchor his perspective while he worked out the character variations with his actors. He found himself chained not to an anchor but to a bobbing buoy going in several directions at once, with montages of the Civil War and talky vignettes by subsidiary characters explaining the progress of the war in Georgia, all of which underwent a daily chain of revisions. Cukor, having spent the past three years with the characters, examining their relationships and their behavior, was now trying to cram this mass of detail into the actors' performances, spending what seemed to Selznick inordinate amounts of time on gestures, inflections, movements, nuances, and the hundred and one other variations of human behavior that a good actor or actress is capable of conveying. Throughout the first two weeks of filming, David kept cautioning Cukor about his tempo and speed, the need for swiftness in the pacing. He became increasingly disappointed with what he was seeing in the rushes. All the careful preparations, the hundreds of sketches for settings and art direction, were not, he felt, being captured on screen. He commented in a note to Menzies and Klune that: "the more I see of our film and compare it with other color pictures such as *Robin Hood,* the more I realize how much we are kidding ourselves in feeling that we could get really effective stuff on the back lot...." By the end of the first ten days' shooting, the combination of Selznick's discontent, his rewriting, and Cukor's near-obsessive attention to detail had resulted in a total accumulated footage of twenty-three minutes, ten minutes of which were scheduled for retakes.

On January 31, Clark Gable joined the company to begin work as Rhett Butler, and the atmosphere on the set, which had begun to smooth down, began to tense up again. Selznick remarked: "Clark was nervous about the gigantic publicity campaign and whether he could live up to it . . . and also he felt that I was introducing a new woman star on his shoulders and would throw the picture to her. I assured him that if he still felt that way when the picture was finished, I would repair it in any way he felt it was necessary, so that calmed him down and he went to work." The first scenes Gable worked in were the complicated ones of the Atlanta charity bazaar, which necessitated his learning the Virginia reel and otherwise acting the dandy, something he was extremely uncomfortable doing. His edginess and insecurities about his role and his abilities were not made easier by the emotional climate on the set. Cukor, Vivien Leigh, and Olivia de Havilland had by now developed a rapport with each other, and Gable, who for years had been pampered and catered to at MGM, felt like an outsider. Because of the complexities of Scarlett's character and her relationship with Melanie, Cukor was spending a great deal of time working with the two actresses, which did little to allay Gable's fears regarding his own role. Cukor's efforts with Gable were directed mainly at loosening him up, trying to get him to give the part a kind of mocking, tongue-in-cheek elegance. But Gable was not what is known as a "quick study." His acting style was more or less an extension of his own personality; anything more than that caused him great torment, in spite of his professionalism. Also, Gable did not understand Cukor's method of working—the personalities and temperaments of the two men were poles apart. Gable was used to specific meat-and-potatoes direction from the likes of Jack Conway and Victor Fleming, men who spoke seldom and right to the point—they knew how to deal with him, how to keep him at ease; in the parlance of the time, they were "men's men," whereas Cukor was cultivated, sensitive, fussy, and maddeningly vague in his instructions. Gable was used to being told specifically what he was doing wrong and how to correct it, and he felt he was not getting this from Cukor.

To Selznick, "Gable was extremely intelligent without being intellectual.... He had no complicated psychological side, his mind was uncluttered.... If he did have problems, he didn't impose them on his performance.... Clark's performances were simply a reproduction of what the author created.... It is conceivable that another actor might have read a different dimension into Rhett, but you wouldn't have had Margaret Mitchell's Rhett. Clark brought precisely to life what she wrote, and what millions of readers wanted.... I don't know of any actor of the past fifty years with the exception of John Barrymore who could have played Rhett as well as Clark did.... If he was dissatisfied with Cukor, he never once mentioned it to me, nor did he ever criticize George." It is not surprising that he didn't mention it to Selznick, as he knew that the

two men were close friends; besides, there was Gable's own dislike of Selznick. At MGM, however, it was different. He let his unhappiness be known to several of the executives there, reportedly telling intimates, "I don't want Cukor; I'm going to have him changed." Gable may have been insecure about his abilities as an actor, but not about his power as a star. There was a clause in his loan-out contract with Selznick that absolved MGM of all responsibility "if the artist refuses to perform," and this was his ace in the hole if the situation became too unbearable for him. Gable was shrewd enough to know that word would get back to Selznick from MGM that he was displeased, and as Selznick later admitted, "I knew about it"—it was just one more straw added to the pressures of the picture. He could not afford to have Gable unhappy, he had given up too much to get him, and the picture would suffer without him. And increasingly, Selznick found himself irritated with Cukor's insistence on doing things his own way. As he felt more and more unhappy about the results of the filming, he began to place the blame on Cukor and to tighten his hold on Cukor's direction, telling him on February 8:

> Before we started this picture we had a long discussion concerning my anxiety to discuss with you in advance the points that I personally saw in each scene; this for many reasons became impossible.... Then we discussed seeing each scene rehearsed, and this idea was in turn lost sight of in the pressure of many things. Now the idea becomes more important than ever because we have little or no opportunity . . . to discuss each rewritten scene before you go into it. I therefore . . . would like to try to work out a system whereby I see each block scene rehearsed in full before you start the shooting on it . . . this would avoid projection room surprises for me and conceivably would be of considerable service to you.

For Cukor, this was very nerve-wracking: "David changed our whole method of working . . . he seemed to trust me less.... I was the director, after all . . . and the director should shoot the scene before the producer sees it.... That's when the producer's opinion is important, when he sees it on the screen for the first time." Just exactly what decided Selznick to replace Cukor will never be known; it was probably a combination of all of the above circumstances.

Matters came to a head on February 13, while the company was filming Rhett, Scarlett, Melanie, and Prissy leaving Aunt Pittypat's house just before the Yankees enter Atlanta. During the lunch break, Cukor went to see Selznick about rewrites for the upcoming scenes involving Ashley's Christmas leave, trying to persuade him once more to return to the Sidney Howard original instead of the more lengthy and wooden Garrett-Selznick rewrite. Cukor later related to Susan Myrick his version of what had transpired, and she in turn wrote to Margaret Mitchell:

> George said he cannot do a job unless he knows it is a good job, and he feels the present job is not right.... For days he has looked at the rushes and felt he was failing. He knew he was a good director and knew the actors were good ones, yet the thing did not click as it should.... He became more and more convinced that the script was the trouble . . . so he told David he would not work any longer if the script was not better and that he wanted the Howard script. David told George he was a director—not an author, and he (David) was the producer and the judge of what is a good script.... George said he was a director and a damn good one and he would not let his name go out over a lousy picture and if they did not go back to the Howard script, he, George, was through. And bullheaded David said, "Okay, get out."

Selznick's version was considerably different:

> George had reached the point where he found it impossible to accept my viewpoint on certain things.... There was no particular dispute or incident, it was just a day by day insistence on my view of the whole concept.... I had to see it through in my way in every single department.... I had to insist that George follow my judgment . . . but he began disagreeing with me on my concept, so I told him that if the picture was to fail, it would fail on my judgment alone. I was careful to keep George on the job until I arranged for him to take over another picture. And neither before or after I made the change did I ever have one word of discussion about the director with Gable.

The novel *Gone With The Wind* had over 150 subsidiary characters who figured prominently throughout the ten-year saga of Scarlett and the South. Selznick and his scriptwriters managed to reduce this to fifty speaking parts—a record number for any production. One of Selznick's greatest strengths was his casting instinct, and he peopled the film with a rich assortment of some of the best character actors from Hollywood and New York. (Top, left) Thomas Mitchell as Gerald O'Hara, master of Tara and father of Scarlett, who taught his daughter that "land is . . . the only thing that lasts." (Top, right) Victor Jory played the obsequious Yankee overseer Jonas Wilkerson, whose affinity for comporting with poor white trash led to his dismissal by Ellen Robillard O'Hara, Scarlett's mother, played by Barbara O'Neil. Oscar Polk was Pork, one of the O'Hara's three household servants. (Middle, left) Melanie and her Aunt "Pittypat" Hamilton.

Laura Hope Crews was cast by George Cukor after Billie Burke had been judged too young. (Middle, right) Scarlett is an unwilling aide to Dr. Meade, played by Harry Davenport, the seventy-three-year-old stage veteran whose film career had begun in 1912; the sergeant behind him is Ed Chandler, and the wounded soldier in pain is George Hackathorne. (Above, left) Carroll Nye was Frank Kennedy, Scarlett's second husband, whom she stole from her sister Suellen because he had $300 to pay the taxes on Tara. Big Sam, her father's ex-foreman, who saved her from being attacked, was played by Everett Brown. (Above, right) Butterfly McQueen, a twenty-eight-year-old New York stage actress, memorably portrayed Scarlett's shrill, dim-witted servant girl Prissy—the one role that Margaret Mitchell wished she herself could have played.

The richest characterization in the entire film was given by Hattie McDaniel as Mammy, the sly, leather-lunged, bossy Emily Post of the O'Hara family and the only person, besides Rhett Butler, who was not fooled by Scarlett's airs and tears. Miss McDaniel was forty-five years old when she played the part and had spent most of her life touring the black theatrical belt, performing in tent shows, cabarets, and vaudeville and on the legitmate stage. Her timing and her comedic and dramatic talents were taken fullest advantage of by Selznick, Cukor, Victor Fleming, and Sam Wood, all of whom gave her some of the juiciest bits in the film. A native of Wichita, Kansas, Miss McDaniel had to be taught by Susan Myrick to speak in the rich dialect of a transplanted Savannah black who had lived in the north Georgia country for twenty years. (Above, left) Mammy's stunned reaction upon hearing Scarlett tell Frank Kennedy that her sister Suellen, to whom he is engaged, "got tired of waiting, was afraid she was going to be an old maid, and is going to marry one of the county boys next month." (Above, right) " 'T'aint fittin'—it just ain't fittin' " is Mammy's disapproving retort to Rhett's declaration that he is going to buy his daughter a blue velvet riding habit.

ke the Dew   SUNDAY, FEBRUARY 12, 1939   7—C

ice

a peep
s, Yan-
.ade by
, seven

the an-
rom the
t owner
n God-
er), who
3, added
nd mod-
e could
-bellum

I like this for Ashley's home

As late as February 1939, Lyle Wheeler, William Cameron Menzies, and Wilbur Kurtz were still wrestling with the concept of Twelve Oaks, Ashley Wilkes's home. Even though she refused to become officially involved in anything to do with the film, Margaret Mitchell did send this newspaper clipping of the Covington, Georgia, home of Mrs. M. S. Turner to Kurtz, noting, "I like this for Ashley's home." (Bottom) Cosgrove's lack of success with this view of the approach to Twelve Oaks was due to the fact that the carriages were photographed in a field outside the studio and then double-printed onto a painting into which Cosgrove had put the shadows of the trees falling across the driveway. There was no time to re-shoot it so that the shadows could be made to ripple across the carriages instead of becoming transparent.

What Selznick refers to as "disagreement on concept" was really a difference of stylistic approach. Selznick and Menzies had decided on a florid theatrical look and feel for the picture, while Cukor was minutely detailing his characters, an approach that Selznick felt did not catch "the big feel, the scope and breadth of the production." In this he was partly right, but it was a moot point, as he had always intended to have someone else direct the larger spectacle scenes. Most of the work that Cukor did on the picture, however, remains in the completed film. His detailing of the O'Hara family, the complex intertwining relationships of the female characters throughout, his attention to the resonances of the time and the place suffuse the early part of the story with a strength and concern for the characters that is so strong and dense that the rest of the picture can proceed on its narrative way without concerning itself about depth of characterizations.

On Monday morning, February 13, the Hollywood film community read in both trade papers that

> George Cukor and David O. Selznick last night issued the following statement: "As a result of a series of disagreements between us over many of the individual scenes of *Gone With The Wind,* we have mutually decided that the only solution is for a new director to be selected at as early a date as is practicable...." [Selznick added:] "Mr. Cukor's withdrawal... is the most regrettable incident of my rather long producing career, the more so because I consider Mr. Cukor one of the very finest directors it has ever been the good fortune of this business to claim. I can only hope that we will be so fortunate as to be able to replace him with a man of comparable talents."

There was nothing new or unusual about directors being replaced on pictures. It was an accepted activity in those days; Selznick himself had been doing it almost his entire career. What was surprising, and what has been made much of all these years, is his supposed ruthlessness in doing this to Cukor. To the world outside Hollywood, the event was news only insofar as everything concerning *Gone With The Wind* had taken on an air of national importance, but in the film community the reaction was one of shocked surprise. Even on Selznick's own staff, the firing was greeted with incredulity: "I never thought David would can George," says Hal Kern. "They were such great friends.... It really took guts to do it." In Kern's opinion, this marked Selznick's emergence as a full-fledged producer—someone to whom the picture was the overriding concern.

Selznick went to extraordinary pains to make sure that there was no misunderstanding in the town that George was being replaced because of inadequacies. He spent the next several days finding another suitable project for him so that he would continue working and not suffer the agony of enforced idleness after what was obviously a tremendous blow to his professional pride and standing. Before the news broke, he asked Louis B. Mayer to assign Cukor to the upcoming film version of *The Women,* Clare Boothe's hit play, which had a cast made up of the studio's biggest female stars. Mayer agreed, and Ernst Lubitsch, who had been scheduled for that, was instead assigned to direct Garbo in *Ninotchka,* the two pictures emerging among the best of the year. Both Selznick and Cukor were highly intelligent, civilized men, and their reactions to the situation were in keeping with their sensibilities: rueful regret, untinged with bitterness or recriminations. While they never worked together again professionally, their friendship and their personal regard for each other remained largely unchanged.

Cukor was still directing the picture, working on the scenes of the birth of Melanie's baby and events leading up to the escape from Atlanta, when news of his removal reached Vivien Leigh and Olivia de Havilland. Their immediate reaction was a hasty call on Selznick; still in their costumes, they begged him to reconsider, arguing with him for close to an hour, following him around the office in their determination to make him change his mind, until finally they cornered him on top of his window seat, while Leigh cajoled, reasoned, and pleaded. She later repeated her remarks to a reporter, telling him: "My test was directed by George.... I would like people to know how grateful I am for the pains George took with me when I was trying to get myself into the character of Scarlett. It was not easy; it was very hard. Or I was stupid. In any case, I've never known anyone to be so patient... as George was with me. He devoted himself for days at a time to teaching me mannerisms, coaching me in voice inflection, and trying to explain to me and implant in me something of the thinking and psychology that made Scarlett what she was. And no matter what happens—whether I do a good job or a bad one I shall be eternally grateful to George Cukor." But in spite of the entreaties of the two actresses, Selznick refused to reconsider. He later remarked: "I have learned that nothing matters except the final picture."

As soon as Cukor left, production was shut down "for several days" while Selznick tried to find another director. To do this, he turned once again to MGM, offering the job to King Vidor, who politely turned him down. Selznick thereupon prevailed upon Mayer to give him Victor Fleming, busy shooting the studio's expensive, troublesome musical fantasy *The Wizard of Oz.* Mayer was agreeable to this providing Fleming was. Fleming had been looking forward to taking a long, relaxing vacation; he wanted no part of the massive problems that obviously would confront him on *Gone With The Wind.* But he and Gable were extremely close friends, and he could not resist Gable's repeated entreaties to come in and help him out of his Rhett Butler predicament. The three-pronged attack of Gable, Mayer, and Selznick finally won Fleming over, and he agreed to leave the last few days of *The Wizard of Oz* to King Vidor, who finished up the picture by filming the "Over the Rainbow" musical sequence.

Saturday, February 18, Fleming spent all day and most of the night at the studio with Selznick, familiarizing himself with the script, the already filmed material, and the production methods that had been devised. "Fleming was another of that extremely masculine breed," remarked Selznick. "I didn't know him well socially.... He was one of the most attractive men, in my opinion, who ever came to Hollywood, physically and in personality.... I enjoyed working with him.... He was an expert craftsman.... He had been a cameraman and knew his cinematics thoroughly." Fleming had started his career as a director in 1920 with one of Douglas Fairbanks's biggest early successes, *When the Clouds Roll By,* which had pretty well defined the Fairbanks personality—breezy, athletic, optimistic, and wearyingly energetic. Fleming's forte seemed to be strong, rugged action, with an emphasis on masculine sensibilities and codes, but he was surprisingly gifted at dealing with the sensitivities of human nature, as proved by his 1927 *The Way of All Flesh* with Emil Jannings; and his wild, outrageous streak made Jean Harlow in *Bombshell* one of the comedic highlights of 1933.

He had not read *Gone With The Wind,* so he had no preconceived idea of the story, and after a look at the completed footage and a careful appraisal of the script itself, he bluntly and forcefully reiterated to Selznick what Cukor had been saying all along: "Your script is no fucking good." This, coming from someone as objective as Fleming, forced Selznick into acknowledging the seriousness of the situation. The immediate problem now became what to do about it, as Fleming refused to direct the script as written; each day that filming was suspended was costing $65,000, just in overhead. Selznick was frantic to find a way out of his script predicament, and as he had so many times before, he turned to Ben Hecht, who coincidentally was just finishing up a writing assignment at MGM. "David and Victor arrived at my house about 8:30 Sunday morning," recalled Hecht.

They knew I always had an early breakfast and they told me they had arranged to borrow me from MGM to write *Gone With The Wind.* I was just about to go back to New York and I didn't want to get involved in all this, and I told David so. We haggled back and forth over coffee, and he offered me $10,000 for two weeks' work, so I thought, "Well, I'll take a chance." I hadn't read the book, I never read those kind of books, and on the way over to the studio, David was denouncing me as a stupid holdout—that I wasn't fit to call myself a writer. We got to the studio [where] we were met by John van Druten, who wrote plays well, but movies not so well. He was going to work with us, so I asked him if he'd read the book. He said, "Yessss"—he was an English boy—and I said, "What did you think of it, is it a good book, Johnnie?" "Oh yess," he said, "It's a fine book— for bellhops"; well, David got furious and fired him on the spot....

There wasn't time for me to read the whole book, so David decided he'd tell me the whole story—which I couldn't follow; it seemed to me to be what we used to call in Chicago as long as a whore's dream—and

(Above) Lyle Wheeler designed this portion of the porch of Twelve Oaks, constructed over the entrance to Stage 11, for the arrival of the guests at the barbecue. The camera followed Scarlett through the door and into the great hall, built inside the stage. (For years tour guides at MGM pointed to a Southern mansion set on the back lot as Twelve Oaks, but this was not true; only one sequence was photographed at MGM—an exterior shot of the Atlanta house showing Rhett teaching Bonnie to ride her pony.) (Below) J. McMillan Johnson's sketch for Scarlett's return to the ruined Twelve Oaks. A portion of the floor, staircase, and ruined wall was built full size; the upper sections of the staircase and the walls were photographed using a "hanging miniature": a miniature construction of the set hung several feet in front of the camera, matching the perspective of the full-sized setting. The combination—if done correctly—is undetectable.

as pointless. So I read the script that they had—it was really a humpty dumpty job—and I asked David if there wasn't a better one, and he dug up the Sidney Howard original, and it was a superb treatment, so I said I'd do the picture based on this script. Of course, I didn't know the characters, so to save time David and Victor decided that they'd act out all the major parts for me—David played Scarlett and somebody named Ashley, and Victor acted Butler and a girl named Melanie. It was very funny, but it . . . kept up till 2:00 A.M., and after a while the humor got a little vague. They'd talk about a scene, then act it out, and I would write it up. I was shrewd enough to involve David in this so there would be no comebacks or rewrites possible, and while their acting seminar went on I'd catch a few winks on the couch. David didn't sleep at all—he was the Dexedrine pioneer of Hollywood, and was getting shots to keep him awake. He was also on some kind of a diet, so we had nothing but bananas and peanuts to eat while all this nonsense was going on.

For five days and nights Hecht cut, rewrote, and straightened out the narrative focus of the story, accomplishing in that time what had eluded Selznick and all the other writers for three years—a tight, concise, visual retelling of the Howard original through the first half. It was strictly a technical job, there was no creative writing involved, and Hecht contributed nothing except the all-important ability to cut through the dense underbrush of numerous rewrites, clearing away the clutter of the minor characters' digressions and loquacity that strangled the main plot line. "On the fifth day," Hecht related, "the blood vessels in Vic Fleming's

right eye exploded and Selznick finally collapsed in what we thought was a coma but turned out to be just a deep sleep. I had finished rewriting everything up to the girl's return to her plantation, which had taken about a week; when he finally woke up David offered me another raise in salary if I stayed beyond the two weeks, but I said there wasn't enough money in the world for this kind of suicidal work—eighteen to twenty hours a day, and after the second week I got out in a hurry."

By now there was enough revised script for Selznick to give orders to restart production, which was done on March 2, after Fleming and Selznick had both recuperated. Literally starting all over, Fleming's first scene was a retake of the opening, with Scarlett once more telling the Tarleton boys that "this war talk is spoiling the fun at every party this spring." Ridgeway Callow, second assistant director, recalls that the day before shooting, "Fleming came onto the set and said to my boss Eric Stacey and myself, 'They tell me that you're supposed to be the best team in the picture business. But I'm going to put both of you in the hospital before this picture is over.'"

The week after production restarted, Selznick got rid of the last of his lingering dissatisfactions when he removed Lee Garmes as director of photography, replacing him with Ernest Haller, who shot the scenes of Scarlett's entrance to the main hall at Twelve Oaks, which Garmes had set up. Garmes commented: "It was very sad. I didn't want to leave the picture. I loved the story and I was very friendly with David, but he just didn't quite understand the softer shades and tones that we were able to get with the new faster stock, so we agreed to disagree." But Selznick had very definite ideas of what he wanted the color to look like:

Neutral colors certainly have their value, and pastel colors . . . make for lovely scenes . . . but this does not mean . . . that the longest picture on record . . . has to deal one hundred percent in these. . . . This picture . . . gives us the opportunity as in Scarlett's costumes, to throw a violent dab of color at the audience to make a dramatic point. . . . The Technicolor experts are here for the purpose of guiding us technically . . . and not for the purpose of dominating the creative side of our picture as to sets, costumes or anything else.

While Selznick fretted over the color, the costumes, and the second half of the script, Fleming took complete control of the production and it had begun to roll down the long road toward getting all the estimated 650 remaining scenes on film. He was doing this at an average rate of three script pages per day, which worked out to about two minutes of footage daily. "The camera rehearsals were what took so long," says Lydia Schiller. "The lighting, steadying the camera, just moving that Technicolor camera was a massive operation, and Mr. Selznick did like his moving camera shots . . . and you know on some of those smaller sets it was just murder to get that camera in there."

With Fleming in charge, Gable's attitude and demeanor changed completely. He relaxed and, under Fleming's careful handling, even began to enjoy the role, although as Ridgeway Callow remembers, "He worked well with everybody, but the crew didn't like him. I know at MGM they were supposed to be crazy about him, but they were not at Selznick. He was very aloof." On March 25, after completing some close-up retakes of the bazaar sequence, Gable left for six days.

Some of Lyle Wheeler's set designs for *Gone With The Wind:*
(Opposite page) Scarlett's bedroom at Tara (top, left): the fresh room of a Southern girl, the "sweet, gentle, beautiful and ornamental" young lady that Scarlett was—at least outwardly. The good taste of Ellen, Scarlett's mother, is evident in the polished floor covered with a brightly colored rug, the simple mahogany furniture, and the white ruffled tester bed. The parlor at Tara (top, right), arranged for Scarlett's wedding to Charles Hamilton. The delicate French marble mantel bespeaks Ellen's Savannah background; Gerald O'Hara's tastes are apparent in the hunting prints above it, and the room is given a rich feeling by the green velvet portieres around the windows. The entrance hall at Twelve Oaks (bottom, left), with its graceful, curved double staircase, copied from a mansion in South Carolina. The beautiful Greek Revival look of Twelve Oaks was enhanced by the series of Corinthian columns that lined the main hallway (bottom, right). Scarlett is standing in the hall leading to the library.
(This page) Rhett's bedroom in the postwar Atlanta house (top, left), dominated by the huge oil portrait of Scarlett painted by Helen Carleton. The parlor in Aunt "Pittypat" Hamilton's Atlanta home during the war (top, right) was the height of fashion with its elegant Victorian furniture and ruffled draperies, but the room, like its "pink-cheeked, fussy" owner, is crowded and overdecorated. The furnishings and other set decorations were by Edward Boyle in collaboration with Joseph Platt, the interior decoration consultant for *House & Garden.* Platt's contributions to the picture are still a subject of controversy. Scarlett's bedroom in the Atlanta house (bottom, left) is in stunning contrast to the simplicity of her room at Tara. The Atlanta house had "more of everything than the governor's mansion," bought with the postwar affluence of Rhett's blockade running. Rhett said it was "a nightmare," but the tufted satin wall and luxurious canopied French bed mirror Scarlett's violent reaction against her bitter wartime poverty. The library at Twelve Oaks (bottom, right) differed markedly from Miss Mitchell's description of "a dim room with towering walls . . . completely filled with books . . . heavy furniture . . . high-backed chairs with deep seats . . . and velvet hassocks for the women."

These twelve frames from *Gone With The Wind* contain some of the most memorable examples of Walter Plunkett's costume designs. (First row, left) Scarlett's white crinoline gown in the opening scenes was a substitution for the green-sprigged muslin that she had originally worn. Selznick felt that the white gown gave her more of a virginal, sixteen-year-old quality. (First row, center) The green-sprigged muslin creation that Scarlett wore to the Wilkes's barbecue was in turn a substitution for the green watered silk festooned with ecru lace visible in the tests on page 263. (First row, right) Scarlett's ivory silk gown for her marriage to Melanie's brother Charles was her mother's wedding dress, hurriedly re-made to fit Scarlett because of the haste with which the wedding was arranged. (Second row, center) Scarlett wore this calico dress, varied in six different ways, throughout the middle portion of the film. Melanie's nightgown in this same shot was used to wrap the bloody head of the Yankee cavalryman Scarlett has just shot. (Second row, right) The most famous costume in the picture—and probably in all motion picture history—was the dress Scarlett made from her mother's green velvet portieres, so that she could "go to Atlanta looking like a queen" in the hopes of borrowing $300 from Rhett to pay the taxes on Tara. She even went so far as to decorate the bonnet with a gilded chicken foot—all to no avail. The spectacular variety of Plunkett's designs for the female characters in *Gone With The Wind* has tended to obscure his outstanding talent for designing for men, as can be seen in several of the shots above, especially those of Rhett Butler. Plunkett's ability to indicate character and attitude through line, color, and fabric remains unsurpassed.

Ona Munson played Belle Watling, the leading madam of Atlanta's red-light district, winning the role over such actresses as Betty Compson and Marjorie Rambeau. (Below, left) Belle's scenes were brief but effective, and, for the time, quite frank in letting the audience know that she was Rhett's mistress. (Below, center) In Atlanta, Scarlett visits Rhett in jail and encounters Belle, who impudently eyes Scarlett and shocks Mammy ("Who dat? Ah ain' never see'd hair dat color in mah life. Does you know a dyed-hair woman?"). (Below, right) Miss Munson's finest moment was her scene with Melanie, in which she tells her that no matter how grateful Melanie is to her for saving Ashley's life, she must not speak to her publicly, as "that wouldn't be fittin'."

Clark Gable with his favorite director and close friend, Victor Fleming. It was Fleming who created the Gable image in the early 1930s, patterning the rather insecure actor after his own tough, honest masculinity and giving him a sense of humor that enhanced Gable's own powerful sexuality.

During his short leave, he and Carole Lombard eloped to Kingman, Arizona; his first day back on the set, there was a small celebration attended by everybody, including Selznick, who was fond of Lombard and truly wished Gable well. Then production resumed at a pace even more hectic than before. The pressure on everybody in the studio was now tremendous, not just from the immense workload but because of Selznick's erratic working habits.

"He was a hard worker," recalls Klune, "but he was not a well-organized man at all. He had great difficulty in organizing his own time properly, and consequently he could never catch up with the things that needed his attention." And the script, no matter how much work was done on it, always needed more attention, like a sick child in the night. Ben Hecht had stayed on the week after the marathon day-and-night sessions that had finally shaped the first half. His second week was spent at a much less frantic pace; he worked during the day trimming the second half down, eliminating everything except the two central stories of Scarlett and Rhett, Melanie and Ashley. He did his best to maintain a smooth narrative flow in the latter half, but the story as trimmed down by Howard lacked the strong action of the first half, and as the plot unraveled itself around Scarlett's love life, it lost much of the epic quality of the book, becoming largely a series of static dialogue sequences between the principals. These weaknesses were readily apparent to Selznick, and he labored over Hecht's work. Dialogue was written, rewritten, and changed again, sequences were altered, dropped, shifted, in a nightmare of schedule revisions and last-minute changes. Klune tried to keep up with these changes, but it was difficult and wearying: "There were days when we didn't even know what we were doing tomorrow. It was not at all uncommon for David to call me at three in the morning and ask me what we were shooting tomorrow. I'd say, 'David, you've got the schedule right there on your desk, so I know that you know.' He'd say, 'Can we change it?' I'd say, 'At this time of the morning?' This happened time and time again."

For Lyle Wheeler, these last-minute changes of Selznick's were particularly frustrating: "I'd have a set all built and ready to go for the next day and David would suddenly decide to shift the scene because it needed rewriting or it wasn't finished yet. He'd tell me, 'We're going to write all night and we need a bedroom set tomorrow morning.' . . . I had a crew that worked many many nights all night long and all day just trying to keep up. We always did, though." One thing that was not keeping up was the money. The constant changes and long overtime hours for the gangs of laborers and other workers were wreaking havoc with the budget, and early in April Selznick realized with a shock that he wouldn't have enough money to finish the picture. Still to come were some of the most expensive scenes, all of which would require thousands of extras, hundreds of workers, and another estimated million and a half dollars. To his rescue once again came the Whitneys, at least Jock and his sister Joan Payson, who advanced some of the money. The balance was to have come from C. V. Whitney, but evidently C. V. declined, for Selznick was forced to turn to MGM for the money, showing Al Lichtman about an hour's worth of completed footage. Lichtman was enthusiastic at what he saw, jubilantly predicting: "This picture will gross nineteen million dollars." He took Selznick's request for more funds back to Mayer, who passed the buck to Nicholas Schenck, knowing that he would turn it down. It was a squeeze play of the most naked kind, for if Selznick could not raise the money, the picture would by default fall into MGM's lap. Not quite stumped, Selznick played his last trump card: Attilio Giannini of the Bank of America. A screening was arranged for him and for Joseph Rosenberg, who was in charge of motion picture loans for the bank. They too were impressed, but bankers can be impressed without being fiscally foolish. All of Selznick International's books were examined and the deficits on the last three pictures stuck out like red flags. Selznick and *Gone With The Wind* were bad risks. The only way the bank would advance the money was if it were guaranteed by the Whitneys. But in order to get the guarantee, Selznick had to give up a portion of his ownership of the company and of his share in the proceeds of *Gone With The Wind*. A straight bank loan of $1.25 million was advanced and the production continued on its seemingly interminable way, safe now from the rapacity of Nick Schenck and MGM.

As soon as the money came through, Selznick gave orders to Klune to schedule the bulk of the spectacular exterior scenes, starting with the panic-stricken populace fleeing Atlanta. The evacuation sequences were scheduled for two days' grueling shooting on April 5 and 6, involving six hundred extras dressed in period costume, carrying every conceivable kind of prop as they struggled to get out of the city while Sherman's army bombarded it. This mass of humanity, animals, props, and explosives had to be carefully organized, not just from the standpoint of the camera but also for the most efficient manner of handling the mobs of extras, getting them costumed, onto the set, and into their places, re-

April 4, 1939—For three days, in 80-degree heat, Vivien Leigh dodged and darted her way through four hundred extras and twenty pieces of horse-drawn equipment, filming the panic-stricken populace fleeing Atlanta.

hearsing their movements, and coordinating the simultaneous levels of action. This last was all-important, for as Lydia Schiller recalls,

> Because she was the center of so much of the action, we couldn't use a stunt double for Vivien Leigh. In the scene where she comes out of the hospital and sees the city going mad, she really took chances. . . . When the army was moving out and there was chaos . . . she ran in between those caissons, they were going at full speed . . . and anything could have happened. . . . There were so many narrow escapes for her. . . . I remember once she was trying to get out of the way of a speeding fire wagon and she ran smack into the path of another wagon coming in from the opposite direction. . . . She just froze, stopped dead in her tracks, and fortunately her hoop skirt flared up and frightened the horses; they reared back and stopped. . . . She took it all in stride, she was a real trouper.

The stress on the actress was not all physical. Her emotional involvement with Olivier led to one particular outburst that helped the scenes she was working in. "Laurence Olivier was leaving to go back East to do a play," says Schiller, "and she wanted to go to the airport to see him off. . . . But Mr. Selznick wouldn't let her go . . . he said it would cost too much . . . so she came in and she'd evidently been crying all night, her eyes were all red and swollen and we wondered if we'd be able to photograph her. So Mr. Selznick scheduled a crying scene for her . . . one right after the death of her first husband, when she's complaining about having to wear widow's weeds, and she threw herself on the bed and sobbed and sobbed. . . . Those were real tears."

Leigh was not the only one who was near cracking up. "We were there working our asses off for fourteen to eighteen hours a day for almost six months," recalls Ridgeway Callow. Selznick himself was going at a killing pace, being fed thyroid extract and Benzedrine to maintain his energy while he worked on the script for the remaining sequences and also on the cutting of the already filmed footage with Hal Kern. Sandwiched in between were conferences on sets and costumes still to come, looking at actors for the small roles, and overseeing the special effects shots that Jack Cosgrove was working on. These were particularly important. They were more time-consuming than anything else in the picture and more critical in terms of the exacting demands not only on Cosgrove but also on his equipment. Cosgrove's technique involved painting with oils on panes of glass 3 to 4 feet wide. "Jack was the

greatest man in the business for these paintings," recalls Hal Kern, "but he was also a pretty heavy drinker. It never affected his work, but I'd go into his workshop and he'd be up on this little platform with no railings, he'd hold on with one hand and he'd be painting with the other, hanging out over twelve feet of nothing and so drunk he didn't even know his own name. . . . Then he'd climb down and maybe fall the last foot or so and go look through the camera finder to see how the match was, and then he'd climb back up there and do it all over again. I was always amazed that he never fell and broke his neck."

One of the shots posed a completely baffling set of problems for Cosgrove. It was the first large "pullback" in the picture, showing Scarlett and her father in silhouette under a tree looking out over Tara nestled in the rolling hills of Georgia, backdropped by a flaming sunset sky. The problem arose from trying to blend the four pieces of film, all of which had been photographed at separate times, combining the live action, two different paintings, and the sunset effect. Cosgrove was going crazy trying to compute the speed of the three separate camera moves necessary to keep the pullback effect in synchronization. Finally, Ray Klune called in the mathematics department at UCLA and they figured it out, using advanced calculus.

On the sets, Vivien Leigh and Fleming were at loggerheads over the interpretation of her role; she was trying to stay as close as possible to the Cukor interpretation, while Fleming wanted her to play Scarlett tougher, making her, in Leigh's opinion, "much more of a bitch," with a consequent loss of sympathy and believability. Leigh, with no one's knowledge, was visiting Cukor on the Sundays she had off to get his help in keeping her perspective about the part, something she later discovered was also being done by Olivia de Havilland, so Cukor managed to keep his finger in the picture even in its advanced stages. Because of the fragmentary nature of the script, Leigh had begun to carry a copy of the book with her everywhere, consulting it before she did a scene to make sure of her bearings and to ascertain that nothing was left out or changed that she felt was important. Selznick began to be irritated by her insistence on consulting the book, yelling at her on several occasions to "please put that damn book away." The tension was beginning to tell on Fleming, who had been working at full steam, nonstop, for well over a year. In mid-April Selznick, alarmed, wrote to Henry Ginsberg:

> We may soon have a serious worry to face . . . that may again halt

This portrait of Clark Gable and Vivien Leigh as Rhett Butler and Scarlett O'Hara was taken by Fred Parrish using the Kodachrome process. *Gone With The Wind* was one of the first productions to use color photographs extensively for publicity purposes.

The city of Atlanta was re-created relatively faithfully from photos and drawings supplied by Wilbur Kurtz. The train station (above, left) was built practically full scale on the back lot from blueprints of the original. This shot of troop trains arriving at Christmas was doctored by Jack Cosgrove, who added the sky and mist in the upper right-hand section of the set; he also added the smoke emerging from the stack of the engine. Only the portion of the engine seen in the shot was actually built; the side not visible to the camera was made of wooden struts and wheels mounted on a dolly. (Above) The populace of the city waiting in front of the *Examiner* office "while two nations came to death grips on the farm lands of Pennsylvania" was a split-screen shot by Cosgrove, who doubled the number of people visible by photographing two hundred extras on one side of the wagon and carriage and then having them change their costumes and stand on the opposite side, giving the impression of the square being jammed with hundreds of people. (Left) No trickery was involved in this shot of the populace fleeing the city as Sherman begins his bombardment. Six hundred extras were used in these sequences, which took three days to film.

production.... I have ... been worried that Fleming would not be able to finish the picture because of his physical condition.... He is so near the breaking point, both physically and mentally from sheer exhaustion, that it would be a miracle in my opinion if he is able to shoot another seven or eight weeks.... Since it would be impossible for any substitute director to step in without taking the time to thoroughly familiarize himself with the book and the scripts, I think we ought to start now selecting an understudy....

While Selznick kept a wary eye on Fleming's health, he decided to break the picture up into three units, one under Fleming, concentrating on the principals, and two second units, one of which, under director Chester Franklin, went to Chico, 100 miles outside of Sacramento, to get the shots of Gerald O'Hara galloping his horse across the fields of Tara, and also to photograph the background shots of Tara devastated after the war. The other unit, under travelogue director James ("as the sun sets in the West") Fitzpatrick, had been dispatched on a three-week tour of five Southern states to obtain atmospheric footage for the titles, montages, and other photographic backgrounds. In addition, William Cameron Menzies, working with Cosgrove at the studio, was occupied filming all the bridging sections, bits and pieces of action, beginnings and endings of sequences, and tying up the photographic and special effects loose ends, while simultaneously laying out and preparing to shoot the still-pending battle scenes.

The breaking point Selznick had predicted for Fleming was finally reached just as he was wrapping a delicate and time-consuming two days' shooting on Melanie's death sequence. Ironically it came when Gable refused to do a sequence in which Rhett Butler cries in Melanie's lap at Scarlett's near death from a miscarriage. Gable was embarrassed, believing that it was "unmanly" to cry; he was adamant, and no amount of persuasion from Fleming could change his mind. Gable left the set at 11:30 A.M., finished for the day, but Fleming's work was just beginning. There was a late night call for a scene between Scarlett, Melanie, and Belle Watling, making her first appearance in the story. It had been planned as an exterior night shot on the back lot set of the Atlanta street. Fleming, still upset at Gable's intransigence, was in no mood for any back talk from other cast members, and when Vivien Leigh made the mistake of arguing with him yet again, Fleming's temper gave way. According to John Lee Mahin, who was on the set, "Vic rolled up his script, threw it at her, and said, 'You can shove this up your royal British ass,'" and stormed off the set. He later confided to Mahin that on his way home to Malibu, he had seriously considered driving his car off one of the Palisades cliffs.

Selznick had not been unprepared for such a development, and when it became clear that Fleming would not return for that night's shooting, he hastily borrowed Sam Wood from MGM. Aided by Menzies, who took care of the set-ups, and armed by Selznick with a detailed description of what the scene should be, Wood began filming the scene at 1:00 A.M. "It was freezing cold that night," recalls Ridgeway Callow, "and every time that Ona Munson as Belle Watling walked over to get into her

"Scarlett O'Hara was not beautiful . . ." wrote Miss Mitchell in the opening sentence of the novel, but David Selznick obviously disagreed, as evidenced by these shots of Vivien Leigh from the film showing the many faces of Scarlett O'Hara, from the opening scene with the sixteen-year-old beauty on the steps of Tara (photographed by Hal Rosson), through war, marriage, poverty, Reconstruction, birth, death, attempted rape, miscarriage, and lost love, until the final image of the tear-stained face of the twenty-eight-year-old Scarlett, who refuses to acknowledge defeat in Rhett's rejection of her, vowing to return to Tara and to "think of some way to get him back. After all, tomorrow is another day."

Clark Gable was the quintessence of the American male movie star. Thirty-eight years old in 1939, he was at the height of his physical appeal, and *Gone With The Wind* marked the apex of his career as a sex object. He was more than a match for Scarlett O'Hara in that department—if not in the final outcome of the battle of the sexes.

May 4, 1939—Director Sam Wood, who had just finished filming *Goodbye, Mr. Chips* in England, took over on *Gone With The Wind* during Victor Fleming's "sickness." He is seen here with Leslie Howard, Vivien Leigh, and a distinguished visitor to the set: Al Smith, former governor of New York and almost president of the United States. (Middle) Susan Myrick (in riding breeches), a friend of Margaret Mitchell's and a forthright, intelligent lady, was brought in from Atlanta to oversee the accuracy of Southern customs and speech in the film and was the final arbiter in all matters pertaining to Southern decorum and manners. (Bottom) The pressure on Vivien Leigh was tremendous. Working six days a week from 7:00 A.M. sometimes until midnight, the actress appeared in almost every one of the picture's ninety sequences. Here she is getting a massage from Isabel Jewell, who played Emmy Slattery, daughter of poor white trash, who was indirectly responsible for the death of Scarlett's mother.

carriage, the horses would decide to take a leak. They must have done it fourteen times, until their bladders finally ran out and we were able to get a good take." They shot till 4:00 A.M., then were back on the set at 9:30 A.M., and Wood directed the shots of a haggard Scarlett, determined to make herself attractive to Rhett Butler, having Mammy make a dress from the green velvet curtains in the Tara parlor.

Wood was a competent, stolid director who could be counted on to put the actors through their paces efficiently and unimaginatively. By now, the performers were well into their roles, so Wood's job was more or less that of a traffic manager. The production began to take on a subdued, clenched-teeth quality, as everybody involved determined to plow through the remaining necessary scenes. But Wood lacked the driving force, the narrative emphasis, and the strong visual storytelling sense that Fleming had brought to the production. Accordingly, Selznick began a concerted campaign to woo Fleming back to work, offering him a share in the profits, to which Fleming is reported to have replied: "What do you think I am, a chump? This picture is going to be the biggest white elephant of all time," a sentiment that did not deter Selznick at all. He enlisted the aid of Gable and Vivien Leigh, and the three of them turned up one Sunday in late April at Fleming's beach home, bearing a large cage of love birds. Leigh was appropriately apologetic, Gable persuasively contrite, and Selznick convincing not only in his concern for Fleming's health but also in his proclamations of how much the picture needed his gifts. After a two-week rest, Fleming returned, Selznick having agreed to keep Wood working as an alternate first unit.

Fleming's first day back had him overseeing the first of five separate attempts to get a dramatic dawn shot of Scarlett's vow in the field of Tara to "never be hungry again." Selznick wanted this to be an affirmation of her indomitability, and her transformation from pampered spoiled child to a mature, determined woman, and it had to be thrilling enough to close the first half of the picture on a highly inspirational note. The scene was scheduled to be filmed on the barren ranchlands called Lasky Mesa near Agoura, several hours from the studio in the San Fernando Valley. To be ready at dawn, the cast and crew had to leave the studio at 1:00 A.M. "We did this several times," recalls Ray Klune,

> because each time David didn't like something about it, either the pullback or the sky or something wasn't right. Vivien and I were not on good terms when we were up there. She hated location. She had to get up so early in the morning, and we'd get out there and sometimes the sun wouldn't come out, it would be all fogged up and a couple of the trips were a waste of time. But then we finally got a good one. It was after an all-night rain, we drove out there and it was pouring and she cursed me out, but the weather prediction had indicated that it would stop before dawn and I knew if it did it would be a beautiful sunrise. Vic thought I was crazy and they were both cursing the hell out of me. But the rain stopped, and even though we were all covered with mud, we got the most wonderful shot. And later she said to me, "Ray, you were right, and I was a bitch," and I said to her, "You're right on both counts."

Klune was now immersed in preparations for the last major production problem in the picture, that of Scarlett's search for Dr. Meade among the wounded and dying soldiers surrounding the Atlanta railroad station. In the book, Margaret Mitchell had used one vivid paragraph to describe Scarlett's reaction to the sight of hundreds of men "lying in the pitiless sun, shoulder to shoulder, head to feet . . . lining the tracks, the sidewalks, stretched out in endless rows under the car shed. Some lay stiff

S.I.P-108-P-269

A harassed Victor Fleming, back at work after two weeks' rest, instructs a tense Vivien Leigh on the dramatic necessities of the scene at hand: Scarlett's search for Dr. Meade among the 1,600 dead and dying Confederate soldiers lying in the Atlanta railroad yards.

(Overleaf) A rehearsal for the massive pullback shot of the Confederate wounded lying in front of the Atlanta train station. A 60-foot construction crane was used to hold the camera, and a special concrete ramp was built for it. On the camera platform are Fleming, cameraman Ernest Haller, and his assistant, Arthur Arling. In addition to eight hundred extras, the scene was populated with eight hundred dummies, who were rocked back and forth by live actors discreetly camouflaging the fraud.

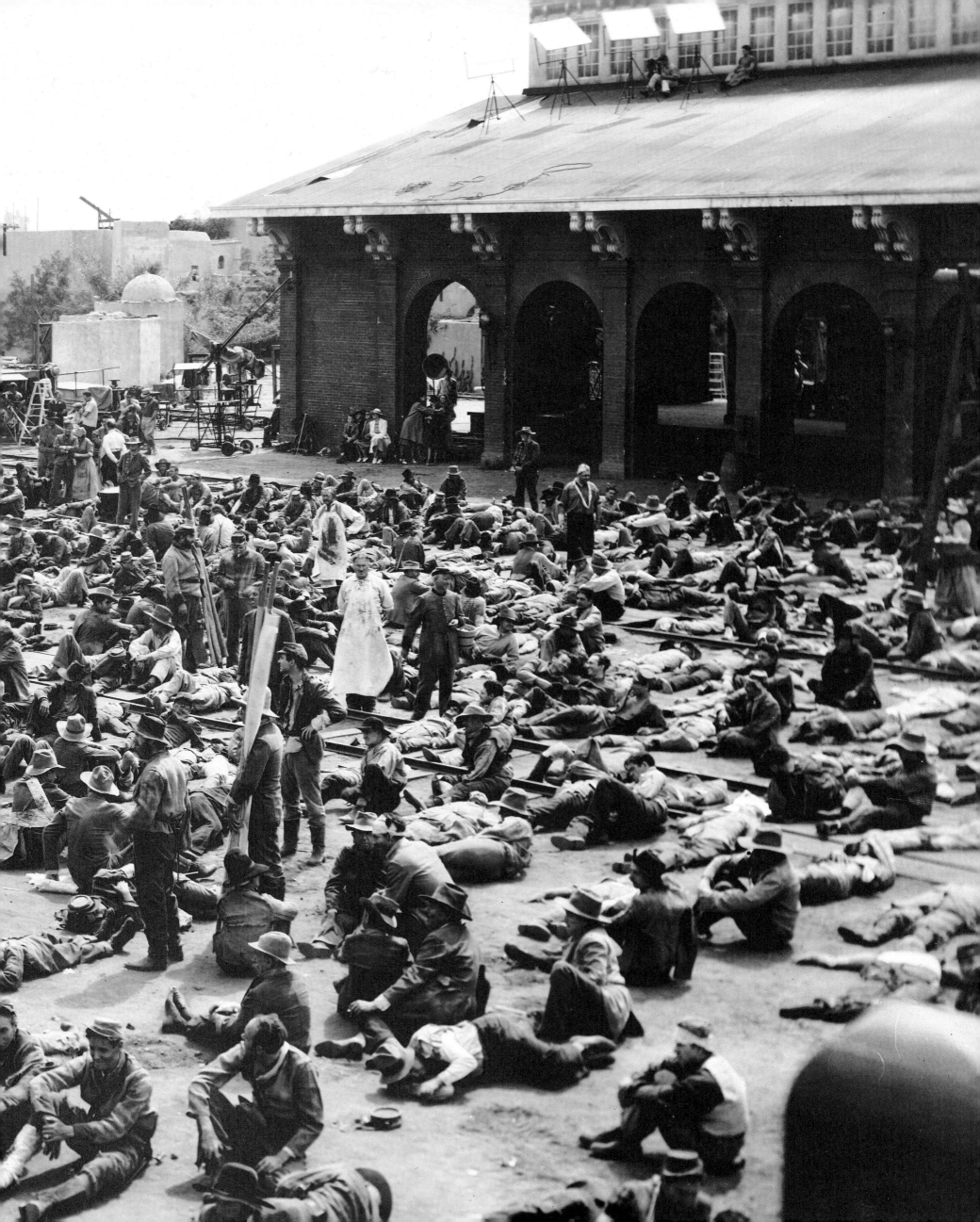

The dramatic high point of Clark Gable's performance in *Gone With The Wind* was this scene of Rhett Butler crying in Melanie's lap over Scarlett's near death from her miscarriage. Rugged leading men, especially romantic heroes, did not cry on screen in the 1930s and forties, and Gable's reluctance to do so was as much from fear of the damage to his image as from his own insecurities as an actor.

and still, but many writhed under the hot sun moaning. Everywhere, swarms of flies hovered over the men . . . everywhere was blood . . . groans, screamed curses of pain. The smell of sweat . . . of unwashed bodies, of excrement rose up in waves of blistering heat until the fetid stench almost nauseated her." Selznick wanted this scene to open on a close-up of Scarlett's horrified reaction to what she sees, then have the camera slowly pull back and up, revealing more and more, literally hundreds of wounded and dying men, with the camera finally coming to a stop on a close-up of the tattered Confederate flag waving over the entire scene. "There was no camera crane large enough to get the kind of a shot David wanted," recalled Klune.

I think that the biggest camera crane in town could only get twenty-five feet off the ground, and we estimated that to take in the expanse of scene that was pictured in the sketches, the camera would have to be about ninety feet off the ground at its highest point. So we found a company that operated the largest construction cranes in southern California, and we got one of their men out to the studio. I showed him the back lot and the scene and explained the problem to him, and he said that they could find us a crane that had an extension range of one hundred and twenty-five feet. Now the problem there is that a camera crane is a precision instrument, whereas a construction crane is anything but. . . . We found that it shook at the very beginning of the movement and at the very end, and as the truck that it was mounted on went into gear and pulled back. The arm itself was pretty smooth during its up and back extension. It was then that I came up with an idea that eliminated the need to use the engine, which was what caused the vibration. We built a concrete ramp about one hundred and fifty feet long—it had to support a piece of steel that weighed ten tons—and these were the days before fast-drying concrete and we couldn't put the damn crane on the ramp for two weeks, but when we finally did, we rehearsed it and the crane slid back down the ramp as smooth as glass while the arm raised and it worked out very smoothly.

Now that the mechanical aspects had been worked out, the sequence needed to be populated with what Klune estimated to be almost two thousand extras, which was just about all that Central Casting had on file. Casting calls usually went out to extras the night before they were needed, and there were several large-scale pictures in production at the same time. "We prepared far enough in advance, we thought," Klune said, " but Central Casting told us the most they could promise us for the next few weeks was about eight hundred people. So we decided to use the eight hundred and intersperse dummies among them, and that'd save us a lot of money. The Screen Extras Guild made a big fuss about it and tried to get us to pay for the eight hundred dummies, and I said, 'No, not one cent,' and they raised all sorts of hell, but we held firm on it and said if you can supply us with real people, we'll pay, otherwise we'll use the dummies. Well, they were only able to come up with a little over eight hundred and that killed the case completely. . . . We never heard another word about it."

Selznick now took on the task of trying to convince Gable to cry in the scene of Rhett's remorse over Scarlett's miscarriage. He was helped in this by Carole Lombard, who persuaded her dubious husband that there was nothing unmanly about an actor crying, that it would be a memorable scene, pointing out that he knew all along he was going to have to do it and couldn't back out now. Selznick relates that "Clark was violently opposed to this and said that nothing was more contemptible than self-pity, that he just could not see himself weeping over this situation. I argued with him and told him that the most universally felt emotion in the world is self-pity, that we all felt sorry for ourselves at one time or another . . . that this would bring public identity with the feeling that he too was vulnerable." Fleming diplomatically offered to film the scene with tears and without, and let Gable decide which one to use. Helped considerably by the design and mood of the scene, a blue-tinged rain-washed night, and by the sympathetic playing of Olivia de Havilland, Gable—under Fleming's sensitive handling—managed to reveal some of the inner torments of Rhett Butler, who up to that point in the film had largely been a charming, superficial cipher. After seeing the rushes, Gable reluctantly agreed that the weeping version was the better of the two, and okayed the use of it in the picture.

This was one of six color photographs taken on the sets of *Gone With The Wind* by a photographer for *House & Garden* magazine. According to Lyle Wheeler, the wallpaper in this shot was the only contribution of Joseph Platt, who is credited with the interiors. Platt, the interior decoration consultant for *House & Garden*, received much publicity in the magazine as the designer for all the film's interiors, something that infuriated Wheeler and Selznick, who immediately put a stop to it.

Olivia de Havilland as Melanie Wilkes in a studio portrait by Fred Parrish.

Leslie Howard as Ashley Wilkes in a studio portrait by Fred Parrish

The intertwining and complex relationships among Scarlett, Ashley, and Melanie de-scribed in the novel were not changed at all in the film. Scarlett loves Ashley, who loves Melanie, who loves Scarlett, who despises Melanie. Scarlett's attitude toward Melanie softens later, for she stays through the siege of Atlanta to help Melanie have Ashley's child and then nurses her back to health at Tara. Scarlett's reluctant admiration for Melanie grows after Melanie helps Scarlett bury the marauding Yankee soldier Scarlett has killed, and on Melanie's deathbed, Scarlett finally sees that Melanie has always been her best friend—and the kind of great lady that Scarlett had wanted to be. Scarlett also realizes that she never really loved Ashley and that she in fact loves Rhett. But it's too late: Melanie dies, Rhett leaves, and Scarlett is left with nothing but Tara and a helpless Ashley, clinging to her skirts and sobbing.

The love scenes between Scarlett and Rhett crackle with a sexual electricity that gives the picture a vibrancy that is one of its main attractions. It begins with their first stormy meeting in the library at Twelve Oaks and intensifies at the Atlanta bazaar (top, left), when Rhett shocks the Confederacy by bidding $100 ("in gold") to dance with the newly widowed Mrs. Hamilton, and Scarlett scandalizes the town by accepting. Their on-again, off-again romance differs slightly from Miss Mitchell's account in that in the film Rhett tells Scarlett several times that he loves her—something he doesn't do in the book until the end. He does try to convince her that "we belong together, being the same sort," and after they finally marry, she taunts him with the fact that "I shall always love another man," whereupon he does the only thing a frustrated husband could do—carries her up the stairs for a night of forced passion. Their scenes have an erotic tension and frankness daring for the time, especially in a costume picture, where everyone usually behaved with decorum and good manners.

Film editor Hal Kern (center) is bent over a Movieola examining a sequence from *Gone With The Wind* with his associate, James Newcom (far left), while assistant film editors Richard van Enger and Ernest Leadly and an unidentified associate editor continue trying to reduce the 160,000 feet of printed film to its final 18,000-foot length.

Production had now been going on for five months; winter had given way to spring, and spring had quickly turned to a blistering summer as the five units struggled to finish up the bulk of the principal photography. On the stages, the heat was aggravated by the huge amounts of light needed for the Technicolor photography. The stages weren't air-conditioned and according to Klune, "It was just brutal. We had great big exhaust fans, but it was still hell." But the production was driving furiously toward the finish date, with Selznick urging everyone to realize that "it is going to take the combined efforts . . . of all of us . . . to speed up the rest of the picture. . . . Quite apart from the cost factor, everybody's nerves are getting on the ragged edge and God only knows what will happen if we don't get this damn thing finished." Finally, on June 27, the last scene was filmed under Fleming's direction. It was, oddly enough, practically the last scene in the picture, Rhett's farewell to Scarlett, and Selznick had revised and rewritten the sequence the night before, bringing the new pages down to the set personally, watching carefully while Fleming set up the shot and rehearsed Vivien Leigh as Scarlett tearfully inquired of Rhett: "If you go, where shall I go, what shall I do?" And he coolly looked at her and replied: "My dear, I don't give a damn." Just before the shot was taken, Selznick added the word "frankly" to the beginning of Rhett's last line, which gave it a kind of lilting, off-handed finality and promptly became as much of a classic catchphrase as Scarlett's "I'll think about it tomorrow." (As a precautionary measure, an alternate version was shot, using the phrase "I just don't care," and this was used at the previews.)

Later that afternoon, Selznick wired Jock Whitney: "Sound the siren. Scarlett O'Hara completed her performance at noon today. Gable finishes tonight or in the morning, and we will be shooting until Friday with bit people. I am going on the boat Friday night and you can all go to the devil." Five months and one day after it had started, *Gone With The Wind* was finished . . . almost.

Now began the arduous, exhausting task of sifting through the mass of filmed material in search of a finished picture. This took up all of July and August, with Selznick running the material over and over with

Hal Kern, who recalls that "Selznick was very interested in editing; he truly believed that a picture could be ruined or made great in the editing. He would talk to me for hours about the pros and cons of doing something in a certain way; he wasn't sure why a person had to keep traveling in the same direction across a screen, if you cut away from them. He thought that the camera could just turn it around and that the audience would still be able to figure it out." These editing sessions with Kern would start early in the afternoon and go on for days.

Kern and his crew had made the first rough assemblage of footage early in July, and found that what with numerous takes and angles of the same scenes, the picture ran almost six hours. All through the sweltering months of summer the editors, Selznick, Barbara Keon, and Lydia Schiller ran the material over and over again. "Every day, it would get a little shorter," recalls Lydia Schiller. "They would make the changes. Mr. Selznick would say, 'Let's not use that shot—let's go to a close-up here.' It just went on forever. We'd be making copious notes so that the cutters could work on these sequences in the morning. Then we'd get them back and he'd want to change this, take that out, put that in, calling for an alternate take or another angle. Then our next session in the projection room he would look at that version and see if he liked it. . . . We worked this way night after night, paring, changing—the night would just disappear—the work was so intense. Bobbie Keon and I would trade off and spell each other, but Mr. Selznick and Hal were at it nonstop, once I think for almost forty-eight hours."

One of the most troublesome sequences in the picture was the very ending of the story, for, as Selznick explained:

We found it impossible to get into script form even the hint that Scarlett might get Rhett back that is inferred in the book. In reaching for a satisfactory ending for motion picture purposes, we tried two or three ways . . . indicating something of the kind after she went back to Tara . . . but none of them worked . . . and I finally cooked up an ending of my own. . . . I felt that the one thing that was really open to us was to stress the Tara thought even more than Miss Mitchell did. . . . Accordingly, after Rhett leaves Scarlett, she turns from the door sobbing, "I can't let him go . . . what is there to do . . . what is there that matters?" Suddenly we hear the ghostlike voice of Gerald saying, "Land's the only thing that matters, it's the only thing that lasts. . . ." Then Ashley's voice saying: "Something you love better than me, though you may not know it. Tara." Then Rhett's voice: "It's this from which you get your strength, the red earth of Tara." The last part of each speech is repeated in turn with increasing tempo and volume . . . during this Scarlett has been emerging from her despair . . . reacting to the realization that she still has Tara . . . and as the camera moves in to a big closeup of her she says, "Home . . . I'll go home . . . and I'll think of some way to get him back. After all, tomorrow is another day." We immediately dissolve to Scarlett standing at Tara in silhouette, the camera pulls back just as it did on Gerald and Scarlett to an extreme long shot as we come to our end. . . . This seemed to give the picture a tremendous lift at the end where it was necessary and where, without something of the kind, we might have ended on a terrifically depressing note.

Working furiously, Selznick and Kern managed to get the film down to five hours by late July. But by that time the cutting continuity was so mangled with cuts, additions, and replacements that neither Selznick, nor Kern, nor any of the editors could make head or tail of it. So Lydia Schiller was assigned to sit down at a Movieola with the cut footage and construct a shot-by-shot description of what had been edited. "I worked on that for about two weeks," she recalls. "I can't remember exactly, it was all such a blur." After she had put it together, the two men spent another hectic month paring the footage down further. While working on the editing, Selznick was also obsessed with the idea of giving the picture a beginning that would live up to the subject, something that would evoke the grandeur and the majesty of the title. He told Hal Kern, "I want the biggest main title that has ever been made." So Kern went off to Pacific Title, the lettering company that specialized in trailers and other kinds of graphic design, and told them he "wanted the letter 'G' to come on and fill the screen, then the same with 'O,' and so on, until each letter had swept across individually. But we found out that the proportion was all wrong, so finally they came up with each of the words individually sweeping across; it took away a little from my first thought, but it was still very impressive, and David loved it when he saw it." To film it, a special dolly had to be borrowed from MGM. It took three men to operate as it moved across the four plate-glass sheets on which the lettering had been hand-painted.

By September 9, Selznick decided that the picture was ready for its first preview, the planning of which he left to Hal Kern, cautioning him not to let anyone know where and when it would take place.

I said to him, "David, the only person who tells about a preview is you, you're always telling all your friends." So I told him that if he didn't know where it was going to be, then he couldn't tell anybody. I told him to tell his secretary that he didn't feel well, that he was going home, and to get in his car, that the chauffeur would know where he was going but David wouldn't. He could make one stop to pick up Mrs. Selznick and Jock Whitney, and that was it. Meanwhile I had taken all the film in a car up to Riverside. . . . I had previewed up there quite a long time and had a couple of good friends who managed the big theatres. . . . So we drove up to the Golden State Theatre, and I looked in and they were playing a Richard Dix picture called *Man of Conquest* and they didn't have more than two hundred people in the place. So then we walked over to the Riverside; they were playing *Beau Geste* and had a full house. . . .

When the picture had ended, the manager stood up in front of the audience and told them there was going to be an unannounced preview, that it was going to be one of the biggest pictures of the year, and that it ran over four hours. He didn't tell them the title; in case anybody left, I didn't want them blabbing. Once some people had gone, I closed the theatre, wouldn't let anybody make phone calls or come back in after they'd left. The manager said, "This is against the law, I can't do it," so I told him I'd do it for him. I'd got hold of the local police department and had cops on every door so that nobody could come in. The manager says, "Hal, I gotta call my wife; she'll kill me if I don't let her know," so I said, "Okay, but I'm going to stand

right by the phone and you tell her nothing except to come right over." Which he did. . . .

By this time the Selznicks had arrived with Whitney, and we made one more announcement that once the picture had started nobody would be allowed to make any phone calls, and that if they left, they wouldn't be allowed back in. So then the lights went down and I was sitting next to David and Mrs. Selznick, and when the curtains opened and Margaret Mitchell's name came on the screen, there was this silence for just a second and then the audience started applauding, and when the title came on and swept across the screen, why I never heard such a sound in my life. . . . The people stood up and cheered and screamed. . . . I had the remote control sound mechanism next to me and I had to turn it up full blast just so you could hear the music. Mrs. Selznick and Jock Whitney started crying like babies and so did David . . . and so did I. Oh, what a thrill it was . . . it was just thunderous, that ovation, and they just wouldn't stop. . . . To this day I still get chills when I remember it. The picture ran four hours and twenty-five minutes, and at the end, the ovation started all over again.

The preview cards unanimously and enthusiastically praised everything about the picture; the phrase that most often leapt out was the cliché "the greatest picture I've ever seen." Selznick carefully tabulated the results of these cards and on the basis of the negative reaction to the question, "Do you think any battle scenes should be added to the picture, or any fuller portrayal of the Civil War, its causes and development?" he jettisoned plans for the filming of these scenes, and decided with much relief that few or no additional scenes would be needed. About his "cooked-up" ending, Selznick remarked that "I tried this out with considerable trepidation, but to my delighted surprise . . . apparently there is no thought in the minds of anyone that this is not exactly faithful to the book, in spirit at least, even though it isn't one hundred percent book material as is true with so much of the picture. . . . Also to my great pleasure, not one preview card mentioned that they wanted to see Rhett and Scarlett together again. I think they still hope they will get together, but it leaves them something to discuss, just as the end of the book did."

For the next month, Selznick and Hal Kern, joined occasionally by Victor Fleming, tried to squeeze another hour out of the picture. They did this by removing a section showing the O'Hara family on their way to the Twelve Oaks barbecue, with Scarlett and her sisters arguing and Mammy scolding them; the dialogue from this was used in a retaken scene showing the girls at the barbecue getting ready for their afternoon naps. Also deleted was a scene showing Twelve Oaks and its guests and servants slumbering after the barbecue; and Scarlett's wedding night with Charles Hamilton, which she made him spend in a chair. The sequences showing the evacuation of Atlanta and the scenes in the hospital were all considerably shortened, as was Scarlett's search for Dr. Meade at the railway station, including her encounter with John Wilkes, Ashley's father, who dies in her arms as she tells him of his impending grandchild. Also cut was a scene of Belle Watling nursing the wounded soldiers, which was not in the novel. A conversation between Scarlett's two sisters was removed in which they discuss what the South will be like after the war with all the best men dead and no one to marry Southern girls. Also deleted was a sequence showing Belle Watling and her "girls" testifying at the inquest into Frank Kennedy's death, and a sequence between Bonnie and Scarlett the morning after Rhett's "rape."

By the second week of October, the combined efforts of the three men and a crew of assistant editors and secretaries had reduced the picture to just under four hours. While Selznick and Kern tinkered with this, Fleming directed three days of retakes and added scenes, tempting fate by directing still another version of the opening scene on Friday, October 13. This time Vivien Leigh, fresh and rested from a two-month vacation, was dressed in the high-necked white gown she wore in the later evening prayer scene, since Selznick felt that it gave her more of a virginal sixteen-year-old quality than did the original green-sprigged muslin dress. The scene went smoothly and quickly. Five days later, Hal Kern called the manager of the Arlington Theatre in Santa Barbara asking him if he could bring up *Intermezzo* to preview. The theatre had just opened *What a Life,* the picture that introduced teenager Henry Aldrich to moviegoers; it was playing with *Charlie Chan at Treasure Island,* and

Some striking examples of Jack Cosgrove's special effects work on *Gone With The Wind*. (Top, left) The shot of Scarlett and her father looking out over the fields of Tara was a combination of two matte paintings of the house and sky, a separately filmed black-and-white silhouette of the two figures, and a third matte painting of the tree. (Top, right) This view of Tara at night was done using one of the miniature models of the plantation, with the sky and surrounding trees added through matte painting. The carriage going up the drive is a miniature, photographed separately and printed onto the final composite shot. (Above) This long shot of Atlanta was a combination of the actual back lot set with the larger vista of Atlanta added through a matte painting done from sketches supplied by Wilbur Kurtz. (Above, right) Scarlett's search for Dr. Meade had her climbing over piles of rubble, with the top of the ruined building added by matte painting; the whole scene was overlaid with wisps of smoke, which were added separately. (Right) Scarlett's trek through the war-torn countryside on her way back to Tara was a combination of three different pieces of film: the wagon with its occupants was filmed on the back lot, the countryside and the clouds was a Cosgrove painting, and the rainbow was a background projection that jiggled a bit.

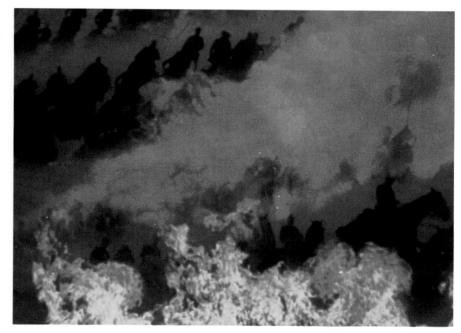

(Top, left) This shot of Atlanta during the fire was achieved by lighting the actual back lot set with red-orange reflectors and smoke pots, while the rear of the scene showing the fire over the tops of the buildings was added by Cosgrove, using process plates projected onto a miniature screen set up behind the foreground screen, on which he projected the previously filmed Atlanta street footage. The two screens were then re-photographed simultaneously using a specially adapted Technicolor camera. (Top, right) This shot of the battlefield was a combination of five separate pieces of film: the wagon and its occupants was filmed separately; the curling black smoke was another piece; the foreground and left side of the frame, with the dead soldiers, was a Cosgrove painting; the overturned canvas wagon was a separate miniature; and the sky was another painting. (Above, left) Three separate shots were necessary for this scene: the burned-out building on the left was a painting, as was the sky and some of the foreground; the water and the wagon were real, photographed separately and added later. (Above) The only special effects shot in the picture not done by Cosgrove was this swirling montage of Sherman's troops marching through Georgia, which opened the second half of the film. As production neared completion, time was running short, and Cosgrove's work load was fierce, so Hal Kern took some unused battle footage, some fire effects, and some Menzies sketches over to the MGM special effects department, where Peter Ballbusch combined them all and came up with this stunningly effective collage, which invariably drew applause when the picture was given its first press and industry screenings. (Left) Rhett and Scarlett's postwar Atlanta house was actually the entrance walk to the Selznick studio combined with a Cosgrove painting—all of which overawed Prissy and Pork, the house servants, standing with Mammy, who was not impressed: "Humph. 'Tain't quality," she sneers.

Gone With The Wind was innovative in many ways in the film industry: cost, length, fidelity to source, and especially the way it pushed the frontiers of Technicolor photography to their limits of excellence. With Selznick's enthusiastic encouragement, William Cameron Menzies constantly devised new visual approaches in the establishing of mood through the use of color, lighting, and composition, as seen in these five frames from the film. (Top, left) The O'Hara family at evening prayer, photographed by Lee Garmes and lit by flickering candles, which gave the scene a hushed, churchlike quality. (Top, right) Selznick originally felt that Menzies had gone too far in his theatricalism in this red-orange-drenched shot of Rhett's farewell to Scarlett on the McDonough Road. Selznick ordered it re-taken, but Fleming, Menzies, and Wheeler convinced him to keep it in the film. (Above) The green teapot, symbol of gossip, jealous old ladies, dominates the scene in which Mrs. Meade and Mrs. Merriwether (Leona Roberts and Jane Darwell), the town dowagers, cluck disapprovingly over Scarlett's postwar conduct. (Above, right) Ernest Haller shot the delicately lit dawn scenes of Scarlett and her father in the study at Tara, when she first discovers her father has lost his mind—one of the most poignant moments in the film. (Right) Rhett proposes to Scarlett in Aunt Pittypat's parlor as the late-afternoon sun suffuses the room with a golden autumnal glow. These shots were photographed by Ernest Haller and Ray Rennahan, both of whom won Academy Awards for their work on the film. There was no precedent for what Menzies had done on *Gone With The Wind,* so in order to give him an appropriate credit, Selznick and Lyle Wheeler together devised the title of production designer. For his "outstanding achievement in the use of color for the enhancement of dramatic mood," Menzies was awarded a special plaque by the Academy of Motion Picture Arts and Sciences.

Margaret Mitchell was reportedly unhappy with Ben Hecht's foreword to the film, which described the Old South as a "land of Cavaliers and cotton fields . . . of Knights and their Ladies Fair, of Master and of Slave. . . ." "I certainly had no intention of writing about cavaliers," she wrote to a friend, feeling that the lines gave a distorted, romantic view of her book. But Selznick's concept of the story was extremely romantic, a larger-than-life depiction of a doomed civilization. These five frames from the film give a good idea of his picture-postcard approach to the idealization of the Old South, including this shot (top, right) of the Mississippi riverboat that carries Rhett and Scarlett to their honeymoon in New Orleans. The boat is a miniature printed onto footage of the river left over from *The Adventures of Tom Sawyer.* The scenes of the barbecue at Twelve Oaks (above, left) and the Atlanta bazaar (above) were the most outstanding pictorial representations of what Miss Mitchell described as a way of life that had "a glamour to it, a perfection, a symmetry like Grecian art." The barbecue was photographed at the old Busch Gardens in Pasadena, soon after converted into an Army training facility. The sequence of the wartime bazaar in the Atlanta Armory was re-done twice at Selznick's insistence: it was re-shot by Victor Fleming after Cukor's departure and the arrival of a new script (and also to eliminate Clark Gable's bogus Southern accent), then re-shot again because Selznick was dissatisfied with Jack Cosgrove's matte painting of the top of the set, which he felt made the whole thing reminiscent of an Italian wedding. (Left) The death throes of the Old South were represented vividly in this classic scene of the Confederate battle flag waving bravely over the remnants of the Army in the last, gray days of the Lost Cause.

Max Steiner (right) goes over a music sheet for *Gone With The Wind* with Lou Forbes, head of the Selznick music department and brother of Leo Forbstein, head of the Warner Bros. music department, from which Steiner was borrowed to work on the film. At the same time that he was composing for *Gone With The Wind*, Steiner was also writing the score for Warner Bros.' *Four Daughters*—and working twenty hours a day trying to finish them both. His doctor was giving him daily injections of thyroid extract and vitamin B-12 shots. With all that, Steiner almost didn't compose the score, as he kept telling Selznick that he couldn't meet the deadline. Selznick was used to hearing that from Steiner, but to ensure that the work would be done, he let it be known that he was thinking of replacing Steiner with Herbert Stothart, the head of the MGM music department. Word of this reached Steiner, who was properly furious, as Selznick knew he would be, and Steiner redoubled his efforts, composing almost all of the three hours and fifteen minutes of music that the picture needed. One of his orchestrators, Hugo Friedhofer, was pressed into service to write the music for the escape from burning Atlanta, while two fragments from Franz Waxman's score for *The Young in Heart*, as well as an ominous bit of music by David Axt from *David Copperfield*, were used for the scene in which Melanie knocks on the door of Bonnie's death chamber. Steiner's score mixes original compositions, folk tunes, and music of the Civil War period to give the film a sumptuous, romantic sound, interspersing it with slyly humorous comments on the action, as in the quotations from "Massa's in de Cold, Cold Ground" at the death of Scarlett's first two husbands.

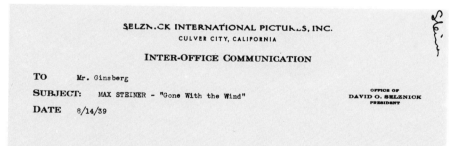

SELZNICK INTERNATIONAL PICTURES, INC.
CULVER CITY, CALIFORNIA

INTER-OFFICE COMMUNICATION

TO   Mr. Ginsberg

SUBJECT: MAX STEINER - "Gone With the Wind"   OFFICE OF
DATE   8/14/39   DAVID O. SELZNICK
                                                                PRESIDENT

In my opinion, Max Steiner should go on our payroll immediately and should start composing all his themes and selecting his basic music for "Gone With the Wind." Bear in mind that the scoring job on the picture is, if only because of its length, exactly twice as big an undertaking as any other picture, and also that no matter how much we speed up Max, obviously we can't overcome what will be his natural desire to do the greatest score ever written, and I don't even think that we should try to overcome this -- so that this also means extra time. A few thousand dollars in Max's salary one way or another is as nothing compared to possibly speeding up the completion of the picture even by a week or two and there is no reason why he couldn't do most of his composing, or in fact all of it, before we turn the picture over to him, and he should be told to do it all even if it involves a certain amount of re-writing and a great deal of rearranging when the picture is finally turned over to him.

If you can arrange for Max to start at once, please do so and have him report to me.

The arrangement should include, if possible, our privilege to use him in whatever capacity we want in connection with the final scoring of "Intermezzo."

And if you could arrange for him to stay here after "Wind" to do the "Rebecca" score, I would like this too.

                                                                DOS

dos*f

Kern was counting on this family-oriented midweek change of bill to guarantee a decent house. "We took *Gone With The Wind* up there," recalls Kern, "and it wasn't put together yet, so it was twenty-four reels of picture and twenty-four reels of sound, and when we carried in this forty-eight reels the manager looked at me and said, 'Hal, you bastard, that's not *Intermezzo* you're bringing in here.' So I did the same thing we did at Riverside, locked the doors and all, and when the picture flashed on the screen, well, it was pandemonium all over again."

The trims and deletions from the first preview had left some scenes without beginnings and endings, while omissions had been bridged with temporary title cards. To smooth out all the rough spots and fill in the gaps, Selznick now put into the works a ten-day shooting schedule of additional scenes and still more retakes designed to fill in the missing linking sequences, and to photograph additional ones made necessary by deletions and Selznick's desire to enhance scenes that lacked dramatic punch. The most elaborate of these additions was a sequence designed to be cut into the trek to Tara, showing Scarlett, Melanie, and Prissy hiding under a bridge during a thunderstorm as a detachment of Yankee cavalry passes overhead. Adding to the filmed drama was a violent clash between Ray Klune and Victor Fleming over the methods of filming the scene. "Vic didn't want to shoot it," recalls Klune. "We were on the back lot, and it actually started to rain and he said it would make it impossible to shoot, that we wouldn't be able to light it properly. I said, 'Vic, we're here, it's supposed to be raining, we've spent the money, let's shoot the damned thing.' Well, he got so mad, he blew up and said, 'You do whatever these Jews want you to do, don't you?' And I said, 'You son of a bitch, if you feel that way, why do you take the money? I'm doing what I think is the right thing to do; I want you to shoot this scene, and if you want to bitch it up by shooting it badly, that's your prerogative, but I don't think you will.'"

Unbeknownst to Klune, Fleming's festering frustration with the whole *Gone With The Wind* production had been brought to a head earlier that day during a meeting with Selznick, who was trying to work out the screen credits. "I asked Vic Fleming," relates Selznick, "whether he would like to see us include a card crediting people who had contributed greatly to the picture ... George Cukor, among them ... Sam Wood ... who had a great many sequences in the picture.... My conversation with Vic on the subject literally didn't last thirty seconds.... He obviously, and no doubt understandably, wasn't happy about the idea, saying in so many words that he didn't think it was necessary to credit them on screen ... and without further discussion I immediately told him to forget about it, that as far as I was concerned it was a closed issue." Fleming, however, brooded over it and the incident began to assume the proportions of a major insult, especially after he saw the program that had been prepared by MGM under Howard Dietz's supervision. Dietz, in an effort to give Selznick as much credit as possible, had inserted a clause stating: "There were five directors on *Gone With The Wind,* all supervised personally by David Selznick." Fleming was enraged at this, assuming that it had been done at Selznick's insistence. No amount of persuasion or explanation by Dietz and Selznick could convince him otherwise, and the unintentional gaffe led to a breach between the two men, with Gable taking Fleming's side—his own reservations about Selznick being reinforced by what he considered to be a betrayal of his closest friend. The coolness between actor and producer turned frigid, with Carole Lombard, who genuinely liked Selznick, trying her best to reconcile them—to no avail.

Selznick was adult enough to be able to shrug off the disappointment of Gable's and Fleming's attitudes; besides, he had more important matters to worry about. One of the most worrisome of these was the Hays office's refusal to allow Rhett Butler's final line to contain the taboo word "damn." The word had not been heard on American screens since the adoption of the Code in 1933; prior to that, there had been several instances of mild profanity on screen, but the new puritanism of the rest of the decade had swept away curse words, nudity, double beds, and unpunished transgressions against the law of man and God. Selznick, however, took the bit between his teeth and, in a lengthy letter to Will Hays, argued persuasively:

The word as used in the picture ... is not an oath or a curse.... The worst that could be said for it is that it is a vulgarism, and it is so described in the Oxford English Dictionary.... Nor do I feel that in asking you to make an exception in this case ... this one sentence will open up the floodgates of [profanity]. I do believe, however, that if you were to permit our using this dramatic word in its rightfully dramatic place, it would establish a helpful precedent ... giving your office discretionary powers to allow the use of certain harmless oaths and ejaculations whenever they are ... not prejudicial to public morals. The omission of this line spoils the punch at the very end of the picture and on our very fade-out gives an impression of unfaithfulness after three hours and forty-five minutes of extreme fidelity to Miss Mitchell's work which has become ... an American Bible.

Selznick's arguments and, at his instigation, the urgings of several other industry leaders convinced Hays to overrule his own board of advisers. Upon payment of a $5000 fine for violation of a Code provision, the picture was allowed to go out equipped with both the "damn" and a Code seal, creating one more sensation in the industry.

The picture had been announced for a December 15 premiere in Atlanta, which was less than a month away, and there were still literally hundreds of production details that needed not only Selznick's constant attention but the staff's as well. Max Steiner poured himself into the completion of a score that equaled the picture's visual magnificence, composing leitmotifs for all the main characters, with a thundering, majestic keynote theme for Tara that leapt up the scale an octave and raised gooseflesh on everyone who heard it. For more than three hours his music sighed, wept, and soared its way through the story, as rich, colorful, and vivid as the Technicolor scenes themselves. Massed descending violins, echoing celeste, and fragrantly scented humming choruses lent an air of redolent nostalgia and evanescent romanticism to the picturization of a way of life that was, as Ben Hecht's title phrase described it, " ... a dream remembered; ... a civilization gone with the wind." Steiner's music for *Gone With The Wind* is one of the most superb scores ever written for any picture at any time, and countless hearings later, even apart from the film, it still has the ability to move and involve the listener. It is the summation and peak of the whole romantic movement in film scoring that Steiner himself had begun earlier in the decade with *Bird of Paradise* and *King Kong,* and it stands as a testament to his spirit as much as the picture itself does to Selznick's genius.

In the last month before the scheduled premiere in Atlanta, work was as intense as ever while everyone tried frantically to get the picture into its final form before Technicolor started making prints. "On the last weeks of *Gone With The Wind,*" relates Hal Kern, "I was working almost twenty hours a day. David just didn't want to let go of it and I would have to threaten him.... I'd say, 'David, unless you let me have this sequence to cut for the lab, we'll never make the premiere date.' I'd literally have to pull it out of his hands. I know just how he felt, though; there were at least three Cosgrove shots that I wish we'd had more time on, because they were the only things in the picture that weren't perfect."

Kern was dividing his time between the studio and the Technicolor laboratories, spending most of the days and nights at the lab, trying to get the color perfectly balanced and matched. Today this is done largely by computer, but in those days it was done by eye, by time-consuming trial and error. Kern recalls: "I told Technicolor, 'You call me at my house any time and I'll come over when you've got a scene ready.' They'd call me at three in the morning, and I'd go over and say, 'This scene is too red, take out some of the magenta, put some more yellow in here....' This went on and on.... David, who was near collapse himself, began to get very concerned about me and he wanted me to stop and rest. I told him I felt fine, that if I stopped or he stopped, we'd be another year getting the picture out, because there were things that we had to do that he wouldn't do unless he had a deadline."

If Kern was working himself to the limit of his endurance, Selznick, in an artificially stimulated state, had gone beyond him. By now he was existing on a steady diet of vitamin B-12 shots, thyroid extract, and Benzedrine, seeming to work more hours than there were in the day to prepare not only for the premiere but also the all-important press preview, now scheduled for December 12. "The man gave his life's blood on this," recalls Lydia Schiller. "He literally went gray trying to finish it in

time." The day before the preview Selznick was still making minor changes; at the last minute, he changed the punctuation of the foreword title, altering a semi-colon to a period in the line, "look for it only in books, for it is no more than a dream remembered. A civilization *Gone With The Wind.*"

As Technicolor frantically printed up this change and spliced it into the first finished print, 750 élite members of the local and national Hollywood press corps and their guests were filling the 1200 seats of the Four Star Theatre on Wilshire Boulevard for the first and one of the most important official screenings of the picture. Their reactions and what they would write about the film would determine to a large extent the attitude audiences would bring to it. The phenomenon that had been building for the last three years, the intense national interest and curiosity about everything connected with the picture, had reached the point where it was estimated that more than 56 million Americans were eagerly awaiting their chance to see *Gone With The Wind.* This was largely a positive curiosity. Everybody wanted to like the picture, hoped that it would live up to their expectations, and the previews had indicated that it probably would. But the first true test would be at the Four Star, before a gathering of individuals whose critical judgments would be shaped not only by the film itself but by the events surrounding it: by their daily exposure to the industry gossip, to the reports of bruised egos, constant changes and uncertainties, to the rumors of power plays within Selznick International and MGM, the bickering, recriminations, and the final massive outlay of money—$4,085,790, more than any picture had ever cost in the entire history of the Hollywood film industry—as well as by an intensive three-year publicity campaign that by now many in the press were convinced could not possibly be lived up to.

The screening was scheduled for noon. Five minutes beforehand an edgy David Selznick and a quiet Victor Fleming slipped into seats in the back row of the theatre. Lydia Schiller was with them, and she recalls:

We went in and sat down quietly.... Mr. Selznick and Fleming were both very nervous ... we were all very intense.... It was a full house with a very hostile attitude.... They were chattering away ... but they quieted down very early.... One thing was the beauty of it ... the scenes behind the titles and the opening scenes for that time were quite extraordinary, and you could sense the tide turning almost immediately. It got so quiet you could almost hear a pin drop, they just all got so totally absorbed, and at the intermission it was very thrilling.... The applause was not polite, it was loud, sustained, and genuinely enthusiastic, and the joy of that was quite something.... Afterwards I don't recall that we went back to the studio ... it's hard to explain that sense of loss we all felt, it sounds silly, I know, but we did ... it was out of our hands now. I remember Mr. Selznick saying that he didn't know whether he'd ever be able to get it out of his system.... He was afraid this was his peak ... not in ability, but in enthusiasm and interest.... He was like the rest of us ... we had lived with it day and night for almost two years and we just felt absolutely lost.

Whitney

AAF12 25 NT
              TDS CULVERCITY CALIF DEC 11 1939
MR. JOHN HAY WHITNEY
THOMASVILLE
GEORGIA
HAVE JUST FINISHED GONE WITH THE WIND. GOD BLESS US ONE AND ALL.
SCREENING AT TWO TOMORROW TUESDAY FOR 750 REPRESENTATIVES OF THE
WORLD PRESS.
          DAVID

The main titles from *Gone With The Wind* utilized a graphic approach unusual in an era when motion picture credits were normally presented quickly and simply: titles were usually announced rapidly, with as much information as possible crammed into several frames. The majesty and excitement of the *Gone With The Wind* credits was apparent from the very first appearance of the title card that announced the cooperative venture of the two studios and the fact that the film was in Technicolor; this dissolved into a full-frame credit for Margaret Mitchell, at which point the main title boomed across the screen, each word filling the entire frame momentarily, perfectly capturing the feeling of romantic grandeur that Selznick wanted the picture to have. The backgrounds for all these titles were carefully selected for mood and beauty. Many of them had been photographed in the South by James Fitzpatrick, while the vistas of the plantations and the city of Atlanta were paintings by Wilbur Kurtz combined with Jack Cosgrove's matte work.

MARGARET MITCHELL'S

STORY OF THE OLD SOUTH

THE WIND

The Players

AT TARA
The O'Hara Plantation in Georgia

Gerald O'Hara . . . . . . THOMAS MITCHELL
Ellen, *his wife* . . . . . . BARBARA O'NEILL

Their Daughters:

Scarlett . . . . . . VIVIEN LEIGH
Suellen . . . . . . EVELYN KEYES
Carreen . . . . . . ANN RUTHERFORD

Scarlett's beaux:

Scarlett's beaux:

Brent Tarleton . . . . . GEORGE REEVES
Stuart Tarleton . . . . . FRED CRANE

The house servants:

Mammy . . . . . . HATTIE McDANIEL
Pork . . . . . . OSCAR POLK
Prissy . . . . . . BUTTERFLY McQUEEN

In the fields:

Jonas Wilkerson, *the overseer* . . VICTOR JORY
Big Sam, *the foreman* . . EVERETT BROWN

AT TWELVE OAKS
The nearby Wilkes Plantation

John Wilkes . . . . . . HOWARD HICKMAN
India, *his daughter* . . . . ALICIA RHETT
Ashley, *his son* . . . . . LESLIE HOWARD
Melanie Hamilton, *their cousin* . OLIVIA de HAVILLAND
Charles Hamilton, *her brother* . RAND BROOKS
Frank Kennedy, *a guest* . . CARROLL NYE

and a visitor from Charleston

Rhett Butler . . . . . . CLARK GABLE

IN ATLANTA

Aunt Pittypat Hamilton . LAURA HOPE CREWS
Uncle Peter, *her coachman* . EDDIE ANDERSON
Dr. Meade . . . . . . HARRY DAVENPORT
Mrs. Meade . . . . . . LEONA ROBERTS
Mrs. Merriwether . . . . JANE DARWELL
Belle Watling . . . . . ONA MUNSON

AND

PAUL HURST	ISABEL JEWELL
CAMMIE KING	ERIC LINDEN
J. M. KERRIGAN	WARD BOND
JACKIE MORAN	CLIFF EDWARDS
L. KEMBLE-COOPER	YAKIMA CANUTT
MARCELLA MARTIN	LOUIS JEAN HEYDT
MICKEY KUHN	OLIN HOWLAND
IRVING BACON	ROBERT ELLIOTT
WILLIAM BAKEWELL	MARY ANDERSON

David Selznick liked to go to costume parties dressed as Teddy Roosevelt, and at the conclusion of production on *Gone With The Wind*, Jock Whitney sent him this oil painting as an affectionate gag gift.

The press preview of *Gone With The Wind* proved to be an inadvertent elegy to the passing of one era of Hollywood history, too, for early that same morning the news came of the sudden, unexpected death of Douglas Fairbanks, Sr., an event that cast a momentary pall over the ecstatic reviews of the picture. Victor Fleming was unable to fully appreciate the extent of the praise coming his way, for Fairbanks had been a very close personal friend—had literally given him his first chance to make a name for himself. In order to serve as a pallbearer at the funeral, Fleming absented himself from the *Gone With The Wind* festivities in Atlanta and refused to comment on anything about the picture, leaving the field completely free to Selznick, who, the night before the press preview, was glibly ambivalent in his attitude toward the film; he was quoted in *Time* magazine as saying: "At noon, I think it's divine, at midnight, I think it's lousy. Sometimes I think it's the greatest picture ever made.... But if it's only a great picture, I'll still be satisfied." With that he flew off to the Atlanta premiere.

Considerably overshadowed by the magnitude and spectacle of the Atlanta and New York openings earlier in the month, the Hollywood premiere of *Gone With The Wind* took place December 27, 1939, at the venerable and prestigious Carthay Circle Theatre out in the flatlands of the Wilshire district. It was the last great movie event of the year and of the decade, and MGM's publicity department under Howard Strickling was determined not to be outdone by the Eastern galas. Searchlights lined both sides of the street for two blocks on either side of San Vicente Boulevard, where the theatre was located, creating a spectacular, blinding display that could be seen for miles. Ten thousand spectators lined the adjacent streets, screaming and roaring their approval as two thousand of Hollywood's élite squeezed their way down the long distinctive garden forecourt and disappeared into the theatre. Inside, the auditorium was rapidly filling up, but Selznick could not understand why a large block of approximately fifty seats in the middle of the theatre remained empty. As the time drew near for the 8:30 curtain, they remained unoccupied. Selznick accosted Russell Birdwell, who had handled the studio's preparations for the opening, and asked him about the blank space, and was a bit shamefaced when Birdwell reminded him that Selznick himself had insisted on holding out a block of tickets for his own personal use. He had been so busy that it had completely slipped his mind; the tickets were still in a desk drawer at Selznick's office. A hurried conference sent several aides scurrying to homes in the neighborhood, inviting fifty startled residents to be the guests of David O. Selznick at the premiere of *Gone With The Wind,* which would start in ten minutes. And so, in the midst of the bejeweled, furred, and tuxedoed throng sat a group of fifty bewildered people in shirtsleeves, sweaters, and sports coats, wide-eyed with delight at their surroundings and this seemingly arbitrary stroke of good fortune. At exactly 8:29, an overwhelming roar from the crowd outside penetrated the inside of the theatre, announcing the arrival of Clark Gable and Carole Lombard. As they swept into the theatre and down the aisle to their seats, the overture started, the lights slowly dimmed to blackness, the curtains parted, and the Selznick International trademark flashed on the screen to a burst of applause. After three years and $4 million worth of work, David Selznick's great gamble, his "folly" and "white elephant," was finally given over to the judgment of his peers.

This was not the first time that *Gone With The Wind* had been on the screen of the Carthay Circle. Late in November, Selznick and Hal Kern had taken the nearly completed picture to the theatre for a private midnight showing to test the sound levels. Selznick was horrified to discover that "as famous a theatre as the Carthay Circle had ... such wretched sound.... The reproduction was simply awful ... the machines weren't even in balance. If this is true ... at the leading showplace of the motion picture capital ... then it is undoubtedly true of 90% of all the theatres in the country ... and it is possible that all our efforts and expense to make *Gone With The Wind* perfect . . . could be ruined through the lack of care and the sloppiness on the part of the exhibitors." To prevent this, Selznick, even while immersed in the round-the-clock details of finishing the picture, began deluging the MGM sales and distribution forces with daily memos and wires on how the picture should be advertised, how it should be sold and be presented, arguing

The Weather
Yesterday: High, 55. Low, 36.
Today: Cloudy. Low, 38.
Complete Weather Details on Page 22.

THE ATLANTA CONSTITUTION

The Constitution Leads in City Home Delivered, Total City and Trading Territory Circulation

The South's Standard Newspaper
Associated Press United Press
North American Newspaper Alliance

VOL. LXXII., No. 187. ONLY MORNING NEWSPAPER PUBLISHED IN ATLANTA ATLANTA, GA., SATURDAY MORNING, DECEMBER 16, 1939. Entered at Atlanta Post Office As Second-Class Matter Single Copies: Daily, 5c; Sunday, 10c. Daily and Sunday: Weekly 25c; Monthly $1.10

'GONE WITH WIND' ENTHRALLS AUDIENCE WITH MAGNIFICENCE

Gable, Miss Mitchell Talk Alone After He Begs a Chat

PETITE ATLANTAN MEETS FILM STARS FOR THE FIRST TIME

'Isn't He Grand? Just What I Expected,' She Exclaims; Their Conversation Kept Secret.

By YOLANDE GWIN.

The man who put $4,000,000 into filming "Gone With the Wind" and the principal stars who put their hearts into it, met the author of the book for the first time yesterday afternoon.

Petite Margaret Mitchell, quiet of voice, smiling somewhat reservedly, save at rare moments, gave her hand to David O. Selznick, the producer; to Clark Gable, Vivien Leigh, Evelyn Keyes, Ann Rutherford and Laura Hope Crews, of the cast, and to Carole Lombard, Gable's glamorous wife, at a cocktail party of the Atlanta Women's Press Club.

"Isn't He Grand?"

Said Mr. Gable: "Do you suppose I could have a few words with her? After all there is a lot I want to tell her."

Said Margaret Mitchell: "Isn't he grand! Just what I expected."

Said Carole Lombard: "Clark has been dying to meet you, Miss Mitchell."

Said Miss Vivien Leigh: "I think she is perfectly marvelous."

It all took place in a room 18x11. There was another room and the bar, into which guests overflowed.

Peggy Mitchell had the spotlight and stole the scene. The greatest names of Hollywood gave it to her willingly.

Gable only wanted to talk to "Peggy" Mitchell, and Gable, as in all his movie roles, found a way to get his girl.

What Did They Say?

They disappeared into a private dining room of the club at 5:16 o'clock. The door was locked. There Gable and Miss Mitchell talked over many things. Both refused to repeat what was said. The world would like to know the things they talked about but probably never will.

Minutes slipped by, but "Peggy" and "Rhett" were still in conference. The clock showed 5:25. Most of the club members were getting a little nervous. What were they saying? Was she telling him she had him in mind for her character when she wrote the book?

When they came out Peggy joined Vivien Leigh and Laura Hope (Aunt Pittypat) Crews in the main room. She confided to them:

"If I sit up too straight, think nothing of it. Somebody jerked a chair back too far today and I sat down too hard on the floor. Now I'm wrapped in adhesive tape."

Carole Lombard slipped into a chair beside her.

Good-byes Said.

Soon Miss Mitchell's husband, John Marsh, beckoned it was time to leave.

It was nearing 6 o'clock. Louis B. Mayer slipped her coat on for her. Mrs. Mayer was there and

Continued in Page 8, Column 7.

Constitution Staff Photo—Bill Wilson.

Margaret Mitchell meets "Scarlett" and "Rhett." Here is the first picture showing the Atlanta author with the movie stars, Vivien Leigh and Clark Gable, who bring the principal characters of her "Gone With the Wind" to life on the screen. The picture was made yesterday afternoon at the party given by the Atlanta Women's Press Club for Margaret Mitchell and not for the stars. All the motion picture people gathered to meet the woman who wrote the story they enact. And it was Gable and Miss Leigh looking for the autographs this time.

EPOCHAL PICTURE MADE BY CROWD AT FIRST SHOWING

Two Brilliant Shows Presented—One Within Theater, the Other a Colorful Drama Outside

A company of ladies and gentlemen, including the city's elite, assembled in De Give's Opera House last evening for the first showing of a cinematograph film named "Gone With the Wind," whose subject matter was the experiences of this city and immediate section during the recent outrogeous assault upon southern rights which is euphemistically termed in some quarters "The Civil War." The entertainment attracted the beauty and chivalry not only of our own people but those from other sections, including the north. It was received with enthusiasm. The picture, or series of pictures in motion, was based upon a book written by one of our talented young matrons, Mrs. John Marsh, nee Margaret Mitchell, who drew from our glory and tragedy a most arresting novel.

By WILLARD COPE.

Even if "Gone With the Wind" had been contemporary with the scenes it depicts, and its review had appeared as this imagined quotation from an issue of The Constitution of the '70's, it premier still would have been the greatest possible news story in Atlanta since Sherman.

In brilliance, in color, in distinction, in action and in plot the premiere last night evidenced what a quiet, bright-eyed somewhat mouselike young feminine person can do in drawing to her home city the notables of America. It was merely one aspect of her remarkable one-book literary career.

Apt Commentary.

If ever there was an apt physical commentary upon an event, it was the presence of the greatest known peacetime concentration of lights—five 800-million candlepower army searchlights—in front of the theater.

They will be talking about the premiere, and its divers eye-arresting, pulse-quickening, heart-warming details when the last small boy there is an old, old boy indeed, biting toothlessly into his porridge.

There was build-up. There was timing. But through it all ran a comforting, kindly, pleasant, even sentimental thread, or strain. The whole brilliant scene had reality.

Held Together.

All present—in an assemblage which drew from every important region and stratum of American life—were held together by the sense of sharing in a common, and most historic, experience.

Sitting with them in seats about the theater were Miss Mitchell, the author; David O. Selznick, the producer; such stars as Gable, Leigh, de Havilland, Munson, Rutherford, Keyes and Crews; the head of the publishing house which brought out the original book, and its associate editor, Lois Dwight Cole, lifelong friend of the author, who might justly have been termed co-author since it was she, as the story runs, who insisted that a literary scout for her firm should look up Miss Mitchell on a now historic southern trip.

It was as if two shows were being presented simultaneously—the fictional "Gone With the

Continued in Page 8, Column 2.

Opportunity Families Call to You for Help

This Is Time To Give Beautiful Christmas Gift for Whole Year.

By FRANK DRAKE.

Today marks the telling of the story of the seventh Opportunity family, Atlanta, and only two have been assured of a break in life thus far.

The fever of "Gone With the Wind" has subsided in the city this morning and the people who were tremendously excited about the visit of all the movie stars are getting back their normal blood pressure. They had a wonderful time welcoming Clark Gable and Vivien Leigh and all the rest but now the "Gone With the Wind" ball and premiere are things of the past.

It's time now, Atlantans, to really think about Christmas and the poor whom you have always aided.

You're planning a bright cheery Christmas for yourself and your family, aren't you? You and your children are looking forward to the day not so distant when everybody in the house will wake up early and shout "Christmas gift" to each other in happy, cheerful voices. Excitement will be rife.

Families in Need.

In the midst of all this merriment, stop for a moment and think about Opportunity families No. 2, No. 3, No. 4 and No. 6, whose tragedies have been told you this last week in The Constitution.

Continued in Page 11, Column 2.

Opportunity 7 Asks Chance

Mrs. Z. is 45, and a widow.

Death and the late unlamented depression makes Mrs. Z. Opportunity No. 7 in this year's Ten Opportunities campaign of The Constitution and the Family Welfare Society.

To help Mrs. Z. fit herself for a job and readjust her life following two terrific shocks, only $18 a month is needed. We believe Atlantans will want to help Mrs. Z.

For the 15 years of her married life Mrs. Z. was as happy as any woman could be. Her husband had a small business of his own and he was a good husband. Perhaps he was a better husband than a business man though. When the depression came along, it eventually wiped out his profits and he operated in the red for a while. Then he had to mortgage their home in an effort to save the business.

No profit, and time finally got the business and the house. The shock of losing everything he had, killed Mr. Z. He died less than a year ago.

Mrs. Z. has carried on as best she could, but the death of her husband and the loss of her home have taken their toll. When all of Mr. Z.'s business affairs were settled a few months ago, Mrs. Z. found that the most she could hope for was about $10 a month. And that only for a short time.

Mrs. Z. believes she has found

Continued in Page 11, Column 2.

A New Film Era

"Gone With the Wind's" Greatness Is Hailed Following Premiere

By LEE ROGERS,
Motion Picture Critic of The Constitution.

It is wonderful.

"Gone With the Wind" opens a new film era. It has everything a great picture could have. It has everything that everybody wanted.

Vivien Leigh is "Scarlett." And Clark Gable is now, more so than ever, the box office public's choice as "Rhett Butler."

All the actors and actresses were marvelously cast and were excellent, but the picture belongs to "Scarlett," just as did the book. Miss Leigh, who changed moods as swiftly as did the character she portrayed, qualifies herself for an Academy Award. Her acting deserves the highest superlatives one wishes to bestow.

Olivia de Havilland as sweet little understanding "Melanie" reached the high spot in her career, and the Gable who portrayed the "Rhett Butler" so wrapped up in his daughter "Bonnie" was completely the character.

Have no fear about the film. It follows closely the story Margaret Mitchell wrote. For three hours and 40 minutes it sticks, in the main, to the plot, situations and story. At times it drags from a motion picture standpoint, but that is overlooked as each new scene is awaited eagerly as Miss Mitchell's printed words come vividly to life.

Ranking with the greatest spectacle scenes in motion picture history is the burning of the ammunition trains, the flight to "Tara," and the wounded yelling soldiers on the tracks at the car shed. Drama is at its height many times. Among the best scenes are when "Scarlett" flies into a rage on finding "Melanie's" baby due and that the negro "Prissy" lied about knowing how to deliver it. Another to Miss Leigh's credit is the closing scene when "Scarlett" learns she loves "Rhett" but for once is unable to hold a man.

The color in the film is almost natural.

Red Cross Grants Finns $250,000

British Hurl New Air Strength Upon Nazis in North Sea Area.

By ROBERT BUNNELLE.

LONDON, Dec. 15.—(AP)—Great Britain's fast-expanding air force was disclosed tonight to have flown boldly to the attack in mass offensives against Germany's boasted air superiority, launching a big-scale war in the air.

With the cold and cloud-blown North sea as the battleground, the British pressed repeated waves of fast long-range planes, capable of both bombing and fighting, against the air and sea escort of a crippled German cruiser, and against Nazi seaplane bases at Borkum, Sylt and Norderney.

These continuing offensive patrols were Britain's answers to persistent Nazi air raids and minelaying forays on British naval anchorages and sealines.

The battle for air mastery, which already has accounted for the loss of some of Britain's and Germany's best fighting aircraft, was expected to turn the North

Continued in Page 2, Column 6.

7
Shopping Days
Till Christmas

Norman Davis Hears Finland Can Hold Out Until Spring, Then Acts.

WASHINGTON, Dec. 15.—(AP)—A prediction that Finland's tiny army could hold out until spring against the overwhelming Soviet forces came today to the American Red Cross, which immediately appropriated $250,000 for Finnish war relief.

Quoting Finnish military authorities, a cable report to the Red Cross added, "if adequate military help is forthcoming, defense can be continued for a long, long time."

The report was written by Wayne Chatfield Taylor, former assistant secretary of the treasury who is now a member of the three-man Red Cross delegation in Europe. He flew to Helsinki from Stockholm three days ago.

Ambulances Ordered.

In response to Taylor's recommendations, Norman Davis, the Red Cross chairman, appropriated $100,000 at once and announced that $150,000 more would be made available as needed.

The first order placed was for 10 light ambulances to be shipped to Finland within 30 days. A large part of the funds remaining from the $100,000, Davis said, will be placed at the disposal of the Finnish Red Cross.

The Red Cross, Davis said, also is canvassing for two doctors trained in the treatment of typhus

Continued in Page 3, Column 1.

In Other Pages

Louisiana Politics

The pot has been brewing for many years in the Cane Belt, but the common man has had little to say. The Gallup Poll has discounted shotguns and other hindrances to bring Constitution readers a true picture of his feelings.

Read the Poll Tomorrow

The premiere of *Gone With The Wind* in Atlanta on December 15, 1939, set a new level in the heights to which motion picture publicity could climb. The spectacle of the premiere, which MGM later boasted had been handled with "magnitude and dignity," was stage managed by the company's publicity head, Howard Dietz, who persuaded the governor of Georgia to declare a three-day holiday in the days before the opening; the mayor closed all the schools and public buildings on the day of the premiere. (Left) More than 300,000 people lined the streets of Atlanta to see the arrival of Laurence Olivier, Irene Selznick, Olivia de Havilland, David Selznick, and Vivien Leigh (below, left). But the biggest reception of all went to Clark Gable and Carole Lombard (below, right), who arrived in a specially chartered American Airlines plane that had "MGM'S GONE WITH THE WIND" emblazoned on the side, much to Selznick's chagrin. Gable was astounded at the hysteria of the screaming thousands who lined the parade route into the city (bottom, left). (Bottom, right) Vivien Leigh is escorted to the Junior League Ball the night before the premiere by Laurence Olivier, who, the newspapers kept insisting, "is in Atlanta on his own business." David Selznick hovers in the background behind Miss Leigh, looking somewhat nonplussed by all the madness around him. The newspaper accounts of the premiere successfully pushed the news of the European war off the front pages for two days. The day after the New York opening (opposite), MGM began calling *Gone With The Wind* "The Greatest Motion Picture Ever Made"—a label that is still appropriate over forty years later.

BROADWAY JAMMED AT TWIN PREMIERES

Thousands at Capitol and Astor to See Celebrities at 'Gone With the Wind'

300 POLICEMEN ON DUTY

Only Persons With Tickets Permitted to Walk Between 50th and 51st Streets

The varied dialects and accents of New Yorkers were commingled last night when thousands of persons impeded pedestrian and vehicular traffic as they stood packed along Broadway, gaping at the celebrities and fanfare attendant upon the premiere of Margaret Mitchell's story of the old South in Technicolor, "Gone With the Wind," at the Capitol and Astor Theatres.

For the first time since the twin premiere of "Hell's Angels," in 1930, pedestrians had to show a movie ticket to walk along a block on Broadway. More than 300 policemen finally reduced the confusion that had been brought on by two batteries of Klieg lights, television sets and hundreds of bejeweled and lavishly gowned women

Politeness toward civilians was the word that was passed around among the uniformed men when they came on duty, shortly after 7 o'clock. But before an hour had passed they had to show more than courtesy to keep the west side of Broadway clear between Fifty-first and Fiftieth Streets, where the Capitol is located, and between Forty-sixth and Forty-fifth Streets, the site of the Astor.

Strict Regulations Set

In the former block the police refused to allow pedestrians unless they had the purple, gray or green tickets which admitted them to the Capitol. Along the latter block the police formed a line down the center of the block, forcing pedestrians to keep moving in two sluggish lanes.

Within the hour before 7 o'clock there was little excitement outside the theatres. As a deputy chief inspector described the affairs complacently: "It's just the old mahooka." One of the harried cab drivers, however, described the event a little bit differently. "And to think a rebel had to start all this," he growled.

As usual the celebrities, famous on the stage, screen and in private business, were late in arriving. This had two results. First, the "curtain" at the Capitol was forty-five minutes late and twenty minutes behind schedule at the Astor.

At the former theatre, where publicity men had gone to work with a vengeance, the early comers took advantage of the delay to examine the Confederate atmosphere. Inside the lobby were two huge portraits of Clark Gable and Vivien Leigh, who play the roles of Rhett and Scarlett.

All along the marble staircase were large vases containing poinsettias, gladoli and roses. Seven professional models, wearing the tight bodiced and hoop skirted dresses of Civil War days, stood outside the foyer distributing programs "to ladies only." An official of the theatre explained there were only 3,000 of these souvenir programs available, with a capacity audience of 5,400 arriving.

Celebrities Chatter Gayly

Finally, a half hour after the show was supposed to have begun, the celebrities began filling the lobby, chattering gayly, while their jewels reflected the huge colored lights installed especially for this occasion. The model dressed as Scarlett tossed aside her cigarette and took her station.

The movies started making history then and there; take David O. Selznick's word, for it. "For three years I have been working and waiting and hoping; waiting for New York to pass judgment on my picture," he said.

Similar sentiments were uttered by James Stewart, Olivia De Havilland, Alice Faye, Constance Bennett, Will Hays and others. Clark Gable and Vivien Leigh said nothing. They were not there.

Finally, at 9 o'clock, after photographers had exploded innumerable bulbs from all parts of the lobby, and the harried theatre officials had been predicting "curtain going up in three minutes" for the tenth time, the curtain did go up.

It went up with an oriental touch that was a sight to the Confederate flags in the lobby. Brass gongs sounded five times and the heavy gold brocade curtain rose slowly. Celebrities hastened to tell their radio audiences how thrilled they were and entered the darkened theatre. At 10:40 there was a ten-minute intermission in the four-hour movie and the audience filled the lobby and lounge, gushing in endurance and complaining of fatigue.

UNITED ARTISTS TO FIGHT

Move by Goldwyn to Terminate to Be Resisted in Court

The move of Samuel Goldwyn to terminate his contract with United Artists will be "resisted in every legal way" by that organization, according to a statement made last night by Murray Silverstone, executive chairman of the United Artists Distributing Corporation. Mr. Goldwyn's intention was announced Monday by Max D. Steuer, his counsel.

Mr. Silverstone's statement said: "We have received this morning a letter from Samuel Goldwyn, Inc., in which it attempts to terminate its exclusive contract with us. We have not breached our contract, it is in full force and effect, and we again reiterate that we shall resist in every legal way any attempt on the part of Samuel Goldwyn, Inc., or Samuel Goldwyn to distribute pictures through any distributor other than United Artists or to terminate any of their other legal obligations to us, prior to Sept. 2, 1945, the expiration date of our present exclusive contract. We will continue to carry out our obligations in the future as we have in the past. The matter has been referred to counsel."

Dramatic Workshop Opened

The dramatic workshop of the New School for Social Research, 66 West Twelfth Street, was opened formally yesterday afternoon with a reception at the school when Dr. Alvin Johnson, director, introduced Erwin Piscator, who will head the new faculty.

THE SCREEN IN REVIEW

David Selznick's 'Gone With the Wind' Has Its Long-Awaited Premiere at Astor and Capitol, Recalling Civil War and Plantation Days of South—Seen as Treating Book With Great Fidelity

GONE WITH THE WIND, as adapted by the late Sidney Howard from Margaret Mitchell's novel; directed by Victor Fleming; musical score by Max Steiner; production designer, William Cameron Menzies; special effects by Jack Cosgrove; fire scenes staged by Lee Zavitz; costumes designed by Walter Plunkett; photography by Ernest Haller, supervised for Technicolor Company by Natalie Kalmus; technical advisers, Susan Myrick and Will Price; historian, Wilbur G. Kurtz; produced by David O. Selznick and released by Metro-Goldwyn-Mayer. At the Capitol and Astor Theatres.

Scarlett O'Hara .... Vivien Leigh
Rhett Butler .... Clark Gable
Ashley Wilkes .... Leslie Howard
Melanie Hamilton .... Olivia de Havilland
Mammy .... Hattie McDaniel
Gerald O'Hara .... Thomas Mitchell
Ellen O'Hara .... Barbara O'Neil
Frank Kennedy .... Carroll Nye
Aunt Pittypat Hamilton Laura Hope Crews
Doctor Meade .... Harry Davenport
Charles Hamilton .... Rand Brooks
Belle Watling .... Ona Munson
Carreen O'Hara ...... Ann Rutherford
Brent Tarleton .... George Reeves
Stuart Tarleton .... Fred Crane
Pork .... Oscar Polk
Prissy .... Butterfly McQueen
Suellen O'Hara .... Evelyn Keyes
Mrs. Merriwether .... Jane Darwell
Mrs. Meade .... Leona Roberts
Big Sam .... Everett Brown
Uncle Peter .... Eddie Anderson
Tom, a Yankee Captain ...... Ward Bond
Bonnie Blue Butler ...... Cammie King
Johnny Gallegher .... J. M. Kerrigan
Emmy Slattery .... Isabel Jewell
India Wilkes .... Alicia Rhett
Jonas Wilkerson .... Victor Jory
John Wilkes .... Howard Hickman
Maybelle Merriwether ... Mary Anderson
A Yankee Looter .... Paul Hurst
Cathleen Calvert ..... Marcella Martin
Beau Wilkes .... Mickey Kuhn
Bonnie's Nurse .. Lillian Kemble Cooper
Reminiscent Soldier ...... Cliff Edwards
Ellah .... Zack Williams

By FRANK S. NUGENT

Clark Gable and Vivien Leigh

Understatement has its uses too, so this morning's report on the event of last night will begin with the casual notation that it was a great show. It ran, and will continue to run, for about 3 hours and 45 minutes, which still is a few days and hours less than its reading time and is a period the spine may prove sooner 'than the eye or ear. It is pure narrative, as the novel was, rather than great drama, as the novel was not. By that we would imply you will leave it, not with the feeling you have undergone a profound emotional experience, but with the warm and grateful remembrance of an interesting story beautifully told. Is it the greatest motion picture ever made? Probably not, although it is the greatest motion mural we have seen and the most ambitious film-making venture in Hollywood's spectacular history.

It—as you must be aware—is "Gone With the Wind," the gargantuan Selznick edition of the Margaret Mitchell novel which swept the country like Charlie McCarthy, "Music Goes 'Round" and similar inexplicable phenomena; which created the national emergency over the selection of a Scarlett O'Hara and which, ultimately, led to the $4,000,000 production that faced the New York public on two Times Square fronts last night, the Astor and the Capitol. It is the picture for which Mr. Gallup's American Institute of Public Opinion has reported a palpitatingly waiting audience of 56,500,000 persons, a few of whom may find encouragement in our opinion that they won't be disappointed in Vivien Leigh's Scarlett, Clark Gable's Rhett Butler or, for that matter, in Mr. Selznick's Miss Mitchell.

For, by any and all standards, Mr. Selznick's film is a handsome, scrupulous and unstinting version of the 1,037-page novel, matching it almost scene for scene with a literalness that not even Shakespeare or Dickens were accorded in Hollywood, casting it so brilliantly one would have to know the history of the production not to suspect that Miss Mitchell had written her story just to provide a vehicle for the stars already assembled under Mr. Selznick's hospitable roof. To have treated so long a book with such astonishing fidelity required courage—the courage of a producer's convictions and of his pocketbook, and yet, so great a hold has Miss Mitchell on her public, it might have taken more courage still to have changed a line or scene of it. But if Selznick has made a virtue of necessity, it does not follow, of necessity, that his transcription is expertly made as well. And yet, on the whole, it has been. Through stunning design, costume and peopling, his film has skillfully and absorbingly recreated Miss Mitchell's mural of the South in that bitter decade when secession, civil war and reconstruction ripped wide the graceful fabric of the plantation age and confronted the men and women who had adorned it with the stern alternative of meeting the new era or dying with the old. It was a large panel she painted, with sections devoted to plantation life, to the siege and the burning of Atlanta, to carpetbaggers and the Ku Klux Klan and, of course, to the Scarlett O'Hara about whom all this changing world was spinning and to whom nothing was important except as it affected her.

Some parts of this extended account have suffered a little in their screen telling, just as others have profited by it. Mr. Selznick's picture-postcard Tara and Twelve Oaks, with a few-score actors posturing on the premises, is scarcely our notion of doing complete justice to an age that had "a glamour to it, a perfection, a symmetry like Grecian art." The siege of Atlanta was splendid and the fire that followed magnificently pyrotechnic, but we do not endorse the superimposed melodramatics of the crates of explosives scorching in the fugitives' path; and we felt cheated, not ungrateful are we, when the battles outside Atlanta were dismissed in a subtitle and Sherman's march to the sea was summed up in a montage shot. We grin understandingly over Mr. Selznick's romantic omission of Scarlett's first two "birthings," and we regret more comic capital was not made of Rhett's scampish trick on the Old Guard of Atlanta when the army men were rounding up the Klansmen.

But if there are faults, they do not extend to the cast. Miss Leigh's Scarlett has vindicated the absurd talent quest that indirectly turned her up. She is so perfectly designed for the part by art and nature that any other actress in the role would be inconceivable. Technicolor finds her beautiful, but Sidney Howard, who wrote the script, and Victor Fleming, who directed it, have found in her something more: the very embodiment of the selfish, hoydenish, slant-eyed miss who tackled life with both claws and a creamy complexion, asked no odds of any one or anything—least of all her conscience—and faced at last a defeat which, by her very unconquerability, neither she nor we can recognize as final.

Miss Leigh's Scarlett is the pivot of the picture, as she was of the novel, and it is a column of strength in a film that is part history, part spectacle and all biography. Yet there are performances around her fully as valid, for all their lesser prominence. Olivia de Havilland's Melanie is a gracious, dignified, tender gem of characterization. Mr. Gable's Rhett Butler (although there is the fine flavor of the smokehouse in a scene or two) is almost as perfect as the grandstand quarterbacks thought he would be. Leslie Howard's Ashley Wilkes is anything but a pallid characterization of a pallid character. Best of all, perhaps, next to Miss Leigh, is Hattie McDaniel's Mammy, who must be personally absolved of responsibility for that most "unfittin'" scene in which she scolds Scarlett from an upstairs window. She played even that one right, however wrong it was.

We haven't time or space for the others, beyond to wave an approving hand at Butterfly McQueen as Prissy, Thomas Mitchell as Gerald, Ona Munson as Belle Watling, Alicia Rhett as India Wilkes, Rand Brooks as Charles Hamilton, Harry Davenport as Doctor Meade, Carroll Nye as Frank Kennedy. And not so approvingly at Laura Hope Crews's Aunt Pitty, Oscar Polk's Pork (bad casting) and "Eddie Anderson's Uncle Peter (oversight). Had we space we'd talk about the tragic scene at the Atlanta terminal, where the wounded are lying, about the dramatic use to which Mr. Fleming has injected his Technicolor—although we still feel that color is hard on the eyes for so long a picture—and about pictures of this length in general. Anyway, "it" has arrived at last, and we cannot get over the shock of not being disappointed; we had almost been looking forward to it.

REMEMBER
The Hundred Neediest!

Candlelight Concert at Center

The Rockefeller Center Choristers will usher in the season's Candlelight concerts today at 5:15 P. M. at Rockefeller Center. The group will sing carols and excerpts from Handel's "Messiah." The choristers have been selected from those who work at the Center and have been rehearsing for months under the direction of John R. Jones. The group will also be heard tomorrow at the same time.

PHOTOPLAYS

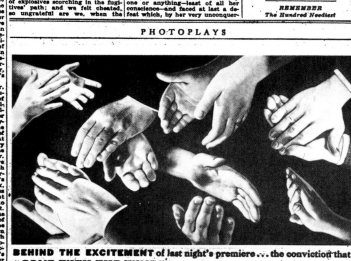

BEHIND THE EXCITEMENT of last night's premiere ... the conviction that **"GONE WITH THE WIND"** is the greatest motion picture ever made!

(See directory on this page for names of theatres and price information.)

Six frames from the original Technicolor coming-attractions trailer for *Gone With The Wind,* produced by Frank Whitbeck of MGM's Culver City publicity department. It was unusual for the time in that it showed no scenes from the film itself, opting instead for a series of paintings done by Wilbur Kurtz based on stills from the film. Variations of this approach were used to sell *Gone With The Wind* for the next fifteen years; it was not until 1954 that actual scenes from the film were used in these "prevue trailers," as they were known in the industry.

heatedly against their plan to present the picture on a continuous performance basis, telling Al Lichtman of MGM:

> I think that not having reserved seats is a shortsighted policy that will kill the goose that promised to lay the golden eggs.... It means that thousands of people are going to be standing in line for a four-hour picture and the repercussions will be terrible. Such greed on the part of the Loew theatres or any other theatre operator can make money for them but hurt us terribly.... This picture represents the greatest work of my life, in the past and very likely in the future.... I am associated with it in the public mind ... and I do not intend without every possible struggle to be blamed for making a miserable botch of its exhibition.

There were two factors in this plan that bothered Selznick. The first, as he pointed out, had to do with

> my cross examination of a number of people in the middle and lower middle class brackets.... One woman told me that she had been saving her money to pay $1.65 for reserved seats to see *Gone With The Wind*... and upon hearing that she would be able to buy the best seats, unreserved, for $1.10, said that she certainly would not do this ... and at that low price, the picture was obviously not what it was cracked up to be ... and that she would wait until it got to the neighborhood houses at regular prices. I believe there are countless thousands of people [just like her] who will be eager to pay advanced prices ... to get reserved seats ... but who will be [disappointed] and even enraged at being gouged for advanced prices and forced to stand in line and scramble for seats ... for something that most of them consider to be a gala event.

The second issue troubling Selznick had to do with his conviction that "everything about *Gone With The Wind* must be set up as separate and apart from any other picture that has ever been made." All motion picture theatres operated on a continuous performance basis, with patrons buying tickets and going in whenever they felt like it, even in the middle of a picture, a practice that gave rise to the phrase, "This is where

we came in." Selznick was terrified that this might happen to *Gone With The Wind,* saying:

> I don't intend to have the picture murdered by allowing any schedule that permitted a large part of the audience to see it backwards, or incomplete, or that they stand in the back of theatres for part or all of its four-hour running time waiting for seats.... We have nothing to gain by several shows a day and a great deal to lose ... since it's obvious that the picture would be ruined by seeing it backwards and the subsequent loss in word of mouth advertising can be ruinous to both Loew's and ourselves.

This ongoing dispute was left unresolved throughout the period of editing and post-production; but at the two previews in Riverside and Santa Barbara, Selznick, via the preview cards, queried the audience about their preferences regarding continuous or reserved performances. Ninety percent replied that they thought seats should be reserved, and armed with these facts, Selznick finally convinced MGM of the wisdom of his logic. After their acquiescence on this, he replied in a conciliatory vein: "Nobody on earth knows how *Gone With The Wind* should be handled, and nobody on earth can find out without experimentation, and that is my principal objection to the present plan, the lack of flexibility in both the distribution and exhibition plans." Now that he had persuaded MGM on these points, he set about to implement what he considered to be the most important aspect of the picture's exhibition: the way in which it was presented to the waiting public.

> I am anxious to do everything possible to see to it that the picture is presented with taste and with showmanship. The old David Belasco tradition of the theatre, the D. W. Griffith and the Samuel Rothafel "Roxy" method of presenting a picture as though it were a jewel have been too long lost.... As in everything else that is offered to the public, the way in which a production is presented is highly important ... doubly important in this case, because I don't think that the members of the audience feel that they're getting something that is worth extra money unless the method of presenting it indicates we feel we have something extraordinary.... I hope that a presentation

FIFTEEN CENTS   DECEMBER 25, 1939

TIME

THE WEEKLY NEWSMAGAZINE

SCARLETT O'HARA

To Dave & Myron, Vivien Leigh.

(Cinema)

VOLUME XXXIV   (REG. U. S. PAT. OFF.)   NUMBER 26

DAVID O. SELZNICK'S *production of* MARGARET MITCHELL'S *Story of the Old South*

GONE WITH THE WIND

in TECHNICOLOR *Starring*

CLARK GABLE
as RHETT BUTLER

LESLIE   OLIVIA
HOWARD ☆ DE HAVILLAND
and presenting

VIVIEN LEIGH
as SCARLETT O'HARA

A SELZNICK INTERNATIONAL PICTURE
DIRECTED BY VICTOR FLEMING
SCREEN PLAY BY SIDNEY HOWARD,
A METRO-GOLDWYN-MAYER *Release*
Music by Max Steiner

D.F.

plan will be worked out that will be uniform throughout the country.... The starting times of the picture should be advertised prominently.... I feel that there should be two or three minutes of music which we will supply, before the main title, which we should not permit any exhibitor to cut off.... The lights should be dimmed as the music continues and as the picture starts all the lights should be out except those required by law, as we have found through long experience that house lights ruin Technicolor... and this again is something that will have to be hammered into the heads of exhibitors.... We have found from experience at our previews that the audience is left absolutely stunned at the conclusion of the picture.... It packs a tremendous emotional wallop... and we must be very careful not to jar this mood by suddenly turning on the lights, playing any kind of inappropriate music or putting anything else on the screen.

All of these suggestions were ultimately contained in an elaborate "presentation manual" prepared by MGM and sent to each theatre in advance of the picture's engagement. Nevertheless, all of Selznick's worst fears about the handling of the picture came true in the initial week of its two Los Angeles engagements. The picture was playing the two-performance, reserved-seat policy at the Carthay Circle and four continuous performances at the downtown United Artists theatre. Both theatres were under the operation of the Skouras brothers, Charlie and Spyros, and at the UA theatre, in spite of careful instructions to the contrary from both Selznick and MGM, the Skourases insisted on running three shorts with the picture, adding forty-five minutes to the length of the show during the day. They also restricted the intermission to one minute between halves, leading one female patron to complain in a letter to Selznick, "I ask you, what can you do in a minute?" On the strength of this and other letters, Selznick sent a member of his staff, Val Lewton, down to the theatre to monitor the shows. His report gives a firsthand account not only of the presentation of the picture, but also of unguarded audience reactions to what they were seeing:

The audience reaction to the picture was as it was at the previews. There was the usual applause at the first appearance of Gable and there was slight applause for Leslie Howard. The audience took the entire first half of the picture well and they took all of the laughs. The intermission was one and one-fourth minutes at this show and pandemonium reigned. There was tremendous confusion in the lobby and aisles when the overture for the second half of the picture started. In the second half the audience really went to work, especially on what we term the rape scene. They liked to have Gable compel Scarlett to sit in the chair and listen to him, and when he picked her up and ran up the stairs with her, the applause was almost equal to that extended to Babe Ruth when he made a home run. They enjoyed the bedroom scene on the following morning immensely. They cried and they cried hard at Melanie's death, and when Rhett gave the tag line they applauded, and at the end of the picture, there was tremendous applause.... Many were crying. I spoke to the manager and he felt very keenly that four shows a day is murder to the picture, that you should not allow theatre operators any discretion as to the length of the intermission but should force them to hold to a ten-minute length. So far as I could determine, the length of the show does not hinder the audience's enjoyment... during one performance only twelve persons got up to go to the lavatories. Dozens of people sat through two showings of the picture and I spoke to one old bird who was going back in to see it a third time.

The situation at the reserved-seat Carthay Circle was even more chaotic and haphazard. The Skouras brothers very cautiously were putting seats on sale only a week in advance; as these were sold, they would put up another block of seats, completely defeating the purpose of advance sales. The confusion was added to by the fact that they had only one small box office and one telephone line, leading to frustration and anger on the part of potential patrons. One of these, a Mrs. Mildred Gregory, wrote an indignant note to Selznick detailing her husband's efforts to obtain tickets for their wedding anniversary and complaining of scalping by ticket agencies. The same sentiments were expressed in an editorial in *The Hollywood Reporter,* and Selznick frantically wired Jock Whitney:

This is our picture and it is high time we brought a few ethics into the business in our relationship with the public.... If ever there was antagonism being built up against an enterprise this is it.... Our obligation to the public must be maintained and fulfilled regardless of whether Loew's considers this interference or not.... The situation at the Carthay is getting worse by the hour and worries me tremendously as an indication of what may be happening elsewhere.

It worried Selznick on another more personal front also, for, as Frank Capra pointed out to him, "The one reason why *Gone With The Wind* might not win the various Academy Awards was because not enough people among the voters will have seen it." Academy procedures in those days were different from today. Studios did not have large private screenings of their pictures for the membership; they went to the theatres and saw them just like everybody else. In spite of the opening night at the Carthay, the bulk of the ten thousand rank-and-file Academy voters had not yet been able to see the picture. This was a potentially serious situation, since Selznick and his staff had worked themselves to exhaustion not only to meet the Atlanta premiere date but also to get the picture finished in order to meet the Academy stipulation that a picture, to be eligible for the Awards, had to open theatrically in the Los Angeles area before the end of the calendar year. After pages of transcontinental wires and letters, the situations at the two local theatres were clarified and smoothed down, with the United Artists theatre changing to two continuous shows a day and one reserved performance at night, while the Carthay Circle installed a new, larger box office, two extra telephones, and put seats on sale for two months in advance. The lessons learned from these first engagements proved extremely valuable in handling the rest of the picture's first year of release across the country, so that by the end of May 1940, *Gone With The Wind* had grossed the astounding amount of $20 million. In the entire history of the film business, no picture had even come close to this. There was some speculation that D. W. Griffith's *The Birth of a Nation* might conceivably have done as well, but it was impossible to tell as that picture had been sold outright to States Rights distributors for a flat fee, and anything that came in to them was not reported. Not until 1938 and the $8 million gross of Disney's *Snow White and the Seven Dwarfs* had any other picture taken in more than $5 million, and Disney's success had been considered an unbeatable fluke by virtue of the novelty of the cartoon form and its broad-based appeal to the family trade.

A large part of the amazing gross of *Gone With The Wind* was due to the very high admission prices; at a time when movie prices seldom went above 50 cents tops, the lowest-priced ticket for *Gone With The Wind*'s first road show engagement was 70 cents. And MGM's sales force demanded and got an unprecedented 70 percent of each dollar that came into the theatre box office, so that out of the initial $20 million, the return to MGM was $13 million. After deducting production costs, advertising and distribution expenses, and the costs of each Technicolor print ($1,100), there was a profit of $8 million to be split evenly between Selznick International and MGM; and this was only from the first road show playoff in some four thousand theatres. Still to come were the "popular price" return engagements, which the picture would play beginning in January of 1941, and which promised to be nearly as lucrative as the original release. And if this pecuniary windfall were not enough, on the evening of February 29, 1940, Selznick's fears about the Academy Awards were put to rest as the picture was voted an unprecedented eight awards by the Academy membership, in almost every major category, with an honorary plaque given to William Cameron Menzies "for outstanding achievement in the use of color," and one to the Selznick studio for "pioneering in the use of co-ordinated equipment" in the production of the film. Strangely enough, the two major awards that it did not win were for two of its most important ingredients: Clark Gable's performance lost out to Robert Donat's in *Goodbye, Mr. Chips,* and Max Steiner's landmark score was passed over in favor of Herbert Stothart's rearrangement of the Harold Arlen melodies for *The Wizard of Oz.* The Awards were not the closely guarded secret they are now, and the Los Angeles *Times* had jumped the gun by publishing the winners even before the ceremony began. Because of this, the Academy subsequently instituted the showmanly gimmick of the sealed envelope.

The Academy Awards for 1939 were almost a clean sweep for *Gone With The Wind*. In addition to two honorary plaques, it received eight awards, including a posthumous one for Sidney Howard's screenplay. Tragically, Howard was killed in an accident on his farm in August 1939, just as the picture was nearing completion. (Above, left) David Selznick received the award for best production in a year that included *Stagecoach, Mr. Smith Goes to Washington,* and *Wuthering Heights.* Vivien Leigh won the award for best performance by an actress, beating out such competition as Bette Davis in *Dark Victory* and Greta Garbo in *Ninotchka.* (Above, right) Victor Fleming won the award for best direction for *Gone With The Wind,* but he wasn't at the ceremony to receive it. This shot was specially posed several days after the event. (Below, left) The most emotional moment of the evening was Hattie McDaniel's award for best performance by a supporting actress, the first time a black had ever been nominated let alone honored. Miss McDaniel's acceptance speech had been ghostwritten by someone at the studio; she carefully memorized it, and after promising to continue "being a credit to my race," she broke down in tears and left the stage. (Below, right) At the Academy Awards ceremony, Ernest Hopkins, president of Dartmouth College, presents David Selznick with the Irving G. Thalberg Memorial Award "for the most consistent high quality of production during 1939." Selznick had originally suggested to the Academy in 1937 that a production award be given in memory of Thalberg, and it was a highly emotional moment for him when he was presented with the bust of his friend.

At the 1939 Academy Awards ceremony: (top) Lyle Wheeler accepting his award for art direction, and (above) Hal Kern (right) and James Newcom receiving their awards for film editing for their work on *Gone With The Wind*.

T he production of *Gone With The Wind* marked the peak of Selznick's career, as he had noted, and also the high point, the full flowering of the romantic era of Hollywood's film industry. It represented not only the maturing of Selznick's powers as a creative filmmaker but the coming together of all the forces that had been shaping the look and style of the Hollywood motion picture in the decade since the advent of sound. In form and content the film embodies the virtues of an age, for embedded in *Gone With The Wind,* but close enough to the surface to be effectively perceptible, are the accumulated values, traditions, and attitudes of the first four decades of twentieth-century America—the romantic, idealistic, yet pragmatic spirit that characterized the two generations that had grown to maturity with the movies, that saw in them a reflection of themselves, of their inarticulated, shared longings, a symbol of their ability to be resilient, to bend with the gale force of the social and economic changes of the times, to take the worst that life had to offer and to overcome it by sheer willpower and determination. By invoking a consciousness of the heritage of the past, *Gone With The Wind* subliminally called up a ringing affirmation of the future of the national character. The ability of Selznick and his associates to respond to these intangibles, and to transmute them into film, is what gives the motion picture *Gone With The Wind* its particular timelessness and its capacity to continue to awaken in its audiences a powerful and positive emotional response. It does this in the best tradition of the newly emergent popular culture, using the kinetic and psychological power of movement, sound, color, humor, and sentiment to evoke in the spectator a subconscious sense of the positive virtues, the enduring nature and indestructibility of the human spirit.

The success of *Gone With The Wind,* the enormous financial and artistic awards that were showered on it and on Selznick, had a long-lasting effect on the industry, only part of which Selznick comprehended in a rather shortsighted comment he made that year to a prominent exhibitor: "... *Gone With The Wind* saved the industry, and gave it new courage to make big pictures, at exactly the right moment—the moment when it looked certain that it was going to be flooded with cheap pictures as a result of panic over the loss of the foreign market." This may have been true, but a much more accurate evaluation of the impact of *Gone With The Wind* on the Hollywood film industry came from the perceptive documentary filmmaker-turned-critic Pare Lorentz, who predicted: "Selznick and Whitney have made a picture that has given the movies enormous prestige ... and they have probably ruined the industry in that the only way that the Napoleons of the West Coast can surpass this one is to do what they did, spend money like generals, take three years and employ the best brains in the industry and cast the best actors on two continents."

It is impossible at this remove to reconstruct the impact of *Gone With The Wind,* the phenomenon that it represented to the industry and to the public. It was the first true "event" movie of the sound era, and its production and marketing set the pattern for all subsequent large-scale efforts in the picture business; the *GWTW* syndrome would dominate the industry's thinking and goals for the next thirty-five years as everybody tried to duplicate its success. Selznick himself, almost as soon as the picture was completed, began trying to follow it up. In December of 1939, he asked Kay Brown to see if Margaret Mitchell would consider either writing a sequel or selling the rights to the characters. Miss Mitchell, weary of the three-ring circus her life had become, replied in a characteristic manner to Kay Brown, who relayed her comments to Selznick:

As to the sequel, Peggy [Miss Mitchell] said quite honestly she did not believe she would do a sequel and that she had, from her point of view, extremely good reasons for not doing it. She said actually in the book when Rhett left Scarlett he was 45 years of age, and furthermore, that she felt that Rhett's words, "I wish I could care what you do or where you go but I can't," are an indication that Rhett had finally lost interest in Scarlett and would never return to her. In the picture that line doesn't appear—but Rhett's last words, "Frankly, my dear, I don't give a damn," implies [*sic*] that this is a fight and that there's always a possibility that a fight can be made up. Therefore Peggy, from her point of view, doesn't believe that Rhett ever would return to Scarlett, and therefore she herself could not write a sequel in which the two would come back together and she believes that this is what the public would want. . . .

Now as to selling us the rights to the characters—she will not do this and she has many reasons for it, which I will outline below. She is hopeful that you can be persuaded also to give up the idea of a sequel. The first reason is that she is not sure that she would like anybody else to create the situations for the characters that she knows so well. . . . Second, she thinks possibly you might suffer very much if you took the characters, of course with her permission, and created a story for them, and advertised that it was by another writer—at least, she thinks, this would hold true in the South, and that you would get reverberations of absolute commercialism culminating in a lack of interest on the part of the people to go and see the picture. Third, she thinks that certain books do allow sequels, but she is afraid that *GWTW* does not. . . . As far as she is concerned, the story of Rhett and Scarlett is ended, and . . . the story of the descendants is not a sequel, or at least not the sequel the public wants and would be prepared to receive. Now, for the last point, and what I consider the most important point . . . a mediocre sequel will damage the re-make rights. . . . I think you can do pretty much anything in pictures, but I would hate to see even you tackle the sequel to *GWTW*. To me it's just like making a sequel to *David Copperfield* or *Les Misérables.*

And with those final words of wisdom from Kay Brown, Selznick reluctantly shrugged off any lingering hope of continuing the saga of Scarlett.

The Forties

SELZNICK'S HERCULEAN EFFORTS in the three years before 1940 had left him physically exhausted and creatively depleted. In addition to the administrative duties inherent in running a studio, he had made 10 films, six of which (*The Adventures of Tom Sawyer, The Prisoner of Zenda, The Young in Heart, Made for Each Other, Intermezzo* and *Rebecca*) he had produced while simultaneously immersing himself in work on *Gone With The Wind*. To an interviewer early in 1940 he had remarked: "Frankly, I think I must have been out of my mind to tackle *Gone With The Wind*...it's the only explanation I have for even attempting something like that...nothing will ever seem hard to me again."

Before he could rest from these labors, however, he had to oversee the breaking up of the Selznick International company. The tremendous returns on *Gone With The Wind* and *Rebecca* had boosted the company's income to such an extraordinarily high level for one year that unless it was reapportioned, most of it would go for taxes. Whitney by now had tired of playing at the movies. While he was very fond of Selznick personally, the man's unorthodox and turbulent methods of moviemaking had become extremely unsettling to a person of Whitney's orderly temperament. So in August 1940 the major stockholders of Selznick International agreed to dissolve the company. After splitting the first wave of profits from *GWTW* and *Rebecca*, Selznick and the Whitney interests ended up with close to $4 million each. In order to help them keep as much of this as possible, Walter Orr, Whitney's tax lawyer, devised a complex and innovative scheme whereby the major partners in the company sold to each other portions of the assets, something that Selznick characterized as "one of our lesser contributions to Hollywood, the introduction of capital gains." There is much less tax paid on the sale of assets, and in order to maximize the benefits of this, the tax lawyers made an agreement with the govern-

ment that the dissolution would be spread out over the next three years. Selznick kept his 44 percent interest in *GWTW*, and took over the contracts of his three female stars, Bergman, Leigh, and Fontaine, those of directors Alfred Hitchcock and Robert Stevenson, and actress Hattie McDaniel. He also assumed Selznick International's commitment to deliver two more pictures for United Artists release, while the Whitney interests, in addition to keeping their 48 percent of *GWTW*, bought the negatives of the nine Selznick International productions, subsequently selling them off to a reissue company called Film Classics, which kept them in circulation all during the forties, the color films being reprinted in the garish two-color tones of Cinecolor.

In 1942, the stockholders of Selznick International, now reduced to Selznick, Jock and C. V. Whitney, David's brother Myron, and Merian C. Cooper, had just received the company's share of the proceeds from the third tour of *Gone With The Wind*. Playing at popular prices—25 to 30 cents—for the first time, it brought in another $1,065,835 to Selznick International. The estimate of the Whitney lawyers and tax accountants was that the public appetite for *Gone With The Wind* had been sated, that there was barely another million left in it. However, as the lawyers and tax accountants forcefully pointed out, the continued possession of the film could jeopardize the carefully worked out capital gains arrangement made with the government. Unless the assets of the company were disposed of by August 1942, the entire tax set-up might be disallowed. Selznick did not want to let go of his share of the picture, no matter how much or how little was left; but on the advice of the attorneys, he made a half-hearted approach to MGM, asking $2 million for his share, and met with a flat turndown.

Jock Whitney was another matter. *GWTW* was complicating his business life, which he desperately wanted to straighten out. With the entry of

America into the war, Whitney enlisted and was commissioned a major; in mid-1942, he was anxious to be off to the fighting, but even this haste did not detract from his business sense. Just before his departure he spent a weekend with the Selznicks, and it was then that the disposition of *Gone With The Wind* was decided upon. According to Selznick:

> Jock and I had a talk in my bedroom, which I deliberately made very brief as I dislike discussing business at home. I told him that I was willing to buy him out rather than sell, but Jock stated flatly that he would only sell at twice what he would buy me out for.... Since Jock was so reluctant to sell to me, I sold to him.... I felt that if anybody should make a profit out of it, it should be Jock, for nothing he could ever do to me in business, and no profits I could possibly make out of my share, could compensate for the magnificent support and help he gave me at the most crucial point in my career, and I shall never forget this.

So Whitney bought out Selznick for $400,000, and a year later, in August 1943, Whitney and his group sold their holdings to MGM for $2.4 million, giving Loew's, Inc., almost complete ownership of the picture except for two small interests held by Myron Selznick and, ironically, C. V. Whitney. At the conclusion of the dissolution, Selznick and Whitney sent a portion of their share of the proceeds to Margaret Mitchell, who replied in a most gracious letter:

> I came home from a long day at the Red Cross, too tired to take my shoes off, and...found your letter and the very generous check.... I had to read it twice before it made any sense and then it almost made me cry. You two and I and hundreds of others have been associated in the most phenomenally successful event in motion picture or theatrical history. I have seen the picture five and a half times now and have examined it from many angles—musical score, costumes, bit players, etc., and I like it better each time. And each time the film reaches out and takes my hand to lead me down paths that seem ever new, for I forget in watching that I was the author of the book and am able to view the film with fresh eyes. At the Grand Theatre here in Atlanta, they play the theme music from *Gone With The Wind* when the last performances of the night are over. Frequently John and I and many other Atlantans remain in our seats to listen to it.... I never hear this music without feeling again the strange mixture of emotions that I experienced on that night nearly three years ago when I sat in the same theatre and saw the film for the first time. I doubt if I could describe those emotions, but they did not include fear that it would not be a great picture. Years before I had seen your picture *David Copperfield* and I realized that here was a producer of...integrity who was breaking all the Hollywood rules by producing the book the author wrote...adding to it his own color, firing it with his own imagination, heightening effects with his own genius. So on the night of the premiere, I knew before the film began to roll that it would be a great picture and before many minutes had passed I knew it was even greater than I could have expected. I have always thought myself fortunate that Selznick International produced *Gone With The Wind*.

By 1947, *Gone With The Wind* had not been seen on American movie screens since November of 1943, when MGM withdrew it after its third reissue had grossed $5.2 million around the country. (It had been playing nonstop in England since April 1940, and in France it had been showing consecutively for four years.) Selznick's office had constantly been receiving requests from individuals and groups who wanted to see the picture again—for instance, the entire student body of Western State High School in Kalamazoo, Michigan, sent him a petition asking for another chance to "enjoy again the superb cast under the direction of David O. Selznick in a supreme film." Margaret Mitchell herself wrote to him, saying, "So many people ask me when the picture will play a return engagement. A number of children who were not old enough to see it when it was last here have requested that I ask you when it will be back. So I am asking for them, and because I'd like to see it myself." Selznick made sure that all this mail was sent to the MGM sales and distribution department. In July 1945, he wrote to J. Robert Rubin, a vice-president of Loew's: "I think the time is about right to revive the film nationally, and I hope you will do this, not merely because of my pride in the film, but also because of what it would mean to [my late brother] Myron's estate, of which I am an executor."

Scarlett in her burgundy gown. A Kodachrome photographed with normal lighting. Compare the difference between the color of the dress in this shot and the way it appeared after Technicolor processing (page 40). MGM put *Gone With The Wind* into general release for the first time in December 1940, a year after its road show openings, giving the picture a gala "birthday" celebration at Loew's Grand Theatre in Atlanta. This popular-priced release grossed $9.7 million, and the picture was voted the most popular of 1940 in the *Film Daily* exhibitors poll.

The poster for the 1942 re-issue—before the drawing of Rhett carrying Scarlett became the dominant advertising image.

(Left) MGM's publicity staff took this photo of the 1947 revival of *Gone With the Wind* in South Africa. It was intended to prove the truth of the new advertising slogan, *"Everybody* wants to see..." This re-issue grossed $9.1 million in the United States alone.

(Myron Selznick had a 6 percent interest in the picture, which after his death was divided between his daughter and his mother.)

Reissuing pictures was an old industry practice, dating back to 1921, when *The Birth of a Nation* startled everyone in the business by being spectacularly successful all over again. Since that time, the distributors had occasionally put back into circulation popular films; *King Kong* was the best known of these, but usually reissues were "fillers," which theatres could throw into their mid-week programming. It wasn't until the amazing success of Walt Disney's reissue of *Snow White and the Seven Dwarfs* in 1944 that the distributors began to be aware that certain pictures did indeed have a marketing life far beyond the few thousand dollars the average reissue brought in. In late 1946, MGM cautiously began experimenting with limited revivals of what they called "masterpiece reprints," offering new prints and ad campaigns for pictures including *The Great Waltz, The Women,* and the 1941 Ingrid Bergman film *Rage in Heaven.* The results were encouraging, and the decision was made early in 1947 to put *Gone With The Wind* back into theatres beginning in July, treating it as a major event with new Technicolor prints, and a huge new ad campaign tailored around a quote from Bosley Crowther in *The New York Times:* "You haven't really seen *GWTW* until you've seen it at least twice"—a remark he had made at the time of the picture's 1942 engagement. Also picked up from that revival was the use of a sketch of Rhett carrying Scarlett in his arms, which became the dominant image for all the subsequent advertising of the film, leading Selznick to remark when he saw the ads that "the art work...is likely to get you into trouble with the Johnston office...it is perfectly ridiculous [for them] to attempt to create salacious art work...when there are so many good stills available."

MGM wanted to cut the film to get in more showings per day, and Selznick halfheartedly assigned Hal Kern the task of trying to eliminate some footage; but after struggling for several weeks, Kern advised Selznick, "It would be impossible to take out [anything] without materially damaging the story," and Selznick told MGM to leave the picture alone, suggesting that they continue to use the phrase "uncut-intact," which had proved so valuable in all the other return engagements. As the re-release date approached, Selznick was insistent that MGM pay scrupulous attention to including the credit billings "David O. Selznick's Production" and "A Selznick International Picture" on all revised ad copy, fearing that they might attempt to call it an MGM picture (which strictly speaking it was, since they now owned most of it). "In view of the tremendous blow to my prestige," Selznick wrote to his lawyers in early 1947, "resulting from the bad press on *Duel in the Sun*, it is extremely important that my name be used exactly as it was on the first release in connection with the reissue of *Wind*...which is to be...very widespread...and one on which they expect a fabulous gross. [MGM] has told me they wouldn't bother to reissue it if they thought they would get less than $5 million...I mention this because of the...extent to which it will be publicized and advertised." As it turned out, it was a conservative estimate, for when the picture opened at Loew's Criterion in Manhattan in September, the crowds that turned out to see it were almost as large as those for the original engagements. These audiences were largely made up of people who had vivid memories of the picture, and now they were not disappointed. Nothing about the film was dated; its craftsmanship and production values were still unequaled by any subsequent Hollywood efforts. And to a new generation of moviegoers who were lining up with their parents, the film was every bit as exciting and satisfying as it had been to their elders. To those who had seen it before, it was more than just a good movie: it represented continuity, a link with their own immediate past—a subliminal repository of memories of themselves in relation to previous screenings.

It was in these original postwar revivals that the picture began to take on the first layers of a patina of nostalgia. The end of the war had brought to moviemaking a new emphasis and appreciation of reality inherited from the documentaries that a number of leading directors had made during the war. As these men returned to commercial filmmaking, the search for a greater realism began to be seen in the widespread use of actual locations for films, and in the choice of stories too; there was a noticeable increase in adult, realistic dramas dealing with themes and topics previously considered taboo. *Crossfire* and *Gentleman's Agreement* were about anti-Semitism, and from anti-Semitism to the problems of racism was a short but courageous step, first taken by independent producer Stanley Kramer in his *Home of the Brave* (1949), followed quickly by *Lost Boundaries, Pinky,* and *Intruder in the Dust.* The novelty of seeing these subjects treated on the screen was fascinating to audiences, but a steady concentration on the unpleasant and the harrowing was more than most moviegoers could absorb, while the escapist films of the time were by now standardized formula, with no surprises and very little satisfaction. Still, moviegoing was a hard habit to break; attendance stayed at its peak level of 90 million all through 1946–47 and into 1948, and *Gone With The Wind* triumphantly rode the crest of this wave. In the last half of 1947 and through most of 1948 it grossed an astounding $9 million, and when Selznick realized what he had sold off five years before he raged: "I could strangle [those tax lawyers] with my bare hands in cold blood."

(Above) Two 11 × 14 theatre lobby cards. These cards were carefully hand-colored and expensively lithographed and were last used for the picture's 1947 re-issue. (Top Right) *Gone With The Wind* opened in London in April 1940. The 3,000th performance of the picture in the West End was given in 1947 and was commemorated with a special scroll presented to David O. Selznick (above) by C. Aubrey Smith and the British Consul General in Los Angeles, J.E.M. Carvell. (Below) Margaret Mitchell sent this clipping to David O. Selznick in 1947. The handwriting at the top of the photo is Miss Mitchell's. She was killed in 1949 by a speeding taxi cab.

"GWTW" REVIVAL BREAKS BOX OFFICE RECORD HERE—All records for popular price admission were shattered at Loew's Grand Wednesday when thousands stood in double lines more than a block long to buy tickets to the "re-premiere" of "Gone With the Wind." Fifty eager fans were standing in front of the box office at 3 a.m. This photo, made at approximately 9:45 a.m., shows the ticket line extending past the rear of the theater in the Loew's Grand by-pass. Wednesday's audience was composed mainly of young people who were not old enough to grasp the movie when it had its gala opening at Loew's Dec. 15, 1939. MGM, which recently bought the film from Producer David O. Selznick, estimate it has taken in $50,000,000. Seeing the crowd above, Loew's Manager Boyd Fry said the planned one-week showing may be extended at least another week.

Margaret Mitchell Dies of Injuries

ATLANTA, Aug. 16. — (P) — Margaret Mitchell, the author of "Gone With The Wind," died today, the victim of a speeding automobile.

Miss Mitchell died at noon in Henry Grady Memorial Hospital as doctors prepared for an emergency operation to try to save her life.

She was struck down last Thursday night as she crossed Atlanta's Peachtree street, scene of much of her famous novel of the South, of the Civil War, and reconstruction days.

RALLIED BRIEFLY—

She had never regained full consciousness after the accident. She rallied briefly at times but never was out of critical danger. Her skull and pelvis were fractured, and she had other injuries.

The driver of the car, Hugh D. Gravitt, 28, had been free on $5000 bond. When the famed author died, he surrendered and was held without bond on a charge of murder.

Atlanta Police Chief Herbert Jenkins said he will seek an immediate grand jury indictment against Gravitt, a cabby, driving his personal car at the time of the accident.

BOOKED 22 TIMES—

Police records show 22 previous traffic charges had been booked against him.

The death of the shy, modest little woman who started out to be a newspaper feature writer and wrote the world's best selling novel brought countless expressions of grief and mourning. The flag at the Georgia Capitol

was lowered to half staff on orders of Governor Herman Talmadge. The Governor said he and all Georgians were shocked by her death.

PRIVATE FUNERAL—

Private funeral services will be held at 10 a.m. Thursday at Spring Hill (Atlanta). Episcopalian Dean Raimundo de Ovies will officiate. Burial will be at Oakland Cemetery.

The family asked that no flowers be sent.

They said Miss Mitchell would have wished instead that offerings be sent to Henry Grady Memorial Hospital where she died. In her lifetime, she had showered the city-owned hospital with many benevolences.

TRUMAN MESSAGE—

President Truman and Hollywood celebrities sent messages. In Hollywood, Clark Gable said: "In the tragic death of Margaret Mitchell I feel a very deep personal loss. She was a woman with a great literary gift, and I shall ever be obligated to her for the finest role I ever played."

Hospital records listed Miss Mitchell's age as 43. She had never revealed it.

Miss Mitchell's husband, John R. Marsh, an advertising executive, was at their apartment when she died. He suffered a heart attack several years ago and has been a semi-invalid since.

MARGARET MITCHELL
—Associated Press wirephoto.

EVERYBODY
WANTS TO SEE
GONE
WITH THE
WIND!

DAVID O. SELZNICK'S PRODUCTION
OF MARGARET MITCHELL'S STORY
OF THE OLD SOUTH

GONE WITH THE WIND
in *Technicolor*
Starring
CLARK GABLE
VIVIEN LEIGH
LESLIE HOWARD
OLIVIA de HAVILLAND

A SELZNICK INTERNATIONAL PICTURE
DIRECTED BY VICTOR FLEMING
Screen Play by Sidney Howard
A METRO-GOLDWYN-MAYER
MASTERPIECE RELEASE
Music by Max Steiner

UNE PRODUCTION
DAVID O. SELZNICK
D'APRÈS LE CÉLÈBRE ROMAN DE
MARGARET MITCHELL

AUTANT EN EMPORTE LE VENT
"GONE WITH THE WIND"

AVEC
CLARK GABLE · VIVIEN LEIGH
LESLIE HOWARD · OLIVIA deHAVILLAND
RÉALISATION de VICTOR FLEMING

SCÉNARIO DE SIDNEY HOWARD   MUSIQUE DE MAX STEINER
UN FILM SELZNICK INTERNATIONAL · TECHNICOLOR®
DISTRIBUÉ PAR METRO·GOLDWYN·MAYER

L'IMMORTEL CHEF D'ŒUVRE
DU CINÉMA

The Fifties

This Belgian poster is from the 1950's.

I N SEPTEMBER, 1953, 20th Century–Fox released *The Robe,* its first production in the new wide screen process CinemaScope. This was the latest development in the technological revolution that had been launched by Merian C. Cooper and Lowell Thomas when they presented "This is Cinerama" in New York in September 1952. The sensation it created caused the film industry to dust off old three-dimensional techniques, introduce stereophonic sound, and other new forms of presenting movies. *The Robe,* well made, spectacular and with the additional widespread curiosity about CinemaScope, immediately became one of the top grossing pictures of the year. Its amazing success led the executives at 20th Century–Fox to predict that it might soon topple *Gone With The Wind* from its fifteen-year reign as the industry's top grosser.

By 1950, when *GWTW* had played its last domestic engagements, the picture had achieved a phenomenal worldwide gross of $62.7 million. Of this total, $46.7 million had come from the United States and Canada (these figures represent what was paid at the box office; the return to the distributor on this was just over $37 million). Fox was claiming grosses for *The Robe* of $26 million, which was box-office gross, not distributor net, and *The Robe* had been playing at greatly advanced prices. It was conceivable that by the time it had played all the theatres that had yet to be converted to CinemaScope, it might indeed overtake *Gone With The Wind.* To MGM and to Selznick, the possibility of losing this longstanding record was unsettling. For Selznick, it would mean losing the prestige of having produced the industry's most successful motion picture, while MGM prided itself on owning the film and seeing it at the top of *Variety's* list of historic top grossers every year. So in the interest of prestige, pride, and, not so incidentally, the money that would come in from another reissue of the film, MGM let Selznick know in late 1953 that they planned to put the picture back into circulation in the spring of 1954—this despite the fact

that it had played its last U.S. theatrical engagement as recently as August 1950. Another reason for issuing it again was that 1954 was the company's thirtieth anniversary, and the picture, even though it had not been made by MGM, was one of its proudest possessions, which could properly be shown off during the birthday celebration. Finally, the sales people felt that exhibiting the picture on the new wide screens that had just come into use would give it a contemporary look and feel, as well as enhancing the spectacle sequences.

The chief difficulty with this latter approach, however, was that most of the maskings of the image necessary to give older pictures a wide-screen proportion were done in the theatre and were largely left up to the projectionists, who took very little care over what they were doing, resulting in heads completely disappearing out of the frame or alternately sitting at the bottom like rows of tenpins. MGM's standards were still the highest in the industry, and many of the people who were working for the company had been entrusted with the care of *GWTW* ever since its original release. They felt an affection for it, and a proprietary interest in its preservation and proper presentation; the thought of its being left to the arbitrary mercies and sloppy projection practices of most theatres was painful in the extreme. So early in 1954, a special assignment was handed to W. D. Kelly of the MGM editorial department: he was to make a survey of the various theatres in the Los Angeles area to determine the proportion in which they projected their image, and how the projectionists framed and centered the picture during a performance. His report to J. Robert Rubin, the vice-president of sales, indicated that "projecting *Gone With The Wind* with present-day standards...could lead to certain scenes being damaged from the photographic and dramatic standpoint." He had made a study of the picture projected through the various ratios, and found that if the image was blown up slightly, to a 1.6-to-1 proportion, only five scenes

Loew's Warfield in San Francisco was one of six test theatres that opened the wide-screen reissue of *Gone With The Wind* in May 1954. Heavily publicized and extensively promoted in the showmanly tradition of MGM (which included having models as Rhett and Scarlett tour the city with signs proclaiming "the return to San Francisco of the greatest motion picture ever made"), the picture did astounding business, outgrossing such current MGM spectaculars as *Knights of the Round Table* and *Executive Suite*. It was a success that was repeated all across the country in the fall of 1954 as the picture opened nationwide, grossing $9 million. To make sure that it would be exhibited properly in wide-screen, MGM carefully masked several scenes in the picture. This shot of the wounded in the Atlanta train station was changed from its original proportion of 1.33-to-1 to a near rectangular 2-to-1 by printing a black strip across the bottom of the image, thereby assuring that audiences would not have the image arbitrarily cut off by careless projectionists. Howard Dietz of the MGM publicity department devised a new slogan for this reissue utilizing the famous initials "GWTW"—only this time it stood for "Greater With the Wide-Screen (and stereophonic—as an added tonic—sound)." Composer Cole Porter liked this latter phrase so much that he appropriated it in 1955 for the song "Stereophonic Sound" in his musical remake of *Ninotchka* called *Silk Stockings*.

in the film would need careful attention from the projectionist: one in the beginning, when Scarlett runs across the lawn at Tara; the first pullback shot of Scarlett and her father standing under the tree looking out over the plantation; two of the spectacular shots in the Atlanta railroad station; and the final pullback shot at the end of the picture. For these, Kelly recommended that the studio itself "reduce the picture aperture ... which would obviate the necessity of having ... theatre projectionists concern themselves with the adjustment." The rest of the picture could be played at the 1.6 ratio with very little loss of the central image.

At the same time that Kelly was making his recommendations, Douglas Shearer of the sound department was concluding arrangements for use of a directional sound process called "Perspecta" in all of MGM's Cinema-Scope and wide-screen features. Once the decision had been made to exhibit *Gone With The Wind* in wide screen, it was also decided that the picture should be adapted for the Perspecta multi-channel sound process. To achieve this, MGM would need the separate music, dialogue and sound effects tracks for the picture, and here they faced a tricky situation. When they had bought the rights to the picture from the Whitney interests, they bought only the physical picture and its finished components, which included the three black-and-white color-separation negatives and a composite sound track. Selznick still owned everything else from the film: costumes, unused footage, and the separate music, dialogue, and other sound tracks. On behalf of his brother's estate, which owned a small part of the picture, David had for years constantly bedeviled MGM over what he felt to be improper accounting in the company's remittances to Myron's heirs. Consequently, they were wary of approaching him for the use of the sound track components for the necessary remix. But when they finally did so, in early February 1954, they found him surprisingly tractable; even more amazing was that he would let them have what they wanted for free. As he stated in a letter to J. Robert Rubin, "I don't want one single penny... I will gladly donate not only [the tracks] but also my own time and effort to assure the preservation of *GWTW* as the biggest and best picture ever made...I will be happy to do this...because my pride and my reputation are at stake and I am not going to have my major effort ruined by [my lack of cooperation]."

Selznick's cooperation in this matter, however, was brought to an outraged halt on the evening of February 14, when Ed Sullivan, on his popular Sunday-night television program "The Toast of the Town," devoted the entire evening to celebrating MGM's thirtieth anniversary. The show was made up of a selection of clips from some of the studio's more memorable films, and Selznick, watching it in New York, was "upset at the complete lack of mention of Louis B. Mayer and Irving Thalberg...the men who built the company...and made most of the pictures that were being excerpted...in the course of the program." His upset turned to fury when, at the program's conclusion, a short sequence from *Gone With The Wind* was shown, after which Ed Sullivan introduced a beaming Dore Schary, MGM's production head, and the following dialogue ensued:

> That's quite a treasury of memories, isn't it, Dore? Incidentally, I understand you are re-releasing *Gone With The Wind*.
> Yes, Ed, it opens in May.
> I remember that picture very well, Dore. I was out there when you made it. It was produced by David O. Selznick and released in 1939... and your MGM team is still leading the league.

Selznick's long-simmering resentment of Schary and his treatment of Mayer now boiled over into sputtering rage, not only at the omission of credits for Mayer, Thalberg, Arthur Freed, and the other producers but also at the implication that Schary had in some way been connected with the making of *GWTW*. Almost immediately after the show ended, Selznick was on the phone with his lawyers, and two days later he issued a lengthy statement:

> Dore Schary, representing the current production management of MGM, failed on The Toast of the Town...to accord the slightest credit, or acknowledge...the past creators whose efforts brought to that studio the eminence it formerly enjoyed.... [These omissions] created the impression that the present studio "team" headed by Dore Schary is responsible for the outstanding films produced years ago by MGM.... I

am also incensed by the startling, and in my opinion, disgraceful and inexcusable attempt on the part of [Schary] to present *Gone With The Wind*…as an MGM production…. *Gone With The Wind* was produced in its every detail and in its entirety by me and for the Selznick International Studio…. [On behalf of] the staff and the team that actually made the picture, and for myself, I deeply resent the attempt to mislead the trade and the public and I have instructed my attorneys to take legal steps toward a correction and damages.

Selznick's lawyers studied a kinescope of the controversial sections and demanded that CBS delete all references to *GWTW* before the show was rebroadcast in other parts of the country.

For the next several weeks, the newspapers gleefully printed all the recriminations, accusations, countercharges, and the flow of statements verging on insults from Selznick, Schary, and even Louis B. Mayer, who from the depths of his involuntary retirement fired several long-overdue salvos in Schary's direction, calling him a "ham…a man who wrecked an institution that ranked as number one." Asked if he intended to file a suit, Mayer retorted, "What kind of a suit could I file? Can I say I'm the great Louis B. Mayer? This is impossible." Of far more concern to Schary and the rest of the MGM hierarchy was the damage the controversy might do to their plans to reissue *GWTW*. Selznick, who could be a legal terror when he felt he had been unfairly treated, might try to stop the re-release through legal action. Howard Dietz meanwhile was enlisting the aid of Ed Sullivan, who was only too happy to be of help. He invited Selznick to appear on his show in the near future to talk about his career and *Gone With The Wind*. On May 23, Selznick went on "Toast of the Town" with two short sequences from the picture, and in a colloquy with Sullivan, he gave Schary an indirect back of the hand. In answer to Sullivan's question, "What has been your overall philosophy in twenty-nine years as the industry's top producer of films?" Selznick commented, "My feeling is that the first and foremost function of motion pictures is entertainment… this is what people pay their money for…and I have small patience with those producers who think it their duty to deliver 'messages' with their pictures…except incidentally and idealistically…. As far as motion pictures are concerned, I think that they must have magic…and that they can

have no higher purpose than to send people back to their homes feeling a little bit better about life in general."

In the two months preceding this broadcast, MGM's technicians had been feverishly working with the sound tracks Selznick had turned over to them, remixing them for the Perspecta effects, and altering the necessary sections of the picture. They did this by rephotographing portions of the original black-and-white negatives onto a new Eastmancolor single-strip color negative. These altered sections were then inserted into the new Technicolor printing matrices and a completely new set of prints run off, which is why, in certain sections of the 1954 reissue, the color suddenly becomes very grainy and washed-out looking. Selznick commented on this during the several weeks he devoted to overseeing the making of the first batch of new Technicolor prints, remarking that "the color seems much harsher than in my original print." There were several reasons for this, the primary one being that the new prints were made on acetate "safety" film, the more volatile nitrate film base having been outlawed in 1949. All of the prints of *GWTW* made in the United States prior to 1950 had been on nitrate-base stock, and these prints, with their delicate, subdued pastel coloring, were destroyed by government order—except for a few that found their way into the hands of private collectors, and one that was presented to the National Archives in 1941 by Selznick and MGM. The new prints made up by Technicolor for the 1954 reissue differed from the originals in several ways. One, of course, was the transparency of the image—it is much denser in these later printings; another was that the color was much more vivid, what technicians call "saturated"—this was an aesthetic decision, made by MGM and Selznick jointly. (In 1940, it was feared that four hours of Technicolor images would be tiring to the eyes of spectators unaccustomed to color movies, so the coloring was purposely kept subdued.) Adding to the change of hues in 1954 was the fact that the Technicolor staff had changed their dye components, using different ingredients in the chemical mixtures that made up their printing colors. The result of all these seemingly insignificant changes was a version of *Gone With The Wind* drenched in color. Even Selznick mentioned that the color seemed "overly bright and vivid," and at his suggestion, whole reels were printed over again to reduce the chromatic richness of the image. For two months prior to the scheduled "repremiere" in Atlanta in May, Selznick fussed and fretted over the new version, spending days with the MGM and Technicolor technicians in an attempt, as he wrote to Eddie Mannix, one of the vice-presidents of MGM, "to duplicate the original color." He was considerably heartened by the attitudes of the MGM staff, commenting to Mannix:

> It seems obvious that they are trying to do a job worthy of the film…but of course none of them has the prior knowledge as to what is necessary to get the full values out of each scene. *GWTW* is a gigantic tapestry, and…its overpowering effect is dependent upon the perfection of its thousands of component parts…no one of these items would seem important to anyone unfamiliar with how the total effect was achieved…. I was very pleased to hear your own staff comment that in all its technical phases [the picture] is still so superior…this is a tribute indeed to my staff and our work, considering that we did the job fifteen years ago!

MGM was still bending over backward to do nothing that might further offend Selznick, and even went to the extraordinary effort and expense of printing up special stickers to paste over the already printed posters and other advertising accessories, replacing the words, "A Metro-Goldwyn-Mayer Masterpiece Release" with the simple phrase, "Released by Loew's Incorporated." The company carefully tested the picture in a series of six "pre-release" engagements, kicking these off with the gala reopening in Atlanta. Howard Dietz sent Selznick a special invitation to take part in the festivities, but he declined, stating, "I am delighted to help to maintain the quality of the picture…but I have no intention of making myself ridiculous by appearing in Atlanta as a member of the 'Schary team' or any other MGM team."

Selznick maintained this standoffish attitude throughout the first months of the picture's revival, softening a bit as letters from moviegoers from all over the country began to arrive at the studio, some from people who had seen it before, but primarily from youngsters, teenagers to whom it was just something their parents had talked about. Some had read the

For the 1954 revival, RCA Victor issued the first recording of the *Gone With The Wind* music. Max Steiner conducted a 30-piece orchestra playing a symphonic suite he had excerpted from his complete score for a 1944 Hollywood Bowl concert. (Also in 1954, "Tara's Theme" was supplied with a lyric by Mack David, and with the title "My Own True Love" was recorded by several vocalists.)

The crumbling facade of Tara as it looked in 1959.

book and were prepared to be critical of the film, but just as with audiences for the past fifteen years, this new generation quickly fell under its spell, many returning to see it several times and leading Selznick to suggest to MGM that they revive the slogan: "How many times have you seen *Gone With The Wind*?" It was the 1954 revival that transmogrified *Gone With The Wind* into more than just an outstanding motion picture, altering its status as the highpoint of the melodramatic, romantic genre. The audiences at the earlier revivals of the picture had been made up largely of people who had seen it before, and their vivid memories were not disappointed in any of the subsequent showings. But in 1954, *Gone With The Wind* was given over to an entirely new generation, who took it for their own as an authentic classic that cut across age and social barriers, its narrative power, the beauty of its images, and its impact potent and undiminished by time, changing attitudes, or technical advances. The 1954 revival turned *Gone With The Wind* into a true folk movie, an heirloom to be handed down from one generation to another.

In August 1954, *Gone With The Wind* finally opened its Hollywood engagement on a glittering, star-studded night at the Egyptian Theatre that was as much a tribute to Selznick as it was to the fifteenth anniversary of the picture. MGM had invited everyone who had worked on the film to attend. Hal Kern, now at MGM as an assistant to Al Lichtman, came to see what had been done to the picture. He hadn't seen it since 1947, and he relates that he was "surprised and disappointed...the wide screen didn't seem to do what it should, and the new sound just ruined it. I didn't get the thrill from it that I had the last time"—sentiments echoed by Lyle Wheeler, who was now supervising art director for 20th Century–Fox: "I thought all of the things we had worked so hard on, the composition...all the money and time we had spent on these were gone...a great deal of it was lost." Absent from the evening's festivities were Victor Fleming, who had died in 1949; Vivien Leigh, who was in England recovering from a nervous breakdown suffered on the set of Paramount's *Elephant Walk*; Olivia de Havilland, who was off making a picture in Europe; and, most conspicuously of all, Clark Gable. Gable and Selznick had patched up

most of their differences immediately after the war when, as Selznick related years later to one of Gable's biographers, "I ran into Clark at a party shortly [after he returned]...he came up, put his arms around me and said, 'I'm so glad to see you...I have an apology to make to you. I was flying over Berlin on my first mission and I was scared to death, sure I was going to die...and for some reason you came into my mind...and I said to myself, What have I got against that man? He has never been anything but kind to me. My best picture was with him...he did me nothing but good. What have I got against him? And I said if I get out of this thing alive and get back to Hollywood, I'm going to apologize to him. I'm now keeping that promise.'"

Selznick continued, "We met several times, afterwards, very cordially ... and he told me that he learned after the fact how much I had to pay for him for *GWTW* and what a fool he had been because they had given him only a bonus." This latter remark is the key to why Gable was not at the 1954 premiere of *Gone With The Wind*. He had just left MGM, after twenty years as their most popular and durable star, and he was bitter at their treatment of him; the *GWTW* windfall to MGM because of him still rankled; and on his last day at the studio, there was not even a farewell party for him, no gesture of parting, of appreciation. A proud man, he resisted all of MGM's efforts to get him to attend the opening. Even Selznick implored Gable's agent, George Chasin at MCA, to urge Gable to attend, saying in a letter that "Clark's appearance at the opening means no more (and no less) to me than it does to him. Neither of us will benefit one penny from how *GWTW* is received. But...it is of great and lasting benefit to us both for *GWTW* to maintain its prestige and its championship. Each of us is likely always to be best remembered for this film...and it would be folly for either of us ever to turn our back on it." Gable, however, remained unmoved and unwavering. The evening went on without him; but even with his absence, and in spite of the wide-screen alterations, the consensus of the celebrity-packed audience that night was that the picture was still "the greatest," a sentiment echoed all across the country.

IN 1958, DAVID SELZNICK had produced *A Farewell to Arms,* starring his second wife, Jennifer Jones, and Rock Hudson. The picture was not a success and Selznick decided to retire after he finished his next picture, *Tender Is the Night,* based on the F. Scott Fitzgerald novel. Because he had sold a large block of his older pictures to British television, English exhibitors banded together and threatened to boycott all future Selznick pictures. This frightened Selznick's distributor into asking him to withdraw as producer of *Tender Is the Night* and instead oversee a young tyro producer named Henry Weinstein. Selznick reluctantly agreed and with his usual vigor began, once again, to prepare a film that would star Jennifer Jones. In the midst of all this preparation came the shocking news of Clark Gable's death from a heart attack at the age of fifty-nine. He had just finished rugged location work on John Huston's *The Misfits* with Marilyn Monroe, and he and his fifth wife, Kay Spreckels, were expecting a child, his first. All over the world, headlines blazoned word of his death, and in Hollywood, the *Citizen-News* covered its entire front page with a black-bordered photograph of the actor. Selznick once again had the sad duty of memorializing someone he had worked with: "Clark Gable was and will for a long time remain the worldwide symbol of American virility. He was unquestionably the greatest male star of our time...."

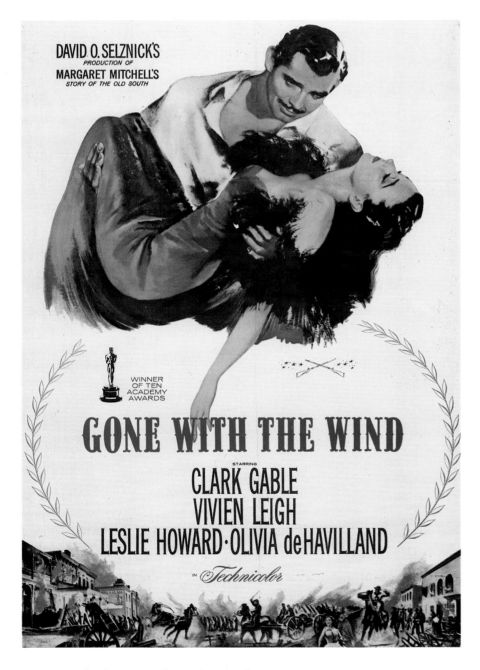

The poster for the 1961 Civil War Centennial.

Almost simultaneously, MGM announced plans to put *Gone With The Wind* into circulation early in 1961, "to commemorate the Civil War centennial." Selznick's attention was pulled away from the frustration and compromises resulting from his not being allowed to work on *Tender Is the Night,* and he was once again faced with the accomplishments of his past. His reaction to the ever-growing legendary status of *Gone With The Wind* had taken on an almost schizoid quality: his pride in it was enormous, and yet he had come to hate the looming shadow of the picture, which seemed to blot out everything else in his professional life. Several times over the years he had caustically remarked to intimates about "that damned picture; when I die, the paper will read 'Producer of *Gone With The Wind* died today.'" If he had owned it, his ambivalence would probably not have been as great, but his resentment toward MGM and the millions of dollars it brought to that company every seven years added greatly to his discontent. Yet all this was tempered by his pride, and the esteem that came to him from having produced the industry's top-grossing picture, a position it held until late 1958, when it was supplanted by Cecil B. DeMille's biblical spectacular *The Ten Comandments.* Consequently, when MGM announced it was putting *GWTW* back into circulation in 1961, Selznick felt bound to cooperate in every way he could to help the picture regain its first-place status. He raised no serious objections when the people at MGM told him in confidence that instead of having Technicolor make new prints for this reissue, the work would be done in MGM's own labs, using the company's "Metro Color" (a trade name for the Eastmancolor process), a quicker, cheaper process that in the fifties had begun to supplant Technicolor as a method for both the photographing and printing of color movies. With careful handling, this process could deliver color that compared favorably with Technicolor's fabled dye transfer system, but it did not offer the control latitude of the Technicolor method, nor did it quite have Technicolor's smoothness and definition in color printing. Finally, it had one distinct disadvantage over the Technicolor dye transfer process: the color, achieved through a chemical process within the layers of the film, was unstable and after several years turned pink as a result of changes in the chemical compositions. The prints made by MGM for the initial 1961 engagements of *Gone With The Wind* lacked the sharpness and definition of the earlier Technicolor prints, and within a year they began to fade, distorting the color values beyond all recognition. When Selznick saw one of these new prints, he was impressed by the lower printing costs but concerned over "the fuzziness and the lack of clarity in some of the exterior scenes and the muddy quality of the interiors, espeically in the shadows and the other delicate areas of color that we took such pains to achieve." Many of the Technicolor prints from the 1954 engagements were still in good enough condition to be used in 1961, so that MGM was able to advertise that the picture was in "Color by Technicolor."

In spite of his reservations about the new prints, Selznick was enough of a pragmatist to realize that the changing quality standards of the industry would have to be lived with, and he allowed himself to be persuaded by MGM to attend a three-day celebration in Atlanta for the reopening of the picture in March of 1961. He tried to convince Jock Whitney to attend, wiring him: "Apparently Atlanta is going mad all over again in connection with the reopening of our opus ... climaxing with a new 'premiere.' I tried to persuade MGM that it would be more like a wake, but they insisted that the Georgians wanted this to be the keystone of their centennial, and finally, if reluctantly — I agreed to be present along with the other principal survivors, Vivien and Olivia. I would feel much better about the whole thing if you and I could be there together and have a few drinks over our recollections. ... [It] should be fun." Whitney evidently had no stomach for nostalgic recollections, for he declined the invitation, and Selznick instead took his younger son, twenty-five-year-old Daniel, who recalls the event: "Loew's Grand was decorated to resemble the way it had looked in 1939.... Inside the theatre Vivien Leigh sat on one side of my father, with Olivia de Havilland on the other. As the main title appeared on the screen, I saw Vivien clutch my father's hand and whisper, 'Oh, David.' When Clark Gable first appeared on the screen, I heard her

For the 1967 reissue of *Gone With The Wind*, MGM converted the image to fit the proportions of the 70 mm process. To do this, it was necessary to recompose every frame for the new ratio. (Left) The original image. (Above) The image as cropped and rephotographed on 70 mm Metro Color (Eastmancolor) stock. (Top) The original, sweeping main title was replaced by this new version for the 70 mm reissue because the wider proportion cropped too much off the tops and bottoms of the letters. Unfortunately, when MGM struck new 35 mm prints of the film, they kept this uninspiring compromise version instead of returning to the original, which they could easily have done. (Above) The projection and masking device showing how this was accomplished.

gasp, 'Oh look at Clark; he looks so young and gorgeous!' My father turned to her at that moment, put his arm around her, and said, 'So do you, Vivien. And you still do.' The applause at the end of the picture was loud and long; all three rose to share in it. My father seemed to be in very high spirits. But when it was time to leave Atlanta to come back to Hollywood, Dad became very wistful, even melancholy. After such a high, there was no place to go but down."

Tender Is the Night proved to be a fiasco for all concerned, and its failure seemed symptomatic of the ailing film business. Through the early 1960's, the movie industry seemed not to be affected by the infectious optimism and general prosperity that had begun to be felt across the country. Selznick, who did not make another picture after the disappointment of *Tender Is the Night,* went on with his business dealings in Hollywood, observing the changes in the industry and the content of contemporary films with the rueful knowledge that he could not work within the new system and could not assimilate the values and attitudes of the new audiences. Because he had enough grace to bow out of the moviemaking process, his dignity and his reputation remained largely intact, unlike those of many of his contemporaries who refused to give up their power or change their methods. He divided his time between his home in Beverly Hills and his suite at the Waldorf-Astoria in New York, busied himself continually marketing his films, selling stories, and acting as behind-the-scenes mentor for the career of Jennifer Jones. The specter of *Gone With The Wind* continued to haunt him, even in semiretirement, and he spent a great deal of time, money, and verbal energy in trying to turn it into a stage musical under the title *Scarlett O'Hara.* Various announcements over the years proclaimed that the songs would be written by Richard Rodgers, Harold Arlen, Leroy Anderson, or Dimitri Tiomkin; each of these had a different set of lyricists announced, from Oscar Hammerstein II to Ogden Nash to Kay Swift and Ben Hecht. None of this ever went beyond the stage of speculation, nor did Selznick's efforts to have NBC mount a television version in six parts.

By 1963, Selznick had given up any further hope of putting *Gone With The Wind* on the stage or on television; MGM was still being deluged with offers for the telecasting of the picture, but Selznick controlled the television rights to the story, so they could not license the picture without making a deal with him. Over a period of years, Selznick had paid the Mitchell estate a total of $250,000 for the maintenance of these rights, and in 1963 he finally succumbed to MGM's blandishments, selling them his remaining rights in the story. This allowed MGM to negotiate with the Mitchell family and to get not only the stage and television rights, but the remake rights as well. Three years later, in 1966, the new president of MGM, Robert O'Brian, asked Ray Klune, now a production executive at the studio, to look into the possibilities of reissuing *Gone With The Wind,* this time using a new big-screen 70 mm process. The C. V. Whitney and Myron Selznick interests still held their shares in the film, and their approval had to be obtained before any part of the picture could be tampered with. These permissions were given quickly, and Ray Klune began working with Merle Chamberlin, the head of MGM's technical department, to solve the problem of fitting *Gone With The Wind's* almost square picture into the long, rectangular shape of the new 70 mm format. Going back to the original black-and-white camera negatives, they were dismayed to find that each negative had shrunk to a different size, meaning that the color would not register without halos. This problem was solved by mounting the negatives on special racks, which could be adjusted individually until they all matched. Having photographed every frame of these black-and-white negatives onto the new Eastman negative stock, Klune, Chamberlin, and the MGM staff then went through every single frame again, laboriously rephotographing each to fit the 70 mm proportion. Unfortunately, this resulted in trimming one-quarter off the top and bottom of the frames, so that the image was cut almost in half, ruining the composition, and in one inexcusable oversight on everyone's part, changing the original main title—"because of technical considera-tion," as Merle Chamberlin put it—and so destroying the grandeur of the sweeping title, which was replaced by four tiny words lumped into the center of the screen. All of this, plus making the new six-track enhanced stereophonic sound to boom along with the new version, took almost two years.*

*For a detailed description of how this was done, see *American Cinematographer,* November 1967.

Early in June 1965, while Selznick was in Los Angeles on legal business, Russell Birdwell, whose publicity company had fallen from its former prominence, began running a series of advertisements in *The Hollywood Reporter*. Largely monologues of reminiscences, written in Birdwell's anecdotal style, they related exploits in his career and talked of some of the famous people he had known. Birdwell started discussing Selznick in ad number 4 and was still hard at it in number 10. As a valedictory to the entire series, Birdwell appended a hand-written note: "COME HOME, DOS, THE INDUSTRY NEEDS YOU!" The ad ran in the morning edition of *The Hollywood Reporter,* on June 22, 1965, across the page from an MGM studio ad announcing proudly that its entire facility was now busy with television work.

The night before the ad appeared, Selznick watched a new film by the French director Jacques Demy, *The Umbrellas of Cherbourg,* and remarked to his son Daniel that the delicately flavored contemporary musical was one of the best made and most entertaining movies he had seen in years. He was due in New York on Thursday for a lunch with Henry Luce to discuss some business ventures, and he wanted to clear up several pending matters, so his schedule for Wednesday included a long session with his attorney Barry Brannen, starting at noon. Their meeting had been going on for an hour when Selznick, according to published accounts, "complained of feeling faint, put his hand on his chest and sat down. An ambulance was called and he was taken to Cedars of Sinai Hospital, where he died at 2:33 P.M. He was 65 years old."

News of his death stunned everyone in the film business. He had been a legend in his own time, one of the authentic giants who was always there as a reminder of what the movies were capable of accomplishing; inactive as he was, Hollywood still felt his presence. To those who had known him or had worked closely with him, the impact of his death was tremendous. Hal Kern remembers the intensity of his disbelief at the news: "I just couldn't believe it. In fact, I think I didn't believe it for two days. You see, I never associated David with death. He had so much life, so much vitality about him, that it just seemed impossible for him to be dead. I think I only finally believed it at the funeral."

A quiet, dignified affair, Selznick's funeral was held on a gray, overcast morning at Forest Lawn Memorial Park in nearby Glendale. At his own request, the services were brief, the eulogies restrained. Newspaper and other media coverage of his death was worldwide and extensive, and the headlines were much as he had predicted: "Producer of 'Gone With the

Wind' Dies." Many of the newspapers concluded their obituaries by quoting a remark he had made in 1959. The set of Tara, still standing on the back lot of what was now Desilu Studios, was about to be dismantled and shipped to Atlanta, where a local promoter intended to reconstruct it on the supposed actual site of the plantation as described by Miss Mitchell. Selznick had presided at a small ceremony as the set was taken down and crated. In one of his more melancholy moods he made a short, untypical speech, saying: "Tara was just a facade; it had no rooms in it. It is symbolic of Hollywood, that once photographed, life here is ended."

But *Gone With The Wind* was not ended. In October 1967, it began its seventh tour of U.S. theatres. Exhibited in the new 70 mm stereophonic version that MGM had spent hundreds of thousands of dollars to prepare, and offered as a reserved-seat attraction for the first time in twenty-seven years, the picture once again demonstrated its unique hold on the imagination of audiences by becoming one of the top-grossing films of the year. The new, younger viewers seeing the film for the first time didn't seem to mind the physical alterations in the look and shape of the film, and were immediately caught up in its narrative drive, its excitement, and the unabashed romanticism. In New York, it stayed at the Rivoli Theatre for almost a year, competing for attention with—and ultimately outgrossing—Stanley Kubrick's masterpiece, *2001: A Space Odyssey.* In Hollywood, *Gone With The Wind* opened at the same Carthay Circle Theatre that had been the scene of its original Hollywood premiere and played there for just over a year; at the conclusion of its run, the theatre was demolished to make way for an office building. Nearly a decade later, MGM, which had always displayed considerable shrewdness in its handling of the picture, finally licensed the rights to NBC for a Bicentennial television presentation. The film was telecast in two parts on the evenings of November 7 and 8, 1976. Reduced to less than lifesize, sandwiched in between endless commercials, with its impact sliced up and delivered like salami and its magnificent color squeezed down to tiny garish blobs, it still had the power, by virtue of its mystique and its craftsmanship, to engage and enthrall 77 million Americans—a record audience that stood until the telecast of *Roots,* a romantic epic of another kind and another sensibility.

THE HOLLYWOOD that David O. Selznick worked in and loved for forty years is gone. Some of the studios still stand, of course, as do many of the landmarks of the town: the Ambassador and Roosevelt hotels, the Hollywood Bowl, Grauman's Chinese and Egyptian theatres. What is gone, and what gave the Hollywood of Selznick's time its vitality and influence, are the people who lived and worked there, the people who made the name Hollywood synonymous with a kind of magic—that mysterious, seemingly inexplicable, and extraordinary power to evoke in the beholder a sense of the inexhaustible resources of the mind and spirit. Remnants of this power can still be found at random moments in the work of some of the newer generation, but by and large the commitment to excellence and the standards of quality to which Selznick and his contemporaries devoted their professional lives are sadly lacking today. The past can never be recaptured, that much is certain. But what can be recaptured, and what makes *Gone With The Wind* live and reverberate with a life beyond its creators, are the same elements that gave the film its appeal to three generations of moviegoers: taste, imagination, idealism, and a concern for the integrity and intelligence of the audience. In an address that Selznick gave at the University of Rochester in May 1940, he spoke of these intangibles and about his love of the moviemaking process, the pride of craftsmanship, and the satisfaction of carefully, painstakingly laboring over the details of a film because of the deeply held conviction that the motion picture was a powerful force for good in the world. At the end of his speech, he expressed just what the movies had meant to him, to me, and to everyone who ever stared in hopeful anticipation at a blank movie screen:

> To you who feel the burning urge to influence the modes and manners, the social and political ideologies of the future through the medium of the motion picture, I say, Here is a challenge, here is a frontier that is and always will be crying for the courage and the energy and the initiative and the genius of American youth. Here is the Southwest Passage to fame and fortune and influence! Here is the El Dorado of the heart, the soul and the mind. □

Now in 70 mm. wide screen and full stereophonic sound!

DAVID O. SELZNICK'S PRODUCTION OF MARGARET MITCHELL'S "GONE WITH THE WIND"

Rambling Reporter

Robert Osborne

On Windy matters of note: This week marks a couple of full-fledged, major landmarks for that one film which, above all others, Hollywood has always used as its final yardstick, David O. Selznick's (and now MGM's) grand and glorious "Gone With the Wind." First off, Crest Labs here in town, acknowledged as one of the best houses in the business for high-quality film-to-tape work, just finished — and yesterday delivered to MGM — the videotape "answer print" which will be used for the home videocassette version of "GWTW." MGM/UA Home Video plans to have it in stores; pushing for sales, by next March 1 (it'll be presented in its full 222 minutes; the price tag will be $89.95 for the double-cassette package). And this transfer, taken from mint archival film elements from MGM's vaults in the salt mines of Hutchinson, Kansas, was no simple by-the-numbers job, either; it's been done in a way even the meticulous Selznick himself would have approved. MGM has backed its desire to turn out the best "GWTW" tape possible with bucks, cueing Crest to go scene by scene to make both visual and audio restoration repairs where necessary. Says Bob Bradford, the supervising mixer on Crest's "Project Wind," "Since the original soundtrack recording on 'Gone With the Wind' was done in 1939, there was a very limited frequency response and dynamic sound range at that time; there are also some ticks and pops that also show up on today's sophisticated sound systems. What we've done in the restoration process is to bring that original soundtrack as close as possible to 1985 sound standards, but without any attempt to change or alter the original sound mix or add any fake stereo sound. We've consistently tried to preserve exactly what the original Selznick sound mixers intended."

To further bring this "Wind" to its fullest flower, consultant Steven St. Croix was brought in with a "magic box" he's invented; it incorporates a technique that actually removes — doesn't just cover up — sound distortion on tracks old and new; such a possibility has never existed until now. Says Bradford, "All past attempts at restoring tracks have been limited to conventional techniques of, say, equalization or single-ended noise reduction, all of which by nature degrade the transparency and frequency response of the film track, and can even introduce additional, unwanted artifacts. So using Steve's distortion-removing device, in combination with the digital acoustic simulation, Crest has been able to make substantial improvements in the 'Gone With the Wind' sound quality." If much of that is too technical for your brain — mine included — having seen a sample of what Crest, St. Croix, Bradford and another mixer, John Pooley, have wrought, I can only say it's sensational. "Gone With the Wind" never looked or sounded better, and in tape form should make additional history when it is eventually unleashed for sale. Who with a VHS or Beta machine wouldn't want a copy? Considering the current financial woes right now at MGM/UA, the only pity it that this "Wind" isn't available as we speak, to cash in on the current splurge of gift buying and giving.

The other "Wind" landmark of note: on Saturday, it'll be a full 45 years since "GWTW" had its world premiere at the (now razed) Loew's Grand Theatre on Peachtree Street in Atlanta. (New York got its first gander four days later, on Dec. 19, at two Broadway houses, the Astor and the Capitol; the L.A. premiere came Dec. 28 at the Carthay Circle. Does it tell you something about the business to note that all four of those theatres where "GWTW" was first shown, have long since also gone with the wind?) But it was that Dec. 15, 1939, night in Atlanta that caused the most furor, and blazed through the most newspaper headlines. The Loew's Grand held only 2,051; tickets were $10, "believed to be the highest in cinema history," so said the Atlanta papers, and even the lower nonpremiere price scale was considered "stiff": $1.10 and $1.50, and all reserved seats. Atlanta was fairly swept with "Scarlett fever": there were parties, celebrations, costume balls and wild receptions for the visiting Hollywood contingent that included stars Clark Gable (with Carole Lombard), Vivien Leigh (with Laurence Olivier), Olivia de Havilland, also Selznick with wife Irene Mayer, "GWTW" author Margaret Mitchell, Evelyn Keyes, Ann Rutherford, Ona Munson, Laura Hope Crews, even Kay Kyser and his orchestra and — also completely unrelated to the film — Claudette Colbert. (Said Selznick, "Poor deluded Claudette came under the notion she was going to have a good time.") Work it was, but spectacular, too, and a grand send-off for the film. And with the upcoming videotape version, it's a cinch "GWTW" will be back making big news again — just as it did 45 years ago.

(Top) A painting by artist Richard Amsell for *TV Guide* the week of November 11-21, 1976 when *Gone With The Wind* made its nationwide television debut. (Below) The ad for the 1984 MGM video release.

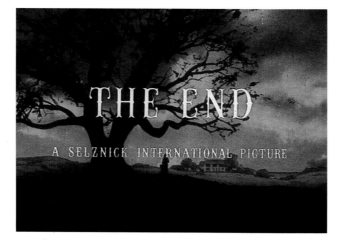

P9-BYB-692

Put any picture you want on any state book cover. Makes a great gift. Go to www.america24-7.com/customcover

MULTNOMAH COUNTY
Benson Bridge, crafted by Italian stone masons in 1914, allows visitors a close-up view of Multnomah Falls. Fed by underground springs on Larch Mountain and by seasonal runoff, the falls plunge 620 feet before flowing into the Columbia River.
Photo by Rhoda Peacher

Oregon 24/7 is the sequel to *The New York Times* bestseller *America 24/7* shot by tens of thousands of digital photographers across America over the course of a single week. We would like to thank the following sponsors, the wonderful people of Oregon, and the talented photojournalists who made this book possible.

LONDON, NEW YORK, MUNICH, MELBOURNE, and DELHI

Created by Rick Smolan and David Elliot Cohen

24/7 Media, LLC
PO Box 1189
Sausalito, CA 94966-1189
www.america24-7.com

First Edition, 2004
04 05 06 07 08 10 9 8 7 6 5 4 3 2 1

Published in the United States by
DK Publishing, Inc.
375 Hudson Street
New York, NY 10014

DK Publishing, Inc. offers special discounts for bulk purchases for sales promo-
tions or premiums. Specific, large-quantity needs can be met with special editions, personalized covers, excerpts of existing guides, and corporate imprints.
For more information, contact:

Special Markets Department
DK Publishing, Inc.
375 Hudson Street
New York, NY 10014
Fax: 212-689-5254

Cataloging-in-Publication data is available
from the Library of Congress
ISBN 0-7566-0078-2

Printed in the UK by Butler & Tanner Limited

First printing, October 2004

CANNON BEACH
Midway along four-mile Cannon Beach,
Haystack Rock (right) is home to nesting col-
onies of tufted puffins and other seabirds.
The 235-foot monolith and the nearby
Needles are among many basalt colossi hob-
bled along the Oregon coast, remnants of
17-million-year-old lava flows.
Photo by Randy S. Corbin

OREGON 24/7

24 Hours. 7 Days.
Extraordinary Images of
One Week in Oregon.

Created by Rick Smolan and David Elliot Cohen

DK Publishing

About the America 24/7 Project

A hundred years hence, historians may pose questions such as: What was America like at the beginning of the third millennium? How did life change after 9/11 and the ensuing war on terrorism? How was America affected by its corporate scandals and the high-tech boom and bust? Could Americans still express themselves freely?

To address these questions, we created *America 24/7*, the largest collaborative photography event in history. We invited Americans to tell their stories with digital pictures. We asked them to shoot a visual memoir of their lives, families, and communities.

During one week in May 2003, more than 25,000 professionals and amateurs shot more than a million pictures. These images, sent to us via the Internet, compose a panoramic yet highly intimate view of Americans in celebration and sadness; in action and contemplation; at work, home, and school. The best of these photographs, more than 6,000, are collected in 51 volumes that make up the *America 24/7* series: the landmark national volume *America 24/7*, published to critical acclaim in 2003, and the 50 state books published in 2004.

Our decision to make *America 24/7* an all-digital project was prompted by the fact that in 2003 digital camera sales overtook film camera sales. This techno-logical evolution allowed us to extend the project to a huge pool of photographers. We were thrilled by the response to our challenge and moved by the insight offered into American life. Sometimes, the amateurs outshot the pros—even the Pulitzer Prize winners.

The exuberant democracy of images visible throughout these books is a revela-tion. The message that emerges is that now, more than ever, America is a supersized idea. A dreamspace, where individuals and families from around the world are free to govern themselves, worship, read, and speak as they wish. Within its wide margins, the polyglot American nation manages to encompass an inexplicably complex yet workable whole. The pictures in this book are dedicated to that idea.

—Rick Smolan and David Elliot Cohen

American nightlight: More than a quarter of a billion people trace a nation with incandescence in this composite satellite photograph.
Photo by Craig Mayhew & Robert Simmon, NASA Goddard Flight Center/Visions of Tomorrow

Small Wonders

By Steve Duin

Big fish. Small pond. Oregon has long worn the tag as a badge of honor. Small wonder. For the longest time, the fish—steelhead and Chinook—were stunning, and their spawning runs relentless.

And if the pond was far off the beaten trail, it was wondrously land-scaped. We could hike and bike and windsurf. We'd ski Mt. Hood and hit the surf at Seaside in the same long, lazy afternoon. At a safe distance from the headaches of Seattle and California, Oregonians could relax in a minor key, convinced our comfort zone was secured by marvelous public beaches, an environmental ethic and an evergreen color scheme, and the right to a doctor-assisted suicide.

For the longest time—note that we are still tethered to past tense—Oregonians gracefully compensated for situational shortfalls. While our state is short on major-league sports franchises—none save the Portland Trail Blazers, who won their lone NBA title during the Carter administration and have been an embarrassment ever since—it is big on participatory athletic extravaganzas like the Hood-to-Coast Relay and Cycle Oregon. Far removed from the halls of power, we're committed to allowing individuals to carve out their own destinies: Voters twice gave autonomy to the terminally ill in making end-of-life decisions. When same-sex marriage licenses recently became problematic for even San Francisco, Multnomah County continued to crank 'em out.

"We do have a progressive tradition, but it's a selective one," says local historian Gordon Dodds. "The progressive things—initiative voting, women's suffrage, the bottle bill, and vote by mail—don't cost anyone any money. If it doesn't require money and work, we'll do it."

WARM SPRINGS RESERVATION
The 173-mile Deschutes River in central Oregon borders the Warm Springs Reservation. A favorite with whitewater rafters, the waterway also has some of the best steelhead fishing in the state.
Photo by Rob Finch, The Oregonian

Dodds calls this habit "adventuresomeness in pursuit of the ordinary." For the longest time, Oregon got by on the ordinary with a light dusting of the extraordinary: Crater Lake and the links course at Bandon Dunes. The Pendleton Round-Up. The best bookstore in the world (Powell's Books in Portland), and urban growth boundaries that discourage quarter-acre sprawls and preserve farmland.

Oregon today is not as boldly diverse as some of the sensational photographs in these pages suggest, but they make clear that it's home for some quirky and artistic individualism. Indie filmmakers and mountain-climbing dogs. Homeschoolers and saddle makers. Refugees who don't want to live by the rules or the traffic patterns of Atlanta or Los Angeles. There is no shortage of small miracles in Oregon.

But where are the big ideas, bold public figures, and ambitious businesses to match the aging icons of the nation's first bottle bill, former Governor Tom McCall, and Nike? Too often we have allowed our inability to improve the landscape to become an unwillingness to generate new landmarks. So it is that Seattle spends millions on a breathtaking, wireless new public library while Portland bitterly laments paying its new library director her $127,000 salary.

Last time I checked, the salmon and steelhead runs had recovered from a dismal decade or two, and the big fish were back. As you review the small wonders of Oregon, a state in which both the fish and the citizenry delight in swimming against the current, you might look for the hook of another big idea. The small pond could stand the excitement.

STEVE DUIN *is the Metro columnist at* The Oregonian *in Portland. He lives with his wife and three children in Oswego.*

PORTLAND

It's recess at Grout Elementary, and 6-year-old Aidan Finnegan is running with it. The 248 Grout students benefit from the public school's rich cultural offerings, including a chess workshop and a Cambodian culture and language program for the school's handful of young Cambodian Americans.
Photo by L.E. Baskow, Portland Tribune

FLORENCE
Princess Ashley Lamb, a member of the
2003 Lebanon Strawberry Court, bestows
her parade wave at the 96th Rhododendron
Festival. When the festival first started in
1908, the population of Florence was just
under 500; now, it's more than 7,000.
Photo by Thomas Boyd

FIELDS

Mike Smit, "jigger boss" at Keuny Ranch, teams up with his daughter Lulu to brand calves at Alvord Ranch. Between the Alvord and Keuny ranches, buckaroos herd 3,500 cows with their calves off the range in groups. "We're fairly traditional. We head and heel," says Smit of the two-rope system. "It takes longer, but it's kind of a social thing."

Photo by Carol Yarrow

ALSEA

Noble firs shape a nine-mile corridor to 4,000-foot Marys Peak in the Coast Range. The area's rapidly changing elevation makes it home to a wide variety of vegetation. Botanists have recorded more than 200 flowering plants, and mushroom lovers descend in the fall for chanterelles.

Photo by Karl Maasdam

BLUE RIVER

Terwilliger Hot Springs, 50 miles east of Eugene, provides a warm soak in the woods for Rene Lehmer, her son Arawen, and her infant daughter Geron. The pools, created by a nearby river that flows through an old lava tube, are evidence of western Oregon's underground volcanic activity.
Photo by Sol Neelman, The Oregonian

Hearth & Home

WARM SPRINGS RESERVATION
Three-month-old Taya Holliday may not agree, but Native American mothers at the Early Childhood Education Center find that traditional beaded cradleboards reassure newborns by providing a secure, womblike sensation. Individually handcrafted for each child, moms traditionally hung the carriers on tree branches while they went about their chores.
Photo by Brian Lanker

PORTLAND

The gentrifying Mississippi Avenue neighborhood is more stroller-friendly these days without the corner drug dealers. Ida Bleu's dad, David Colombo, opened the Fresh Pot coffee shop and is one of several young entrepreneurs making a difference. "It was the first service business on a notorious corner," says Colombo. He adds, "We're trying to get the whole street Wi-Fi'd."
Photo by John Klicker

PORTLAND

Tatiana (foreground) likes to visit friends—her family lives in a one-room shack. After arriving in Oregon from Puebla, Mexico, her father got work as a landscaper, but the family is struggling and still owes the *coyote* for their crossing. Her mother says it is worth it, though, because in America the children can go to school and hope for a better life.
Photo by Faith Cathcart, The Oregonian

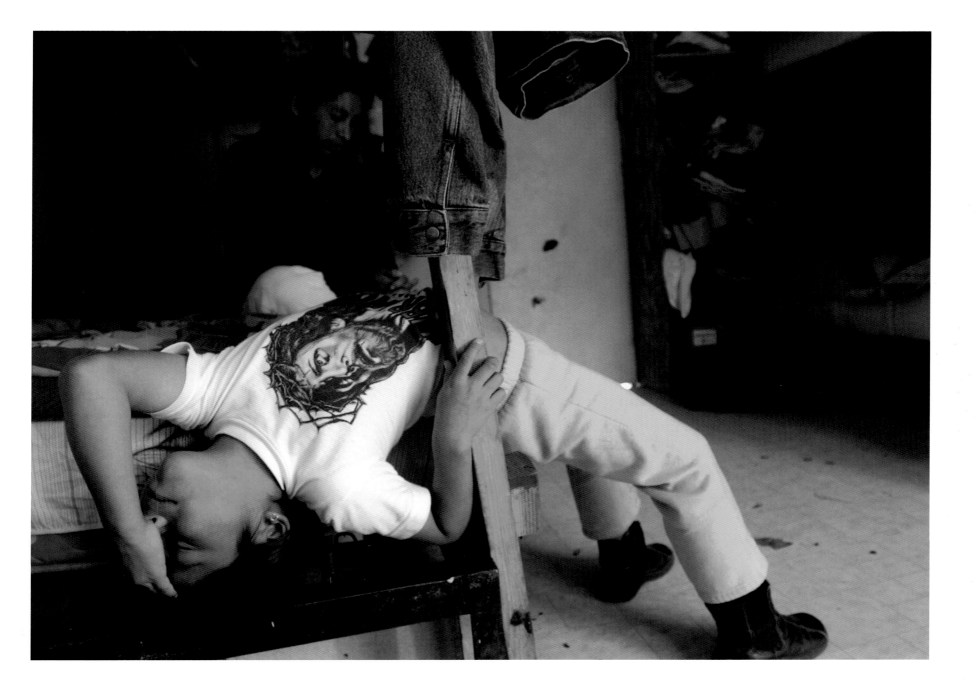

PORTLAND

Dawn Thalacker hangs with a tribe of street kids around Pioneer Square who help keep her daughter Emma fed and in clean clothes. The estimated 2,000 homeless youth in the city tend to form families that have codes for responsible behavior, including sharing food, maintaining good relationships with local businesses, and taking care of each other. Nonprofit organizations provide jobs, counseling, and medical support.
Photo by Joni Kabana

TUALATIN

On May 14 at 7:37 p.m., Marlena and Trevor Williams welcome their son Carter Alan (8 pounds, 12 ounces) into the world at the Andaluz Waterbirth Center. Warm water is said to relieve labor pains and increase oxygen to the baby.
Photo by Julie Keefe

JOSEPH
Midwife Sherry Dress determines the position of Colleen Whelan's baby, due in June. The expectant mother is opting for a water birth in her home. Says Dress, "That's where the baby was made and that's where it should be delivered."
Photo by Stephanie Yao, The Oregonian

PORTLAND

Brynn Opsahl is often overshadowed by two older brothers, but she has learned to be proactive—even mischievous—to get in on the action. She might tell a joke, throw a tantrum, or impress with a high dance kick. Biding her time while her dad and brothers play ball in their Sellwood neighborhood street, Brynn waits for her chance.
Photo by Joni Kabana

PORTLAND

The Klicker sisters respond differently to waking up early. Morning-person Lucinda gets down to the business of breakfast, but night-owl Sophie resists the pull of morning duties—such as getting ready for school.

Photo by Julie Keefe

GREEN

Linnea Witt's husband James works mornings as a logger in order to homeschool their kids in the afternoons. A teacher by training, he decided he could do better educating their nine kids than the local Christian school. "I'm not really a home-school mom," says Linnea. "I'm married to a homeschool dad." She spends afternoons helping the younger kids with their reading.

Photo by Stephen Brashear

CORVALLIS

Chris and Kelly Manhard had a third child and needed more room, but Silicon Valley's sky-high home prices forced them to look elsewhere. In Corvallis, they doubled their square footage at half the price. Kelly's employer, Silicon Graphics, lets her telecommute; Chris takes care of the kids. When Samantha, 5, got to decorate her room, she chose pink.

Photo by Karl Maasdam

CORVALLIS
Alicen Bartholomeusz noticed that Sofia, 18 months, and Rachel, 6 months, calmed down when her husband mowed the lawn. Faced with two crying babies and a husband at work, she cuts the grass with babies on board. Hopefully, she has an equally clever solution for back pain.
Photo by Karl Maasdam

MILWAUKIE
Jamie Peery, a senior at Putnam High School, waits for her boyfriend Mike Suchy's umbrella as rain descends on prom night. This was Suchy's first prom—he is a freshman at Clackamas Community College and never attended his prom—but it was Peery's third. "I love dressing up and dancing with all my friends around," she enthuses.
Photo by Faith Cathcart, The Oregonian

PORTLAND

Working with Holt International Children's Services, Lee and Kathy Moore have created a global family. Their daughters Lily and Meena are from Thailand and Manisha is from India. Holt International was founded in 1956 by two Oregon residents who went to Korea after the war to provide homes for orphans. Since then, the agency has placed 60,000 children all over the world.
Photo by Steven Bloch

WARM SPRINGS RESERVATION
Adeline Miller, 83, has done beadwork most
of her life at her reservation home. The
Warm Springs Reservation was established
in 1855 and is home to Wasco, Walla Walla
(Warm Springs), and Paiute Indians, and
stretches from the Cascade Mountains to
the palisades above the Deschutes River in
central Oregon.
Photo by Brian Lanker

HARNEY COUNTY
Jet, a border collie pup, helps Whitehorse Ranch buckaroo Matt Rice unwind after a long day of moving cattle. At 4 months, Jet is still too young to help move the herd of 2,000 cows from pasture to pasture.
Photo by Carol Yarrow

EUGENE
Tuna gets his morning tummy rub while Randi Bjornstad catches up on current events.
Photo by Paul Carter

WASHINGTON COUNTY

Elyssa LaFlamme, 10, rushes home after school to play with her eight hens. Buttercup, a 2-month-old Golden Sex-Link, is the family favorite. The LaFlammes, who raise the hens for eggs, are allowed up to eight chickens because they live outside the city limits. Within Portland, the family limit is three.

Photo by Rhoda Peacher

TUALATIN

"I am the happiest man in Oregon," says Roy Lumber, 84. "Jean and I are healthy, and this job gives me something to do every day." Lumber and his wife bought Schulz Clearwater, a porta-potty business, in 1984. He says their 31 employees take care of the real work, while he takes clients to lunch and plays with Tia, their toy poodle.

Photo by Steven Bloch

FALLS CITY
Melody Le May of Dallas feeds the rabbits, peacocks, and chickens on the farm belonging to her friends the Vincents. The Vincents are Winnimem Wintu Indians and let the animals roam free. The rabbits, or *po-kel-ils*, represent gentleness and peace, Steve Vincent says.
Photo by L.E. Baskow, Portland Tribune

PORTLAND

Friends Diana Perkins, Kieren Connolly, and Mark Ruskamp check out what's new at Mike Hockman's house. Hockman cleans homes and businesses in the Portland area and takes home whatever his clients don't want. He never sells the items but keeps them around as conversation pieces.

Photo by Steven Bloch

CORVALLIS
Brody Lowe plays his latest composition, "Daddy," for housemate Justin Reed. Lowe, a junior at Oregon State University, describes his music as "rock with an acoustic touch" and mentions Ben Harper and Jack Johnson as influences. He performs with the brodylowe band all around the state and hopes to produce an album soon. In the meantime, he works part-time as a graphic designer.
Photo by Karl Maasdam

PORTLAND

At her dress fitting, LaTonya Mitchell and her mother Laura consult with tailor Kim-Dung Vu at Kim's Kreations. In June, LaTonya will make her debut at Les Femmes Society's debutante ball. The Society was founded 52 years ago to do good works and to instruct girls in all things ladylike.
Photo by Julie Keefe

NEWBERG

Although their hot-air balloon cannot take flight, Dave and Gloria Ludlow's hearts are soaring. Their plans to be married in the skies above Sportsman Park were grounded by fog. Rather than wait for favorable weather, they go ahead with a down-to-earth wedding.

Photo by L.E. Baskow, Portland Tribune

The year 2003 marked a turning point in the history of photography: It was the first year that digital cameras outsold film cameras. To celebrate this unprecedented sea change, the *America 24/7* project invited amateur photographers—along with students and professionals—to shoot and, via the Internet, submit digital images. Think of it as audience participation. Their visions of community are interspersed with the professional frames throughout this book. On the following four pages, however, we present a gallery produced exclusively by amateur photographers.

PORTLAND Night, a black Lab, watches over Anna Setter during a lazy morning on the sun porch.
Photo by Jannine Setter

PORTLAND Even when he's not getting a bath, Graeme Setter likes this spot in the sink where he can see the trees. *Photo by Jannine Setter*

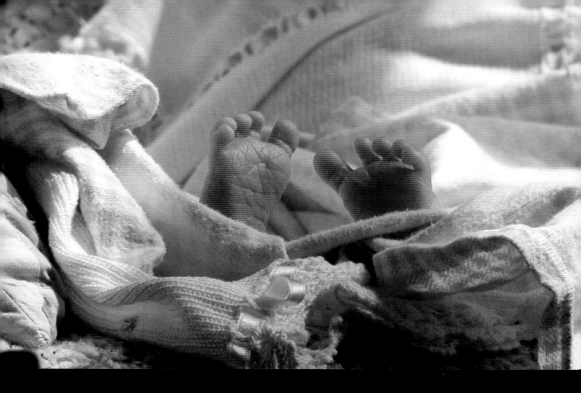

PORTLAND Adele Baughman, age 3 days, tests her new environment with a wiggle and a curl of her toes. *Photo by Justin Baughman*

PORTLAND Eeny, meeny, miny, moe—which one of you gets to come in the tub with me? Anaga Srinivas, 3, doesn't like to pla—f——ites. *Photo by Bindu Malini*

BEAVERTON Getting the morning paper can be a drizzly affair given Beaverton's 36 inches of rain per year. *Photo by M. Schoen*

BORING Like most cats, Feather is a sun worshipper. Ron Ingemunson's living room windowsill is where she heads for her morning nap. *Photo by Ron Ingemunson*

MT. BACHELOR Alex, an avalanche-rescue dog, gets a ride up the Pine Marten chair lift to her Ski Patrol station on the 9,065-foot mountain. *Photo by David L. Williams*

PORTLAND Bride's-eye view: Rachel Edmonson spies on her wedding guests being seated in the auditorium at Parkrose Deliverance Tabernacle. Her grandfather, pastor of the Pentecostal church, will perform the ceremony. *Photo by Maura Donis*

WARM SPRINGS RESERVATION
Punching a vegetable garden out of the high
desert where Angie David and her husband
Butch live is no easy task. "I wanted to watch
the playoffs," says NBA fan Butch, "but she
hauled me out to the garden." From their
land, they can see the Three Sisters, Mt.
Hood, and Mt. Jefferson.
Photo by Rob Finch, The Oregonian

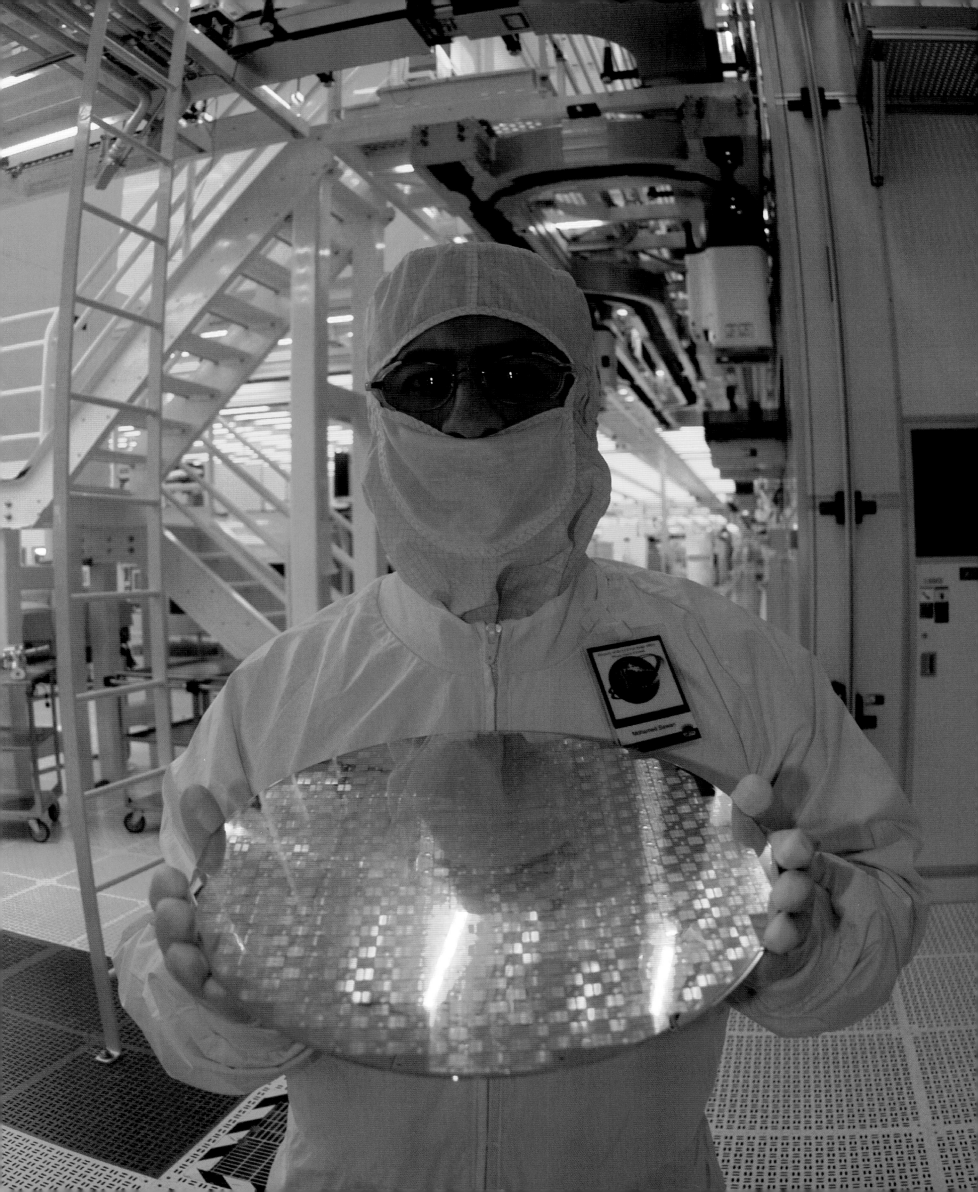

HILLSBORO

Intel employee Mohamed Sawan, decked out in his clean-room suit, holds a 300 mm wafer containing hundreds of Pentium 4 chips at the company's newest fabrication facility in Hillsboro. Although based in California, the chip maker has its biggest operation in Washington County—seven campuses, 14,500 employees—making it one of the largest employers in the state.

Photo by C. Bruce Forster

PORTLAND

The Standard Insurance Company management team takes a break during an out-of-the-office planning session. Top execs of the company, founded in 1906, support its president and CEO Eric Parsons. Wouldn't you trust these folks with your life?

Photo by Joni Kabana

WALLOWA COUNTY

Brazilian exchange students Lucas DeCastro Sakr and Lucas Ferrante Fonseca learn what it takes to brand a calf on the 2,000-acre Duncan Ranch. The Duncan family invited the students, who attend a local school, to experience life on their spread for a few days.

Photo by Michael Durham, www.DurmPhoto.com

HARNEY COUNTY

Whitehorse Ranch buckaroos Matt Rice, Ray Hardy, and Joe Draper, and cow boss Tim Draper start branding at 5 a.m. Cowboys in the Great Basin have their own distinctive style. They wear fringed "chinks," favor braided rawhide ropes and reins, and use silver spade bits. The buckaroo subculture originated in California, where conquistadors called early stockmen *vaqueros*, Anglicized to "buckaroos."

Photo by Carol Yarrow

WARM SPRINGS RESERVATION

Riding bucking broncs up and down the northwest rodeo circuit for more than 50 years, Sterling Green has broken a lot of bones, tangled with plenty of bulls, and roped his share of calves. These days, he builds bronc saddles and trains rodeo horses. "You have to train 'em to buck," he says.

Photo by Rob Finch, The Oregonian

PENDLETON

Saddle making runs in the Severe family. Randy learned the art from his dad Bill and uncle Duff, who started Severe Brothers Saddlery in 1955. "They wouldn't teach me until I got married, since they figured that meant I was ready to settle down," Randy says with a laugh. "I've been at it ever since." A custom saddle takes between 80 and 180 hours.

Photo by C. Bruce Forster

EUGENE
Howard Pazdral of Deadwood, 30 miles west of Eugene, prefers nonmotorized methods for removing Douglas fir logs from his property. Ruby and Roma, experienced Percheron mares, will pull the downed tree out of the woods—just as soon as they can get their legs over it.
Photo by Paul Carter

BEND

The surgery team at Bend Equine Medical Center performs a neurectomy on a horse. The laser procedure removes a nerve in the front foot to give the animal instant relief from chronic pain. The 2,000-pound horse was hoisted onto the operating table with a series of pulleys in the ceiling. The surgery costs approximately $1,000.
Photo by Dean Guernsey

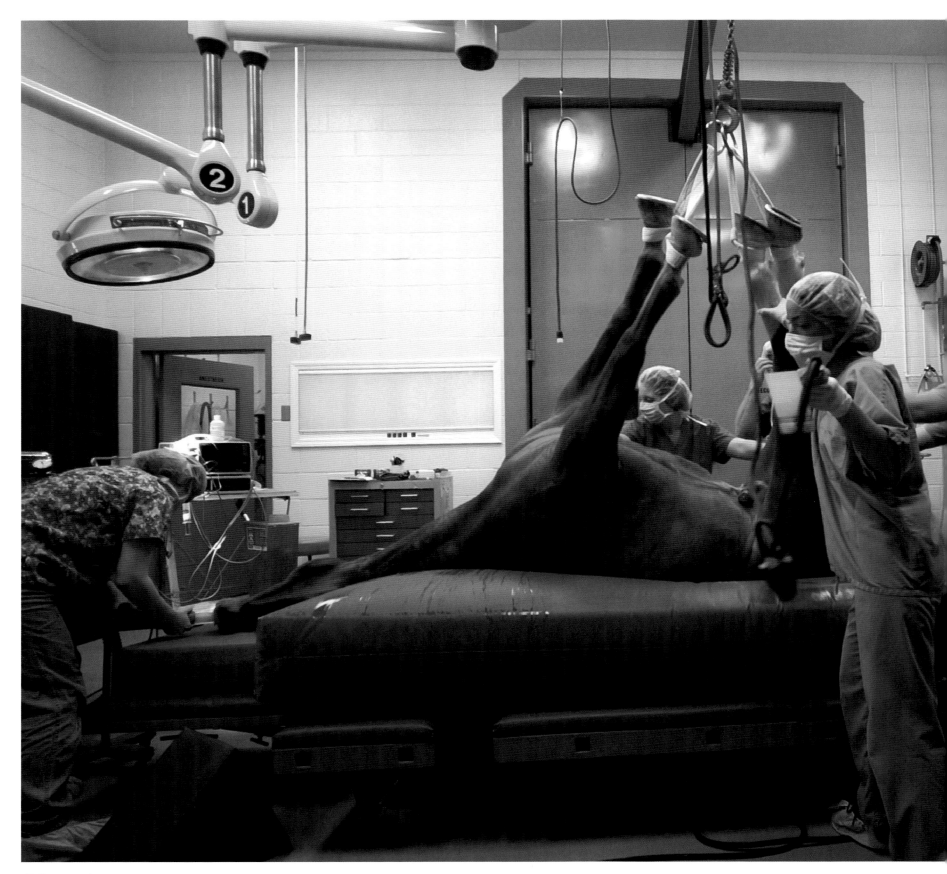

OLNEY

"My priorities changed," explains Sharnelle Fee, who walked away from a high-paying legal job seven years ago to found the nonprofit Wildlife Rehab Center of the North Coast. The organization cares for injured wild birds like this brown pelican named Netarts. Most are rehabilitated and released, but Netarts lost a wing, so she stars in the center's educational programs.

Photo by Gary Braasch

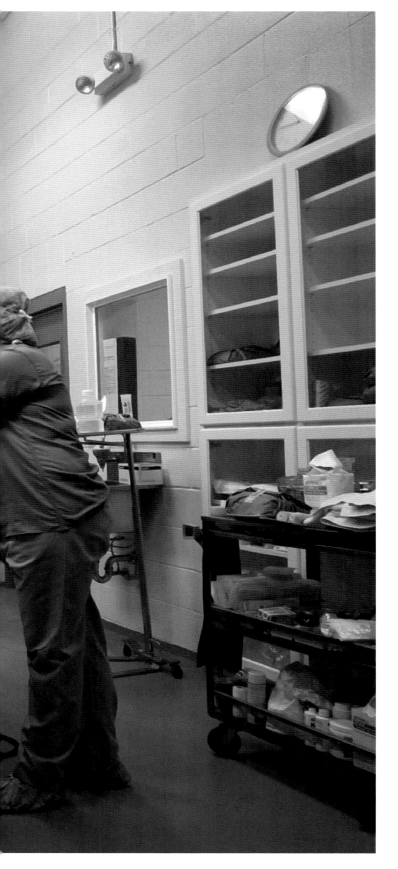

PORT ORFORD

After cleaning the day's halibut catch, fisherman Jeremy Knapp shares a carcass with the birds. Knapp is on a wharf at Port Orford, one of only two "dolly dock" marinas in America. To prevent damage from coastal storms, large yellow cranes hoist boats 25 feet up from the water and nest them in dollies (trailers) out of harm's way.

Photo by Lou Sennick, The World

MAUPIN

At first light, Robert Charley, Sr., a Warm Springs Indian, dunks for Chinook near Shearer's Falls on the Deschutes River. He uses his tribe's tried-and-true method of dip-netting atop wooden platforms that hover over the rushing waters.

Photo by L.E. Baskow, Portland Tribune

CELILO

Grant Meanus, a Yakama Indian, dries his family's fishing nets along the side of their home. Each day, his father, uncles, and older brothers fish for salmon on the Columbia River. Their catch is distributed to markets statewide through their village's fish buyer. Says Grant's mother, "Fishing runs in the family."

Photo by L.E. Baskow, Portland Tribune

PORTLAND

Film buffs looking for obscure works will likely find plenty to feed their passion among the 45,000 titles at Mike's Movie Madness on Belmont Street. Store clerk Angela Baldwin digs the murals and "the vibe and soul of the clientele." The southeast Portland shop has 86,000 accounts.

Photo by Joni Kabana

PORTLAND

For his newest works, Portland artist Stephen Hayes found inspiration in the common tragedy of children who disappear in America. His show "Last Seen" at the Elizabeth Leach Gallery consists of more than 100 monoprint portraits of real missing children.

Photo by Julie Keefe

Takaya and Kiyo Hanamoto emigrated from
Osaka, Japan, to the Oregon coast in 1989. Both
chefs, they opened their restaurant Yuzen in 1990
and set about fusing their native cuisine with the
Pacific Northwest's shellfish, mushrooms, and
strawberries.
Photo by Brian Lanker

PARKDALE

Looking for another use for fruit from his family's orchard, Steve McCarthy picked European-style fruit spirits. One of his favorites is pear-in-the-bottle. The process starts in May, with bottles being hung on the infant fruit. In late August, when the pears are fully grown, the bottles are harvested, painstakingly cleaned, and filled with pear eau-de-vie, the clear distillate of the fermented fruit.

Photo by C. Bruce Forster

ENTERPRISE
The Nature Conservancy's Zumwalt Prairie Preserve is one of the last sizable bunchgrass prairies in the country. Hefting the rock is Preserve Steward Andi Mitchell, who explains that "some places are so hard, you can't drive a T-post in, so we use rock jacks to keep the posts in place."
Photo by Michael Durham,
www.DurmPhoto.com

PORTLAND

Claude Ferris has worked the same route for 20 years. During this time, he's found a murdered woman in a burning house and helped police corner a burglar. For real excitement, though, he goes to rodeos. "I'm too old to compete, but I get a rush from watching the shows," he says. "My friends call me a wanna-be cowboy."

Photos by Steven Bloch

TUALATIN

Chadwick Thomas and Daniel Lee Huft are known as the "Yard Dogs" at Schulz Clearwater. They make sure the company's 4,000 portable restrooms are clean and fully equipped before being shipped to clients. Thomas says their biggest headache is vandalism. "We spend a lot of time washing off graffiti and repairing toilets."

PORTLAND
Sea lion ballet: The Stellar Cove Exhibit is a prime attraction at the Oregon Zoo, drawing in more than 1.3 million kids and adults each year.
Photo by L.E. Baskow, Portland Tribune

Oregon At Play

MT. HOOD
When speed climber Dan Howitt ascends 11,237-foot Mt. Hood, he competes against himself. He and his yellow Lab, Caddis, made it in 1 hour and 55 minutes from Timberline Lodge, a climb that takes most mountaineers 8 to 10 hours. "It's a hybrid sport—running and climbing," says Howitt. "I'm trying to make it a more official sport." On the southern horizon: Mt. Jefferson.
Photo by Bruce Ely

SCIO

A couple of Flora Dora Girls, Carol Bates and Marian Anderson, take a moment along the 68th annual Linn County Lamb and Wool Fair parade route to strum their stringless ukuleles for the crowd. During World War II, Bates was part of a dance ensemble called the Flora Dora Girls that entertained the troops. She resurrected the group 20 years ago.
Photos by L.E. Baskow, Portland Tribune

SCIO

Parade watchers put 'em up for gunslinger Rocky Meadows. Since 1935, the fair has showcased sheep and wool products. Activities other than the parade include the Northwest Champion Sheepdog Trials, a carnival, and a fleece and fiber show.

SCIO

Reuben and Isaac Jantzi of Sweet Home hoped their lambs' costumes (cowboy and lumberjack, respectively) would put them at the top of the flock in the Best-Dressed Lamb contest, but their younger sister's snow-suited lamb walked away with the first-place ribbon.

BEND

Shawn Snyder practices "slacking" between two ponderosa pines in Drake Park. Slackline enthusiasts can string their ropes between canyon walls, 2,700 feet above a river, or 3 feet off the ground. Staying on requires balance, concentration, and strength, no matter how high the rope is.
Photo by Robert M. Kerr

PORTLAND

The province of gangs only a few years ago, Mississippi Avenue now has more places for kids like Lucinda Klicker and Elly Warner to play safely: a large park and a playground created by a local merchant out of a vacant lot.
Photo by John Klicker

EUGENE
Mapleton High School freshman Justin Burt gives it all he's got as he nears the finish line of the 1,500-meter race at the Mountain West track and field championship. He finished sixth.
Photo by Sol Neelman, The Oregonian

BANDON

"The best golf courses are organic, evolving from the ground they inhabit," says Tom Doak. The designer, who has studied more than 1,000 courses around the world, applied this belief to the "walker only" Pacific Dunes, based on traditional Scottish-style courses. Four holes play right along the Pacific Ocean; the rest wander among sand dunes and shore grass.

Photo by Sol Neelman, The Oregonian

John Benenate (in car) checks in with Lyndon Owens, Jr., Karim Brown, and Johnson Don, members of b.i.k.e., or Bicycles and Ideas for Kids' Empowerment. Benenate founded the nonprofit in 1995 to give at-risk children an alternative to hanging out on the streets. Not only do kids learn about racing bicycles, they also get year-round tutoring and mentoring.
Photo by Julie Keefe

PORTLAND

Madre Stocker races for b.i.k.e.—an organization that helps kids build confidence and values by developing their physical skills. Training at the Alpenrose Velodrome, an Olympic-style, 268-meter track with a 45-degree bank, Stocker prepares for the upcoming Alpenrose challenge.
Photo by John Klicker

PORTLAND

Aaron Opsahl catches air in his new 'hood. His family recently pulled up stakes from the suburbs and moved into town so the kids could circulate in a more diverse milieu. "My world feels bigger," says Aaron, who left a big yard and wide sidewalks for a new set of curbs to conquer.
Photo by Joni Kabana

CULVER
Warm Springs Stars players Rosey Twostarrs
Suppah (third from left), Mallory Smith, and
Chandra Robinson do a dugout-rooftop victory
jig after winning their baseball game.
Photo by L.E. Baskow, Portland Tribune

PORTLAND
The sweet spot: Future U.S. Open contenders—
maybe—Andrea Chan and Lindsey Carter warm
up before rallying at the Grout Elementary School
tennis courts.
Photo by L.E. Baskow, Portland Tribune

BLUE RIVER
Students from Mohawk and McKenzie high schools compete in the annual donkey basketball fundraiser for athletic programs. The mounts were provided by Donkey Sports, Inc., which trucks donkeys around the Pacific Northwest for games and exhibitions. According to Donkey Sports, the cost of training the animals to play basketball is "food and a whip."
Photo by Thomas Boyd

HOOD RIVER

American Windsurfer Magazine Publisher John Chao takes some time out of his day to catch the famous Columbia Gorge wind. Many locals, including Chao, consider Hood River one of the best windsurfing spots in the world. "The winds are constant and predictable," he says, "and the variety of waves on the river is simply radical."

Photo by Brian Lanker

BEND

Rocketman: Brian Walker dreamed of becoming an astronaut but didn't think he could get into NASA, so he took matters into his own hands. Walker is building a rocket and plans to launch himself 50 miles into space. His successful toy development business is funding his quest, which he dubbed Project RUSH, for Rapid Up Super High.

Photo by Dean Guernsey

BEND

NASA doesn't sell space suits or time in simulators, so Walker went to Russia, where he trained with cosmonauts and bought a space suit for $15,000. "I'm living the American dream," he says. "If you are determined and work hard enough, you can do anything." He hasn't set a launch date, yet.

Photo by Dean Guernsey

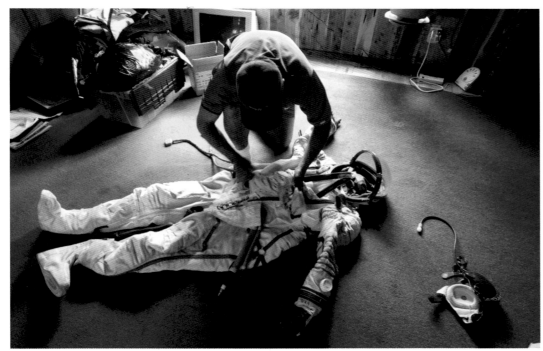

PORTLAND

Jim Colvill, a chef who started Klingon Karaoke, gets into character as the macho Qaolin. Every Thursday night at Bodacious Classics sports bar Galactic crooners translate well-known tunes like Sinatra's "My Way" into the Klingon language. Trekkies claim that the 2,000-word language created by linguist Marc Okrand for the *Star Trek* TV series, is the fastest-growing tongue on Earth.
Photo by Bruce Ely

PORTLAND

"Art is being inspired by the endlessly familiar but surprising limitations of life." Thus Miranda July describes her work. The multimedia artist, who assumes unusual poses to work on her scripts, makes a special effort to stage shows in high schools. "It is important to let young people know that other forms of expression are open to them."

Photo by Steven Bloch

ROSEBURG

Tyler Minnis, Taniesha Moore, and Billie Eveland sing for their burgers. The kara-oke experiment was short-lived at the local Carl's Jr., but preteen girls loved it.

Photo by Andy Bronson

FLORENCE

Traveler's Cove, a bar and restaurant on the Siuslaw River in Florence's Old Town, has live music three nights a week. Not satisfied with the dance-floor stage, Barb Roberts belts it out from a booth in the bar.

Photo by Thomas Boyd

A dancer adjusts her outfit before performing in the Sinferno Cabaret at Dante's Cafe & Cocktail Lounge. Between 300 and 500 people crowd the club on Sunday nights for the Cabaret, which offers a stage to fire walkers, sword swallowers, jugglers, comedians, strippers, and trapeze artists.
Photo by Steven Bloch

EUGENE

"Delta Gamma, yes I amma!" At a nightclub near the University of Oregon campus, Delta Gamma sorority sisters Emily Perkins, Pamela Hobson, Megan Dobson, Lindsay Wood, and Jen Guptil sing along to the Olivia Newton-John and John Travolta duet "Summer Nights" from the musical *Grease*. The movie was released in 1978, five years before these women were born.

Photo by Sol Neelman, The Oregonian

WARM SPRINGS RESERVATION
Joe Tuckta, a Warm Springs and Paiute
Indian of the Quartz Creek Drum and Dance
Group, spent two years designing his traditional regalia outfit. But once he started
working on it, the eagle-feather, beadwork,
and otter-skin costume took him only two
months to make. The Smithsonian once offered him "a lot of money" for it, but Tuckta
declined the offer.
Photo by Brian Lanker

Reason To Believe

PORTLAND
Francisca Gabriel, a resident of the Park Terrace apartments, believes personal power can come through photographs, so she surrounds herself with pictures of her heroes—popes, priests, President John F. Kennedy, Robert Kennedy, and Martin Luther King, Jr. Born in the British West Indies, Gabriel came to Oregon with other family members and worked for many years as a nurse's assistant.
Photo by Steven Bloch

PHILOMATH

James Yarbrough accepts the communion grape juice from Kris Calaba at Church of the Nazarene. Special Sunday afternoon services, called My Church by the attendees, are held for people with physical and mental disabilities. The congregants range in age from 20 to 79.

Photo by Karl Maasdam

PORTLAND

At the Mississippi Street Fair, members of Yahweh Youth Drill, Mime, and Sign for Jesus wrap up their routine in sync. The group was founded by residents of the McCoy Village Apartments, a low-income housing complex on Martin Luther King, Jr., Boulevard.

Photo by Julie Keefe

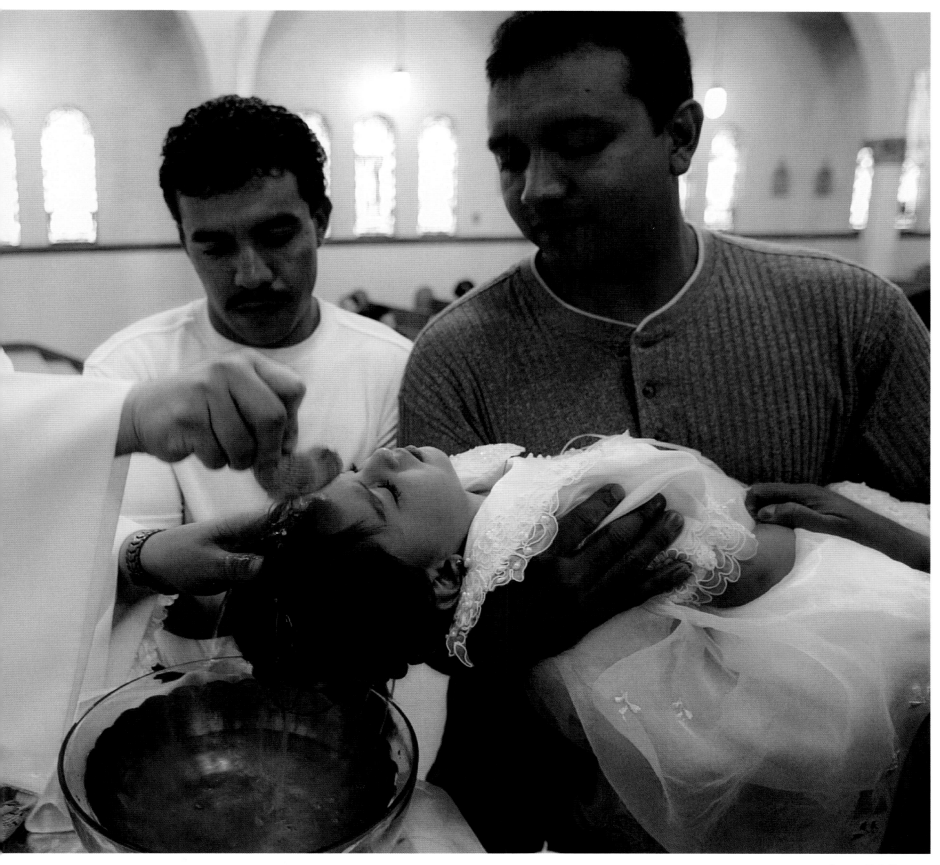

KLAMATH FALLS
Father Saul Alba-Infante baptizes three-year-old Karina Sandoval as she rests in the arms of her uncle, Salvador Cazarez, at Sacred Heart Church. Her father, Gerardo Cazarez (center), is especially overcome. Gerardo wanted to baptize Karina when she was born, but her mother kept putting it off. Now that the two are no longer together, he is finally able to christen his daughter.
Photo by Ron Winn

PORTLAND

Pastor Amzie Bailey founded New United Christian Church Family in north Portland in 2001. Soon, his group will relocate from their temporary Mississippi Avenue location to a new neighborhood. "We are a predominantly African-American congregation, but not by choice," Bailey says. "We're trying to reach out to other groups because we believe serving all humanity is our mission."

Photo by Julie Keefe

PORTLAND

The 265 members of the celebrated Oregon Repertory Singers are volunteers. Founded in 1974, the group has grown from a single adult choir to six choirs with members ranging in age from 5 to 65. The company, shown here at St. Mary's Cathedral, sings a variety of sacred and secular music.

Photo by Paige Baker

MT. VERNON
Pastor Sharon Miller leads a prayer during an evening service at the Living Word Christian Center.
Photo by Stephanie Yao, The Oregonian

JOSEPH
Sadie the dog sits by midwife Sherry Dress's Subaru station wagon. As the only midwife east of Bend, Dress puts thousands of miles on her odometer.
Photo by Stephanie Yao, The Oregonian

PORTLAND
Jack Tafari is chairman of Dignity Village, a tent city of 65 to 80 homeless people. The villagers use a website to raise money for the purchase of a "permasite." For now, the camp's location is Sunderland Yard.
Photo by L.E. Baskow, Portland Tribune

PORTLAND
David Deese rakes precise patterns representing water in *Hiraniwa*, the Flat Garden, one of five landscapes in the Japanese Garden. The gourd shape symbolizes happiness, and the circle, or "sake cup," connotes enlightenment. Designed by Takuma Tono and opened to the public in 1967, Portland's garden is considered by experts the best example of a Japanese garden outside of Japan.
Photo by L.E. Baskow, Portland Tribune

CORVALLIS
Nancy Link and her mother Mary, who is visiting from Wisconsin, walk the labyrinth at the First United Methodist Church. This is her mother's first visit since Nancy's father passed away. Nancy says the meditation helps them navigate through this difficult period. "Walking the labyrinth shows you that no matter how lost you feel, you will eventually find your way."
Photo by Karl Maasdam

PORTLAND

Asian students find connections in an exercise at the Asian American Youth Leadership Conference at Lewis & Clark College. The students create a web of common experiences by tying their personal stories to universal themes, such as being an outsider, balancing the values of differing cultures, and handling conflicts between family and society.

Photo by Rich Iwasaki

UMPQUA

Devotees of the spiritual practice Sant Mat are asked to pay whatever they can when they stay at the Lighthouse Center retreat and farm. Here practitioners like Holger Kypke can meditate 12 hours a day without distraction. Sant Mat follows the teaching of Indian guru Sant Thakar Singh.

Photo by Stephen Brashear

PORTLAND

Steve Vincent, head fire keeper of the Winnimem Wintu Indians, calls forth the spirits with his elk hide drum. He says the rhythmic beats match the heartbeat of Mother Earth. For thousands of years, Vincent's people have lit the sacred fire to communicate with the world's creator.
Photo by L.E. Baskow, Portland Tribune

WARM SPRINGS RESERVATION

Roberta Kirk, a Warm Springs Indian, sewed her dentalium and seed-bead buckskin dress by hand. For the fan, a friend assembled the eagle feathers and Kirk did the beadwork. "The feather in my hair signifies that I am a native woman, and that I have respect for the eagle feather and all that it represents to our people," she says.

Photo by Brian Lanker

EUGENE

Frank Merrill, an elder of the Karuk tribe, uses an eagle feather to bless the Meadowlark Prairie in west Eugene. The 400-acre native prairie wetland, bounded by Royal Avenue and Greenhill Road, has been recently restored. The work took several years and $6 million.

Photo by Paul Carter

PORTLAND

A couple views downtown from the Eastside Esplanade along the Willamette River. A 1972 city ordinance requires that buildings reduce in height as they approach the river. An easy transit system, parks and plazas, and revitalized warehouse districts help make Portland one of the most civilized urban centers in America.

Photo by Rhoda Peacher

Our Town

PORTLAND
John Replinger placed a personal ad in 1997;
Valerie Wildman answered it, and two years
later they were married. When triplets Zara,
Ian, and Deirdra turned 5 months, the couple ordered this custom-made trailer. The
family logged 1,200 miles in 2002, riding
every weekend and some evenings.
Photo by Rhoda Peacher

Been there, done that: State Senator Peter Courtney (D-Salem) faces another budget crisis. For the eighth straight quarter, Oregon has less money than it was budgeting for—$650 million less. "It never gets easier," Courtney says. "If it's not budget shortfalls, it's same-sex marriage or tax reform." The senator has served the citizens of Oregon for 19 years.
Photo by Michael Lloyd, The Oregonian

JOSEPH

"In a small area, you do what you can to survive," says Mayor Kevin Warnock, who works full-time at a bronze foundry. Warnock is also an EMT and volunteer fireman in the town of 1,054, which was named for the Nez Perce Chief Joseph, who was born in the Wallawa Valley in 1840.
Photo by Michael Durham, www.DurmPhoto.com

ENTERPRISE

An old farmhouse, newly outfitted with solar power and plumbing, is a summer home for volunteers and researchers on the 27,000-acre Zumwalt Prairie Preserve.
Photo by Michael Durham, www.DurmPhoto.com

HILLSBORO

The Truman Show? No, Jim Carrey's not going to walk out of one of these new homes in the Arbor Ridge subdivision, but members of 500 families do every day. The high-density cluster homes are mandated by state and local governments in an effort to prevent urban sprawl and preserve farmland around Portland.
Photo by Gary Braasch

PORTLAND
Alex Bennett rides his scooter up Mississippi
Avenue's "killer hill" in north Portland.
Photo by Julie Keefe

ALBANY

Ted Hill tidies up his memorial garden. Hill, a former mill worker, bought the land in 1976. When a family member dies, he plants their favorite flower and adds their name to the board. The first person so honored was his dad, Harry Deady Hill (1892–1961). Now 84, Hill also grows vegetables, including cabbage, carrots, and beets.
Photo by Karl Maasdam

FLORENCE

Lane County motorcycle officers assist Florence police during the annual Rhododendron, aka Rhody, Festival. Law enforcement gears up when 9,000 people come to party in the county with the highest rate of traffic fatalities in the state.

Photo by Thomas Boyd

DOUGLAS COUNTY

A team from Plikat Logging, in business for four generations, cuts Douglas firs near Anlauf. David Murphy, Justin Murphy, and Dan Parker set the chokers—steel cables—on a felled tree to pull it out of the cutting area. The Oregon timber industry harvests 3.9 billion board feet annually, employing 5,300 people in logging operations and mill work.

Photo by Stephen Brashear

WASHINGTON COUNTY

Colorful, yes, but calendula and forget-me-nots are weeds to Sheri LaFlamme. Since moving just outside Portland with her husband and two daughters, LaFlamme, a painter, has devoted much time to growing organic herbs, vegetables, and unusual fruits, including goumi, feijoa, aronia, and shipova. She even set up houses (wooden posts with holes) for nonstinging orchard mason bees, which help pollinate the garden.

Photo by Rhoda Peacher

PORTLAND

After living on the streets for a year in Arkansas, Robert moved to Oregon to find fishing work, but in vain. Oregon's fishing industry is depressed, and the state has an 8.5 percent unemployment rate. Portland provides food and shelter for the homeless, but Robert has had his possessions stolen in shelters, so he panhandles for the $13 a night he needs to stay at a hotel.

Photo by Stephen Voss

WESTLAKE
Facing east on Siltcoos Lake, Bob Jackson's Mini Marina moors 20 boats. A floatplane pilot convinced Jackson to get an airport designation for his dock in 1995. "When the FAA calls and asks me about the facilities, I tell them there are no facilities," says Jackson, who piloted flying boats during World War II.
Photo by Thomas Boyd

YACHATS
A harbor seal wakes up with the barnacles and starfish at Cape Perpetua.
Photo by Brian Lanker

FLORENCE

Heceta Head Lighthouse sits 205 feet above the sea, its Fresnel lens casting a beam for 21 miles to warn ships of the rocky point. The headland was named for Portuguese sea captain Bruno Heceta.
Photo by Thomas Boyd

CASCADE LOCKS

A tug pushes a barge down the Columbia River after passing through the Bonneville Lock and Dam. Beacon Rock is in the background. The 850-foot-high peak was named by Lewis and Clark, who camped at its base in 1805. The water spray at right helps keep predatory birds away as salmon from a nearby hatchery travel through the dam's bypass system.

Photo by C. Bruce Forster

ENTERPRISE

Most of the farm buildings still standing on the Zumwalt Prairie Preserve were constructed at the turn of the 19th century. This old barn has stalls for 11 teams of draft horses. After World War I, the remote farms in the area prospered, as the demand for grain was high and several years of abundant rain made dryland oats, rye, and barley profitable crops.

Photo by Michael Durham, www.DurmPhoto.com

NEWPORT

The Yaquina Bay Bridge is one of Oregon's most beloved spans. Designed in 1936 by Conde B. McCullough, the lacy structure of steel and concrete arches carries Highway 101 across Yaquina Bay at Newport. McCullough, who attended Oregon State University, became internationally acclaimed for the beauty of his bridges.

Photo by Gary Braasch

In eastern Oregon, the weathering of volcanic ash over millennia has resulted in the undulating, striated Painted Hills in the John Day Fossil Beds National Monument.
Photo by Stephanie Yao, The Oregonian

BEND
South of the Three Sisters in the Cascade Range, Broken Top is a stratovolcano first formed in the Pleistocene era and carved by centuries of glaciers. Part of the Pacific Ring of Fire, the Cascades stretch from British Columbia to California and have erupted as recently as 1911 (Mt. Lassen) and 1980 (Mt. St. Helens).
Photo by Robert M. Kerr

EUGENE
At the Cascades Raptor Center, a northern
spotted owl recovers after being rescued.
The owl, which prefers to nest in old-growth
forests, has long been the crux of a controversy between environmentalists and the
logging industry in the Pacific Northwest.
Currently, the species is considered threatened and is on federal and state endangered
species lists.
Photos by Brian Lanker

EUGENE

Pan, a Swainson hawk, is a permanent resident at the center. In 1997, he was stolen as an egg from a Colorado nest and raised illegally. He was rescued and brought to the center two years later. Because he has imprinted on humans, Pan cannot be released to the plains, where his kin glide on thermals hunting rodents.

PENDLETON

Interstate 84 snakes northwest toward Portland, where it concludes its 770-mile journey from Salt Lake City, Utah. The route transports modern-day wagons over much of the same territory that Oregon Trail pioneers crossed in covered wagons on their journey from Missouri to Oregon more than 160 years ago.

Photo by C. Bruce Forster

PORTLAND

The lights of Portland sparkle on the Willamette River as it flows under the Hawthorne Bridge. The 244-foot-long vertical lift bridge, which opened in 1910, was renovated in 1998. The sidewalks were widened, the lift system upgraded, and the steel-grate deck replaced.

Photo by Rhoda Peacher

How It Worked

The week of May 12-18, 2003, more than 25,000 professional and amateur photographers spread out across the nation to shoot over a million digital photographs with the goal of capturing the essence of daily life in America.

The professional photographers were equipped with Adobe Photoshop and Adobe Album software, Olympus C-5050 digital cameras, and Lexar Media's high-speed compact flash cards.

The 1,000 professional contract photographers plus another 5,000 stringers and students sent their images via FTP (file transfer protocol) directly to the *America 24/7* website. Meanwhile, thousands of amateur photographers uploaded their images to Snapfish's servers.

At *America 24/7*'s Mission Control headquarters, located at CNET in San Francisco, dozens of picture editors from the nation's most prestigious publications culled the images down to 25,000 of the very best, using Photo Mechanic by Camera Bits. These photos were transferred into Webware's ActiveMedia Digital Asset Management (DAM) system, which served as a central image library and enabled the designers to track, search, distribute, and reformat the images for the creation of the 51 books, foreign language editions, web and magazine syndication, posters, and exhibitions.

Once in the DAM, images were optimized (and in some cases resampled to increase image resolution) using Adobe Photoshop. Adobe InDesign and Adobe InCopy were used to design and produce the 51 books, which were edited and reviewed in multiple locations around the world in the form of Adobe Acrobat PDFs. Epson Stylus printers were used for photo proofing and to produce large-format images for exhibitions. The companies providing support for the *America 24/7* project offer many of the essential components for anyone building a digital darkroom. We encourage you to read more on the following pages about their respective roles in making *America 24/7* possible.

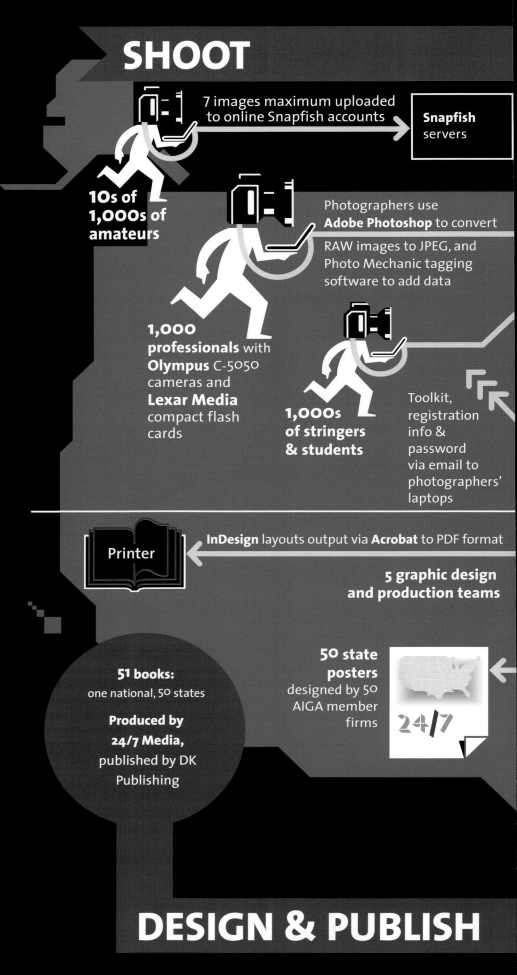

SHOOT

7 images maximum uploaded to online Snapfish accounts → **Snapfish** servers

10s of 1,000s of amateurs

Photographers use **Adobe Photoshop** to convert RAW images to JPEG, and Photo Mechanic tagging software to add data

1,000 professionals with **Olympus** C-5050 cameras and **Lexar Media** compact flash cards

1,000s of stringers & students

Toolkit, registration info & password via email to photographers' laptops

Printer ← **InDesign** layouts output via **Acrobat** to PDF format

5 graphic design and production teams

51 books: one national, 50 states

Produced by 24/7 Media, published by DK Publishing

50 state posters designed by 50 AIGA member firms

24/7

DESIGN & PUBLISH

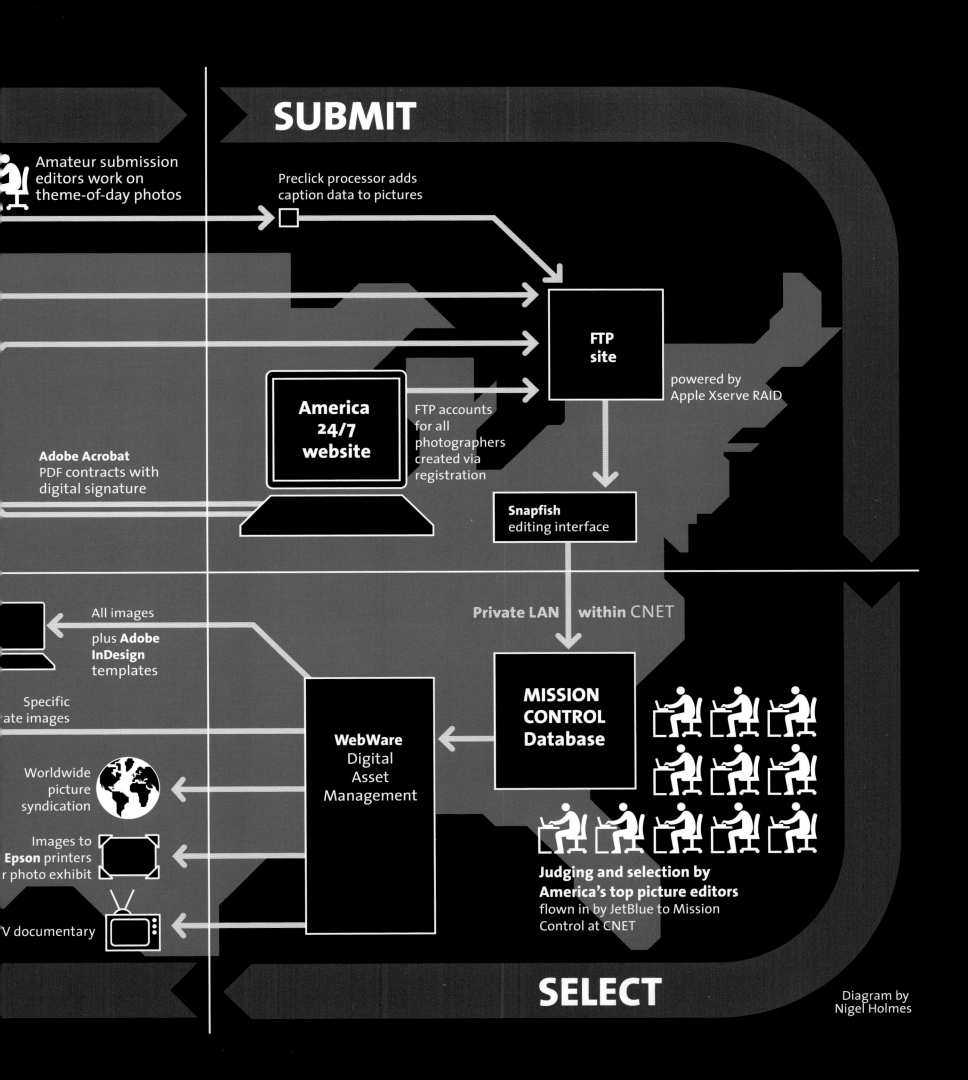

SUBMIT

Amateur submission editors work on theme-of-day photos

Preclick processor adds caption data to pictures

FTP site

powered by Apple Xserve RAID

America 24/7 website

FTP accounts for all photographers created via registration

Adobe Acrobat PDF contracts with digital signature

Snapfish editing interface

All images plus **Adobe InDesign** templates

Private LAN within CNET

Specific ate images

WebWare Digital Asset Management

MISSION CONTROL Database

Worldwide picture syndication

Images to **Epson** printers r photo exhibit

Judging and selection by America's top picture editors flown in by JetBlue to Mission Control at CNET

V documentary

SELECT

Diagram by Nigel Holmes

About Our Sponsors

Adobe

America 24/7 gave digital photographers of all levels the opportunity to share their visions of what it means to live in the United States. This project was made possible by a digital photography revolution that is dramatically changing and improving picture-taking for professionals and amateurs alike. And an Adobe product, Photoshop®, has been at the center of this sea change.

Adobe's products reflect our customers' passion for the creative process, be it the photographer, graphic designer, layout artist, or printer. Adobe is the Publishing and Imaging Software Partner for *America 24/7* and products such as Adobe InDesign®, Photoshop, Acrobat®, and Illustrator® were used to produce this stunning book in a matter of weeks. We hope that our software has helped do justice to the mythic images, contributed by well-known photographers and the inspired hobbyist.

Adobe is proud to be a lead sponsor of *America 24/7*, a project that celebrates the vibrancy of the American spirit: the same spirit that helped found Adobe and inspires our employees and customers to deliver the very best.

Bruce Chizen
President and CEO
Adobe Systems Incorporated

OLYMPUS

Olympus, a global technology leader in designing precision healthcare solutions and innovative consumer electronics, is proud to be the official digital camera sponsor of *America 24/7*. The opportunity to introduce Americans from coast to coast to the thrill, excitement, and possibility of digital photography makes the vision behind this book a perfect fit for Olympus, a leader in digital cameras since 1996.

For most people, the essence of digital photography is best grasped through firsthand experience with the technology, which is precisely what *America 24/7* is about. We understand that direct experience is the pathway to inspiration, and welcome opportunities like this sponsorship to bring the power of the digital experience into the lives of people everywhere. To Olympus, *America 24/7* offers a platform to help realize a core mission: to deliver and make accessible the power of the digital experience to millions of American photographers, amateurs, and professionals alike.

The 1,000 professional photographers contracted to shoot on the America 24/7 project were all equipped with Olympus C-5050 digital cameras. Like all Olympus products, the C-5050 is offered by a company well known for designing, manufacturing, and servicing products used by professionals to perform their work, every day. Olympus is a customer-centric company committed to working one-to-one with a diverse group of professionals. From biomedical researchers who use our clinical microscopes, to doctors who perform life-saving procedures with our endoscopes, to professional photographers who use cameras in their daily work, Olympus is a trusted brand.

The digital imaging technology involved with *America 24/7* has enabled the soul of America to be visually conveyed, not just by professional observers, but by the American public who participated in this project—the very people who collectively breath life into this country's existence each day.

We are proud to be enabling so many photographers to capture the pictures on these pages that tell the story of who we are as a nation. From sea to shining sea, digital imagery allows us to connect to one another in ways we never dreamed possible.

At Olympus, our ideas have proliferated as rapidly as technology has evolved. We have channeled these visions into breakthrough products and solutions to meet the demands of our changing world—products like microscopes, endoscopes, and digital voice recorders, supported by the highly regarded training, educational, and consulting services we offer our customers.

Today, 83 years after we introduced our first microscope, we remain as young, as curious, and as committed as ever.

LEXAR
Media™

Lexar Media has grown from the digital photography revolution, which is why we are proud to have supplied the digital memory cards used in the America 24/7 project. Lexar Media's high-performance memory cards utilize our unique and patented controller coupled with high-speed flash memory from Samsung, the world's largest flash memory supplier. This powerful combination brings out the ultimate performance of any digital camera.

Photographers who demand the most from their equipment choose our products for their advanced features like write speeds up to 40X, Write Acceleration technology for enabled cameras, and Image Rescue, which recovers previously deleted or lost images. Leading camera manufacturers bundle Lexar Media digital memory cards with their cameras because they value its performance and reliability.

Lexar Media is at the forefront of digital photography as it transforms picture-taking worldwide, and we will continue to be a leader with new and innovative solutions for professionals and amateurs alike.

Snapfish, which developed the technology behind the *America 24/7* amateur photo event, is a leading online photo service, with more than 5 million members and 100 million photos posted online. Snapfish enables both film and digital camera owners to share, print, and store their most important photo memories, at prices that cannot be equaled. Digital camera users upload photos into a password-protected online album for free. Users can also order film-quality prints on professional photographic paper for as low as 25¢. Film camera users get a full set of prints, plus online sharing and storage, for just $2.99 per roll.

Founded in 1995, eBay created a powerful platform for the sale of goods and services by a passionate community of individuals and businesses. On any given day, there are millions of items across thousands of categories for sale on eBay. eBay enables trade on a local, national and international basis with customized sites in markets around the world.

Through an array of services, such as its payment solution provider PayPal, eBay is enabling global e-commerce for an ever-growing online community.

JetBlue Airways is proud to be *America 24/7's* preferred carrier, flying photographers, photo editors, and organizers across the United States.

Winner of Condé Nast Traveler's Readers' Choice Awards for Best Domestic Airline 2002, JetBlue provides friendly service and low fares for travelers in 22 cities in nine states across America.

On behalf of JetBlue's 5,000 crew members, we're excited to be involved in this remarkable project, and for the opportunity to serve American travelers each and every day, coast to coast, 24/7.

Digital Pond has been a leading creator of large graphic displays for museums, corporations, trade shows, retail environments and fine art since 1992.

We were proud to bring together our creative, print and display capabilities to produce signage and displays for mission control, critical retouching for numerous key images for the book, and art galleries for the New York Public Library and Bryant Park.

The Pond's team and SplashPic® Online service enabled us to nimbly design, produce and install over 200 large graphic panels in two NYC locations within the truly "24/7" production schedule of less than ten days.

WebWare Corporation is pleased to be a major sponsor of the America 24/7 project. We take pride in being part of a groundbreaking adventure that is stretching the boundaries—and the imagination—in digital photography, digital asset management, publishing, news, and global events.

Our ActiveMedia Enterprise™ digital asset management software is the "nerve center" of *America 24/7*, the central repository for managing, sharing, and collaborating on the project's photographs. From photo editors and book publishers to 24/7's media relations and marketing personnel, ActiveMedia provides the application support that links all facets of the project team to the content worldwide.

WebWare helps Global 2000 firms securely manage, reuse, and distribute media assets locally or globally. Its suite of ActiveMedia software products provide powerful media services platforms for integrating rich media into content management systems marketing and communication portals; web publishing systems; and e-commerce portals.

Google

Google's mission is to organize the world's information and make it universally accessible and useful.

With our focus on plucking just the right answer from an ocean of data, we were naturally drawn to the America 24/7 project. The book you hold is a compendium of images of American life distilled from thousands of photographs and infinite possibilities. Are you looking for emotion? Narrative? Shadows? Light? It's all here, thanks to a multitude of photographers and writers creating links between you, the reader, and a sea of wonderful stories. We celebrate the connections that constitute the human experience and are pleased to help engender them. And we're pleased to have been a small part of this project, which captures the results of that interaction so vividly, so dynamically, and so dramatically.

Special thanks to additional contributors: FileMaker, Apple, Camera Bits, LaCie, Now Software, Preclick, Outpost Digital, Xerox, Microsoft, WoodWing Software, net-linx Publishing Solutions, and Radical Media. The Savoy Hotel, San Francisco; The Pan Pacific, San Francisco; Four Seasons Hotel, San Francisco; and The Queen Anne Hotel. Photography editing facilities were generously hosted by CNET Networks, Inc.

Participating Photographers

Coordinator: Michael Lloyd, *The Oregonian*

Paige Baker
L.E. Baskow, *Portland Tribune*
Justin Baughman
Steven Bloch
Thomas Boyd
Gary Braasch
Stephen Brashear
Andy Bronson
Paul Carter
Faith Cathcart, *The Oregonian*
Randy S. Corbin
Maura Donis
Michael Durham,
www.DurmPhoto.com
Bruce Ely
Rob Finch, *The Oregonian*
C. Bruce Forster
Dean Guernsey
Ron Ingemunson
Rich Iwasaki

Joni Kabana
Julie Keefe
Robert M. Kerr
John Klicker
Brian Lanker*
Michael Lloyd, *The Oregonian*
Karl Maasdam
Bindu Malini
Sol Neelman, *The Oregonian*
Rhoda Peacher
M. Schoen
Lou Sennick, *The World*
Jannine Setter
Stephen Voss
David L. Williams
Ron Winn
Stephanie Yao, *The Oregonian*
Carol Yarrow

*Pulitzer Prize winner

Thumbnail Picture Credits

Credits for thumbnail photographs are listed by the page number and are in order from left to right.

21 Karl Maasdam
John Klicker
John Klicker
Michael Lloyd, *The Oregonian*
Faith Cathcart, *The Oregonian*
Julie Keefe
Dennis Walker, Camera Bits, Inc.

22 Julie Keefe
Joni Kabana
Dennis Walker, Camera Bits, Inc.
Ron Winn
Julie Keefe
Michael Durham, www.DurmPhoto.com
Julie Keefe

26 Carol Yarrow
Rhoda Peacher
Joni Kabana
Greg Ebersole, *Longview Daily News*
John Klicker
Ron Winn
L.E. Baskow, *Portland Tribune*

27 Joni Kabana
Rhoda Peacher
Julie Keefe
Thomas Boyd
Stewart Martin
Terry L. Aichele
Dennis Walker, Camera Bits, Inc.

28 Dennis Walker, Camera Bits, Inc.
Stephen Brashear
Dennis Walker, Camera Bits, Inc.
Rob Finch, *The Oregonian*
Michael Durham, www.DurmPhoto.com
Karl Maasdam
Karl Maasdam

29 M.D. Sullivan
Thomas Boyd
Rhoda Peacher
Karl Maasdam

Stephanie Yao, *The Oregonian*
Karl Maasdam
Dennis Walker, Camera Bits, Inc.

32 Tiffany M. Brown
Michael Durham, www.DurmPhoto.com
Faith Cathcart, *The Oregonian*
Faith Cathcart, *The Oregonian*
Thomas Boyd
M.D. Sullivan
Michael Lloyd, *The Oregonian*

33 Sol Neelman, *The Oregonian*
Michael Durham, www.DurmPhoto.com
Steven Bloch
Tiffany M. Brown
Rhoda Peacher
Stephen Brashear
Faith Cathcart, *The Oregonian*

36 L.E. Baskow, *Portland Tribune*
Carol Yarrow
Michael Durham, www.DurmPhoto.com
Heather Lavoie
Paul Carter
Andy Bronson
Dennis Walker, Camera Bits, Inc.

37 John Klicker
Rhoda Peacher
L.E. Baskow, *Portland Tribune*
Stephanie Yao, *The Oregonian*
Steven Bloch
John Klicker
Julie Keefe

40 Steven Bloch
Joni Kabana
Thomas Boyd
John Klicker
Steven Bloch
L.E. Baskow, *Portland Tribune*
Steven Bloch

41 Julie Keefe
Stephen Voss
Stephen Voss
Joni Kabana
Karl Maasdam
Joni Kabana
L.E. Baskow, *Portland Tribune*

42 Brian Lanker
Brian Lanker
L.E. Baskow, *Portland Tribune*
Julie Keefe
John Klicker
Steven Bloch
Michael Durham, www.DurmPhoto.com

43 Julie Keefe
L.E. Baskow, *Portland Tribune*
Michael Durham, www.DurmPhoto.com
Steven Bloch
Brian Lanker
Stewart Martin
Thomas Boyd

51 John Klicker
C. Bruce Forster
Tiffany M. Brown
Stephanie Yao, *The Oregonian*
Joni Kabana
Tiffany M. Brown
Tiffany M. Brown

52 Carol Yarrow
Michael Durham, www.DurmPhoto.com
Carol Yarrow
Carol Yarrow
Carol Yarrow
Michael Durham, www.DurmPhoto.com

53 Carol Yarrow
Carol Yarrow
Michael Durham, www.DurmPhoto.com
L.E. Baskow, *Portland Tribune*
Carol Yarrow
Michael Durham, www.DurmPhoto.com
Michael Durham, www.DurmPhoto.com

55 C. Bruce Forster
Rob Finch, *The Oregonian*
C. Bruce Forster
Rob Finch, *The Oregonian*
C. Bruce Forster
C. Bruce Forster
C. Bruce Forster

58 Brian Lanker
Dean Guernsey
Dean Guernsey
Stephen Voss
John Klicker
Dean Guernsey
Dean Guernsey

59 Stephanie Yao, *The Oregonian*
Gary Braasch
Gary Braasch
Stephanie Yao, *The Oregonian*
Stephanie Yao, *The Oregonian*
Stephanie Yao, *The Oregonian*
Rhoda Peacher

60 C. Bruce Forster
Lou Sennick, *The World*
Bruce Ely
Lou Sennick, *The World*
L.E. Baskow, *Portland Tribune*
Lou Sennick, *The World*
Lou Sennick, *The World*

64 Joni Kabana
Andy Bronson
Joni Kabana
Frank Lynch
John Klicker
Stewart Martin
Michael Durham, www.DurmPhoto.com

65 Frank Lynch
Julie Keefe
Rhoda Peacher
Stewart Martin
Rhoda Peacher
Stephen Voss
Rhoda Peacher

66 C. Bruce Forster
Carol Yarrow
Brian Lanker
C. Bruce Forster
John Klicker
Steven Bloch
Joni Kabana

67 Michael Durham,
www.DurmPhoto.com
Stephen Voss
Stephen Voss
C. Bruce Forster
Stephen Voss
Stephen Voss
Stephen Brashear

70 Stephen Voss
Steven Bloch
Michael Durham, www.DurmPhoto.com
Steven Bloch
Andy Bronson
C. Bruce Forster
Lou Sennick, *The World*

71 Paul Carter
Steven Bloch
Tiffany M. Brown
Robert M. Kerr
Stephanie Yao, *The Oregonian*
Michael Durham, www.DurmPhoto.com
Thomas Boyd

76 Julie Keefe
L.E. Baskow, *Portland Tribune*
L.E. Baskow, *Portland Tribune*
L.E. Baskow, *Portland Tribune*
L.E. Baskow, *Portland Tribune*
Steven Bloch
L.E. Baskow, *Portland Tribune*

77 M.D. Sullivan
L.E. Baskow, *Portland Tribune*
Thomas Boyd
L.E. Baskow, *Portland Tribune*
M.D. Sullivan
Thomas Boyd
Thomas Boyd

78 Bruce Ely
Robert M. Kerr
Brian Lanker
John Klicker
Michael Lloyd, *The Oregonian*
John Klicker
John Klicker

79 Joni Kabana
Stephen Voss
L.E. Baskow, *Portland Tribune*
Joni Kabana
Sol Neelman, *The Oregonian*
L.E. Baskow, *Portland Tribune*
Julie Keefe

82 Julie Keefe
Julie Keefe
Robert M. Kerr
Julie Keefe
Julie Keefe
Robert M. Kerr
L.E. Baskow, *Portland Tribune*

83 John Klicker
John Klicker
Robert M. Kerr
Julie Keefe
Joni Kabana
Steven Bloch
Thomas Boyd

84 Thomas Boyd
L.E. Baskow, *Portland Tribune*
Andy Bronson
Dennis Walker, Camera Bits, Inc.
L.E. Baskow, *Portland Tribune*
Thomas Boyd
L.E. Baskow, *Portland Tribune*

85 Tiffany M. Brown
Rob Finch, *The Oregonian*
Andy Bronson
Andy Bronson
Thomas Boyd
Rhoda Peacher
L.E. Baskow, *Portland Tribune*

88 Bruce Ely
Dean Guernsey
Dean Guernsey
L.E. Baskow, *Portland Tribune*
Dean Guernsey
Karl Maasdam
Dean Guernsey

89 Dennis Walker, Camera Bits, Inc.
John Klicker
Stewart Martin
Bruce Ely
Rich Iwasaki
Bruce Ely
Steven Bloch

91 Thomas Boyd
Steven Bloch
Thomas Boyd
Andy Bronson
Karl Maasdam
Thomas Boyd
Joni Kabana

92 Steven Bloch
Stephen Voss
L.E. Baskow, *Portland Tribune*
Steven Bloch
L.E. Baskow, *Portland Tribune*
Dennis Walker, Camera Bits, Inc.
Steven Bloch

93 Gary Braasch
Sol Neelman, *The Oregonian*
Karl Maasdam
Thomas Boyd
Dennis Walker, Camera Bits, Inc.
Gary Braasch
Steven Bloch

98 Ron Winn
Karl Maasdam
Ron Winn
Faith Cathcart, *The Oregonian*
Julie Keefe
Faith Cathcart, *The Oregonian*
Tony Sibley

99 Karl Maasdam
Stephen Voss
Michael Lloyd, *The Oregonian*
Karl Maasdam
Ron Winn
Karl Maasdam
Faith Cathcart, *The Oregonian*

100 C. Bruce Forster
Julie Keefe
Gary Braasch
Bruce Ely
Julie Keefe
Joni Kabana
Bruce Ely

101 John Klicker
John Klicker
Julie Keefe
Julie Keefe
Paige Baker
Terry L. Aichele
Julie Keefe

102 C. Bruce Forster
Stephanie Yao, *The Oregonian*
John Klicker
Stephanie Yao, *The Oregonian*
Steven Bloch
L.E. Baskow, *Portland Tribune*
C. Bruce Forster

106 Stephen Brashear
Karl Maasdam
Karl Maasdam
Faith Cathcart, *The Oregonian*
Paige Baker
Stephen Brashear
Gary Braasch

107 Stephanie Yao, *The Oregonian*
Rich Iwasaki
L.E. Baskow, *Portland Tribune*
L.E. Baskow, *Portland Tribune*
Stephen Brashear
C. Bruce Forster
L.E. Baskow, *Portland Tribune*

108 Brian Lanker
Brian Lanker
Brian Lanker
C. Bruce Forster
L.E. Baskow, *Portland Tribune*
C. Bruce Forster
Stephanie Yao, *The Oregonian*

109 L.E. Baskow, *Portland Tribune*
Brian Lanker
Michael Durham, www.DurmPhoto.com
Brian Lanker
Paul Carter
Rich Iwasaki
L.E. Baskow, *Portland Tribune*

114 C. Bruce Forster
C. Bruce Forster
Michael Lloyd, *The Oregonian*
L.E. Baskow, *Portland Tribune*
Michael Lloyd, *The Oregonian*
C. Bruce Forster
Michael Lloyd, *The Oregonian*

115 Michael Lloyd, *The Oregonian*
Michael Lloyd, *The Oregonian*
Ricky Cleave
M.D. Sullivan
Michael Durham, www.DurmPhoto.com
Patrick Ezard
Stephen Voss

116 Heather Lavoie
Michael Durham, www.DurmPhoto.com
C. Bruce Forster
Gary Braasch
Gary Braasch
Heather Lavoie
Paige Baker

117 Michael Durham,
www.DurmPhoto.com
Joni Kabana
Joni Kabana
Rhoda Peacher
Julie Keefe
Thomas Boyd
Karl Maasdam

120 Carol Yarrow
Thomas Boyd
Michael Durham, www.DurmPhoto.com
John Klicker
Stephen Brashear
Joni Kabana
Julie Keefe

121 Joni Kabana
Rhoda Peacher
Michael Lloyd, *The Oregonian*
Michael Lloyd, *The Oregonian*
Stephen Voss
John Klicker
Stephen Brashear

124 Gary Braasch
C. Bruce Forster
Brian Lanker
Cassidy Lena Brock
Gary Braasch
Lou Sennick, *The World*
Gary Braasch

125 Ron Winn
Thomas Boyd
Stewart Martin
Rich Iwasaki
Lou Sennick, *The World*
Thomas Boyd
L.E. Baskow, *Portland Tribune*

128 Brian Lanker
Michael Durham, www.DurmPhoto.com
Gary Braasch
Stephanie Yao, *The Oregonian*
Gary Braasch
Cassidy Lena Brock
Gary Braasch

129 Michael Durham,
www.DurmPhoto.com
Cassidy Lena Brock
Bob Russell, Camera Bits, Inc.
Stephen Brashear
Stephanie Yao, *The Oregonian*
Elsa Holmquist LaBaw
Brian Lanker

Staff

The *America 24/7* series was imagined years ago by our friend Oscar Dystel, a publishing legend whose vision and enthusiasm have been a source of great inspiration.

We also wish to express our gratitude to our truly visionary publisher, DK.

Rick Smolan, Project Director
David Elliot Cohen, Project Director

Administrative
Katya Able, Operations Director
Gina Privitere, Communications Director
Chuck Gathard, Technology Director
Kim Shannon, Photographer Relations Director
Erin O'Connor, Photographer Relations Intern
Leslie Hunter, Partnership Director
Annie Polk, Publicity Manager
John McAlester, Website Manager
Alex Notides, Office Manager
C. Thomas Hardin, State Photography Coordinator

Design
Brad Zucroff, Creative Director
Karen Mullarkey, Photography Director
Judy Zimola, Production Manager
David Simoni, Production Designer
Mary Dias, Production Designer
Heidi Madison, Associate Picture Editor
Don McCartney, Production Designer
Diane Dempsey Murray, Production Designer
Jan Rogers, Associate Picture Editor
Bill Shore, Production Designer and Image Artist
Larry Nighswander, Senior Picture Editor
Bill Marr, Sarah Leen, Senior Picture Editors
Peter Truskier, Workflow Consultant
Jim Birkenseer, Workflow Consultant

Editorial
Maggie Canon, Managing Editor
Curt Sanburn, Senior Editor
Teresa L. Trego, Production Editor
Lea Aschkenas, Writer
Olivia Boler, Writer
Korey Capozza, Writer
Beverly Hanly, Writer
Bridgett Novak, Writer
Alison Owings, Writer
Fred Raker, Writer
Joe Wolff, Writer
Elise O'Keefe, Copy Chief
Daisy Hernández, Copy Editor
Jennifer Wolfe, Copy Editor

Infographic Design
Nigel Holmes

Literary Agent
Carol Mann, The Carol Mann Agency

Legal Counsel
Barry Reder, Coblentz, Patch, Duffy & Bass, LLP
Phil Feldman, Coblentz, Patch, Duffy & Bass, LLP
Gabe Perle, Ohlandt, Greeley, Ruggiero & Perle, LLP
Jon Hart, Dow, Lohnes & Albertson, PLLC
Mike Hays, Dow, Lohnes & Albertson, PLLC
Stephen Pollen, Warshaw Burstein, Cohen, Schlesinger & Kuh, LLP
Rick Pappas

Accounting and Finance
Rita Dulebohn, Accountant
Robert Powers, Calegari, Morris & Co. Accountants
Eugene Blumberg, Blumberg & Associates
Arthur Langhaus, KLS Professional Advisors Group, Inc.

Picture Editors
J. David Ake, Associated Press
Caren Alpert, formerly *Health* magazine
Simon Barnett, *Newsweek*
Caroline Couig, *San Jose Mercury News*
Mike Davis, formerly *National Geographic*
Michel duCille, *Washington Post*
Deborah Dragon, *Rolling Stone*
Victor Fisher, formerly Associated Press
Frank Folwell, *USA Today*
MaryAnne Golon, *Time*
Liz Grady, formerly *National Geographic*
Randall Greenwell, *San Francisco Chronicle*
C. Thomas Hardin, formerly *Louisville Courier-Journal*
Kathleen Hennessy, *San Francisco Chronicle*
Scot Jahn, *U.S. News & World Report*
Steve Jessmore, *Flint Journal*
John Kaplan, University of Florida
Kim Komenich, *San Francisco Chronicle*
Eliane Laffont, *Hachette Filipacchi Media*
Jean-Pierre Laffont, *Hachette Filipacchi Media*
Andrew Locke, MSNBC
Jose Lopez, *The New York Times*
Maria Mann, formerly AFP
Bill Marr, formerly *National Geographic*
Michele McNally, *Fortune*
James Merithew, *San Francisco Chronicle*
Eric Meskauskas, *New York Daily News*
Maddy Miller, *People* magazine
Michelle Molloy, *Newsweek*
Dolores Morrison, *New York Daily News*
Karen Mullarkey, formerly *Newsweek, Rolling Stone, Sports Illustrated*
Larry Nighswander, Ohio University School of Visual Communication
Jim Preston, *Baltimore Sun*
Sarah Rozen, formerly *Entertainment Weekly*
Mike Smith, *The New York Times*
Neal Ulevich, formerly Associated Press

Website and Digital Systems
Jeff Burchell, Applications Engineer

Television Documentary
Sandy Smolan, Producer/Director
Rick King, Producer/Director
Bill Medsker, Producer

Video News Release
Mike Cerre, Producer/Director

Digital Pond
Peter Hogg
Kris Knight
Roger Graham
Philip Bond
Frank De Pace
Lisa Li

Senior Advisors
Jennifer Erwitt, Strategic Advisor
Tom Walker, Creative Advisor
Megan Smith, Technology Advisor
Jon Kamen, Media and Partnership Advisor
Mark Greenberg, Partnership Advisor
Patti Richards, Publicity Advisor
Cotton Coulson, Mission Control Advisor

Executive Advisors
Sonia Land
George Craig
Carole Bidnick

Advisors
Chris Anderson
Samir Arora
Russell Brown
Craig Cline
Gayle Cline
Harlan Felt
George Fisher
Phillip Moffitt
Clement Mok
Laureen Seeger
Richard Saul Wurman

DK Publishing
Bill Barry
Joanna Bull
Therese Burke
Sarah Coltman
Christopher Davis
Todd Fries
Dick Heffernan
Jay Henry
Stuart Jackman
Stephanie Jackson
Chuck Lang
Sharon Lucas
Cathy Melnicki
Nicola Munro
Eunice Paterson
Andrew Welham

Colourscan
Jimmy Tsao
Eddie Chia
Richard Law
Josephine Yam
Paul Koh
Chee Cheng Yeong
Dan Kang

Chief Morale Officer
Goose, the dog